Born and Raised Under a Straw Roof:
A True Legacy of the Human Spirit

Printed in Canada by Hignell Printing Limited, 2001

Canadian Cataloguing in Publication Data

Drzewiecki, Mary Anna, 1953-
Born and raised under a straw roof: a true legacy of the human spirit

Includes bibliographical references and index.
ISBN 0-9687458-0-6

1. Drzewiecki, Sylwester 2. Horoszkiewicz-Drzewiecki, Janina
3. Poles--British Columbia--Vancouver Island--Biography. 4. Polish
Canadians--British Columbia--Vancouver Island--Biography.
5. Immigrants--British Columbia--Vancouver Island--Biography.
6. World War, 1939-1945--Personal narratives, Polish. I. Title.

FC3849.C39Z7 2000   971.1'20049185   C00-900870-5
F1089.7.P6D79 2000

Dedication

With love and gratitude to my parents, Janina and Sylwester
Drzewiecki, who lived this remarkable legacy, and spent countless hours recounting their stories to me; and to my daughters,
Annette and Marysia, who are the wind beneath my wings,
and whom I shall forever love up to the stars and back.

Acknowledgements

Thank you to all who touched my work in their own special way, for there were many whom I cannot begin to list. Your contributions were greatly appreciated, no matter how big or how small, and helped mold *Born and Raised Under a Straw Roof .... A True Legacy of the Human Spirit*, into what it is today. A very special thank you to my parents, my daughters, and my sisters, for their unconditional love and support.

Narratives:
My parents: Sylwester and Janina Drzewiecki.
My grandparents: Adam and Filipina Horoszkiewicz.
My aunt: Stanisława Regulant.

Head Editor:
My daughter: Annette Drzewiecki-Dykes.

Main Previewers:
My daughters: Annette and Marysia Drzewiecki-Dykes.
My sisters: Daeina Thomson, Wandzia Thomson, and Krystyna Groholski.
Friends: Horst Kimler, Janet McIver, Raman Grewal, and Corina Messerschmidt.

Main Translators:
Polish: My parents, aunt, and Anna Dubienski.
German: Horst Kimler.
Russian and Ukranian: Rev. Fr. Andriy Werbowy.

Preface

One of my earliest childhood memories is of sitting around the double barrel furnace in our basement with its door wide open, watching the fire as my father told stories of his youth. My sisters and brothers all gathered around, seated on wooden benches and chairs. My mother would come downstairs and join us with mugs of hot chocolate and freshly baked treats. We were captivated by Dad's amazing tales of growing up in Eastern Poland and surviving the labor camps in Germany in the Second World War. It was difficult for us to relate our peaceful and comfortable lives to his of poverty, starvation, and war. Here we were in Canada, only one generation later, with comforts my father could only dream of as a child: plenty of food, warm clothes, medical care, and education. My mother had her share of stories as well, but she did not like to relive them, and buried many of them deep in memory. My father had a photographic memory and he told the stories in vivid detail, retelling events, locations, and dates. He could recite poems, and sing songs in Polish and in Russian that he had learned in the 1930s as a young school boy, more than sixty-five years earlier. He never used the Russian, German or Ukrainian languages after the Second World War, yet could speak them on demand without hesitation for the rest of his life. His memory was truly remarkable.

There was a small Polish community on Vancouver Island where I grew up. Sunday brought many Polish-Canadian visitors to our home in Cedar, British Columbia, just south of Nanaimo. Stories of combat, Siberia, Auschwitz, starvation, and brutality abounded. It was fascinating and horrible at the same time; a very real part of their lives. They were all survivors of war. I remember nightmares haunting my father for years.

The entire Polish community gathered by the Nanaimo River behind our house in Cedar every summer for a Polish picnic. The adults sat on blankets talking and singing Polish songs, while the children played and ate as much ice cream as they wanted. My father had a natural gift for harmony, and would add the depth of his resonance to the songs. The picnic was a feast of Polish dishes: Gołąbki - Cabbage rolls, Naleśniki - Cheese Crepes, Pierogi - dumplings, only to name a few. Polish picnics were memorable days of much food and fun.

The old barrel furnace that presided in our basement was eventually replaced by an oil furnace, and the days of gathering around the old relic ended, but the incredible tales continued over the years around our kitchen table. I could not let my parents' remarkable legacy die, as so many unwritten legacies have in the past. I was compelled to research, write and record. I am hopeful the readers will find this an incredible journey into the extraordinary lives of my parents, Sylwester Drzewiecki and Janina Horoszkiewicz, (pronounced: Sylvester Jev-yet-ski and Yu-nee-na Ho-ro-shke-veech), and learn never to take freedom and peace for granted.

Sylwester and Janina
Moje Rodzice....My Parents
Germany 1947

Historical Explanation

Before reading this book, it may be helpful for the reader to understand that Poland has been a country ravaged by war from its earliest records. The country has no natural barriers to prevent mass invasions from the West and East, and its borders have changed many times. Except for the rolling Carpathian Mountains in the south, Poland is quite flat. In fact the word *pole* in Polish means field. Poland has been an easy target over the centuries. From 1795 to 1918, it was divided amongst Russia in the East, Prussia in the West, and Austria in the South, and was not recognized as a country during this 123 year period. Some key family figures in this book lived during this time. Poland was reinstated as a country when the First World War ended in 1918.

In September 1939, the Second World War began when Germany attacked Poland from the West, and Russia attacked from the East. The country was taken and divided between the two powers. My parents resided in Eastern Poland and lived under the laws of Russian occupation from 1939 to 1941. Germany attacked its Russian ally in 1941. In 1942 my father was taken from his home in Rudnia by the Germans, to work in their forced labor camps in Germany; he was sixteen years old. All Poles from Eastern Poland were considered Russian, and my father was stationed to work with Russian prisoners and lived in the *Russisches Arbeits Lager* - Russian Work Camps. He slaved and starved for three long years. He and all the Russian workers had to wear a badge identifying their origin. The badge read OST - meaning "East" in German.

In 1943 Ukrainian dissidents revolted within Eastern Poland, trying to reclaim the land they believed rightfully theirs. Entire villages were destroyed and thousands of Poles were slaughtered. The world did not hear the cries, nor see the genocide of the Polish civilians killed during the Ukrainian uprising.

In 1943, my mother's village of Omelanka was attacked by Ukrainian dissidents. She was sixteen years old when her family fled their home and hid in the forest for one week. To escape imminent slaughter, my grandfa-

ther lead his family on a perilous journey all night through the forest, to the village of Rachwaluwka. He knew Rachwaluwka was occupied by the Germans; they were guarding the train station there. They were taken by train to work as forced laborers on German farms.

That same year, while my father was working in Germany, his home village of Rudnia was also attacked by the Ukrainians. His family fled to Przebraże. His sisters and younger brothers survived, but his father and eldest brother did not. His mother had died in 1933 when Sylwester was only seven years old. No one knows the fate of his step-mother and his three step-siblings. Rudnia, Omelanka, and many other villages in the province of Wołyn were completely destroyed during the Ukrainian uprising in 1943.

My parents' home villages were only forty kilometers apart. They did not meet until 1947 in a Polish refugee camp in Raderhorst near Lahde, Germany. Neither of my parents ever returned to the places where they grew up after their tragic departures in 1942 and 1943.

The Polish border shifted west after the Second World War, and Eastern Poland was claimed within the Russian border. The flat land that was once Rudnia and Omelanka was erased from the map, and was turned into pasture. Today, the area where my parents were *Born and Raised Under a Straw Roof*, is in the Ukraine. The towns of Łuck, Kołki, Kostopol, and Rachwaluwka, which were near my parent's villages, still exist, and can be located on modern day maps.

Overview

Born and Raised Under a Straw Roof is a true account told to me by my parents, Sylwester and Janina Drzewiecki; my grandparents, Adam and Filipina Horoszkiewicz; and my aunt, Stanisława Regulant. It is an accumulation of years of research and countless hours of writing. To ensure accurate documentation, stories were recorded on tape, and written in detail. I made two trips to Poland which gave me the opportunity to meet and interview elderly relatives, and also to experience the country and its culture.

Born and Raised Under a Straw Roof is a story of the endurance of the human spirit; of war and peace; of love and forgiveness. It follows my parents' separate journeys from Eastern Poland to Germany during the Second World War. It continues to their chance meeting in 1947, in a refugee camp in Raderhorst near Lahde, Germany. It then follows their immigration to Canada in 1949, and their new lives in their new homeland. They are true Canadians and love Canada with a passion.

My mother and father were faced with learning many different languages in their journeys: Russian, Ukrainian, German, French, and English. To add authenticity, and to help the reader understand the feeling of being immersed in unfamiliar languages, I had the dialogues translated into the languages that were spoken, followed by the English translations. I have devoted the first sections of Parts I and IV, to introducing my parents' childhoods, family members, and the family dynamics under which they grew up.

PART I Sylwester Drzewiecki
      Rudnia, Eastern Poland
      Under Russian Occupation 1939 - 1941

PART II Sylwester Drzewiecki 1942 - 1945
      German Forced Labour Camps

PART III Sylwester Drzewiecki 1945 - 1947
      Germany - Chaos After the War

PART IV   Janina Horoszkiewicz   1943 -1945
                Omelanka, Eastern Poland to Germany

PART V   Sylwester and Janina 1947 - 1949
                Raderhorst near Lahde, Germany

PART VI   Sylwester and Janina - CANADA

My parents and I emphasize that the intent of this book is **NOT** to condemn the nations as a whole under whom they suffered. My parents and their families, endured many injustices during World War II by hands that were fueled by ignorance, hatred, and fear. *We emphasize the importance of forgiving the perpetrators of their crimes. Peace can only come through forgiveness.*

Sadly, prejudice and discrimination continue today between ethnic, religious and racial groups, and thus history continues. Since the Second World War, and the Ukrainian uprising within it, the world has seen more wars, uprisings, and slaughterings of hundreds of thousands of innocent people. The weapons change, and shamefully the atrocities continue. Mankind's record has not been kind. Let it change with each person who reads this book. Learn from my parents' past.

When I first began writing *Born and Raised Under a Straw Roof,* I wrote to document my family's history, with the intended audience being my family. As I wrote, I became immersed in the characters and lived each word. I felt the fear and the joy my parents would have felt. As my work developed and progressed, I shared excerpts with friends. Upon reading, and learning the overwhelming chain of stories that brought my parents to Canada, I was encouraged to go public. My parents and family supported me in this venture wholeheartedly. I hope you enjoy reading *Born and Raised Under a Straw Roof*, a family history which became a documented legacy.

Polish Pronunciations

Every letter or combination of letters is sounded in the pronunciation of Polish words. There are no silent letters as there are in English. Unfortunately the combination of letters in Polish that make up the various sounds, are different from those used in English. The following list might be helpful in assisting the reader with Polish names.

Polish	*Similar English Letter Sound*
a	short u
ch	h
cz ci ć	ch
dz drz	j
i	long e - ee
j	y
sz si ś	sh
u ó	oo
w	v
zi ż	jh

Note:
The titles of Aunt and Uncle are addressed two ways in Polish;
1. Stryjenka - Aunt, and Stryjek - Uncle
2. Ciocia - Aunt, and Wujek - Uncle
Stryjenka and Stryjek are only used when the uncle is a brother of the father. Ciocia and Wujek are used in all other cases.

Pronunciations:

Stryjek	Stri-yek	Uncle
Stryjenka	Stri-yen-ka	Aunt
Wujek	Voo-yek	Uncle
Ciocia	Cho-cha	Aunt

Note:
Girls' names in Polish usually end in A.

Boys' names in Polish usually end in EK.
examples:
Bolka   female
Bolek   male

Grandmother - Babcia   bub-cha
Grandfather - Dziadziuś   Ja-joosh
Mr. or Sir - Pan   Pun
Mrs - Pani   Panee

Polish Currency:
dollars - złoty   zwoty
pennies - groszy   gro-shee

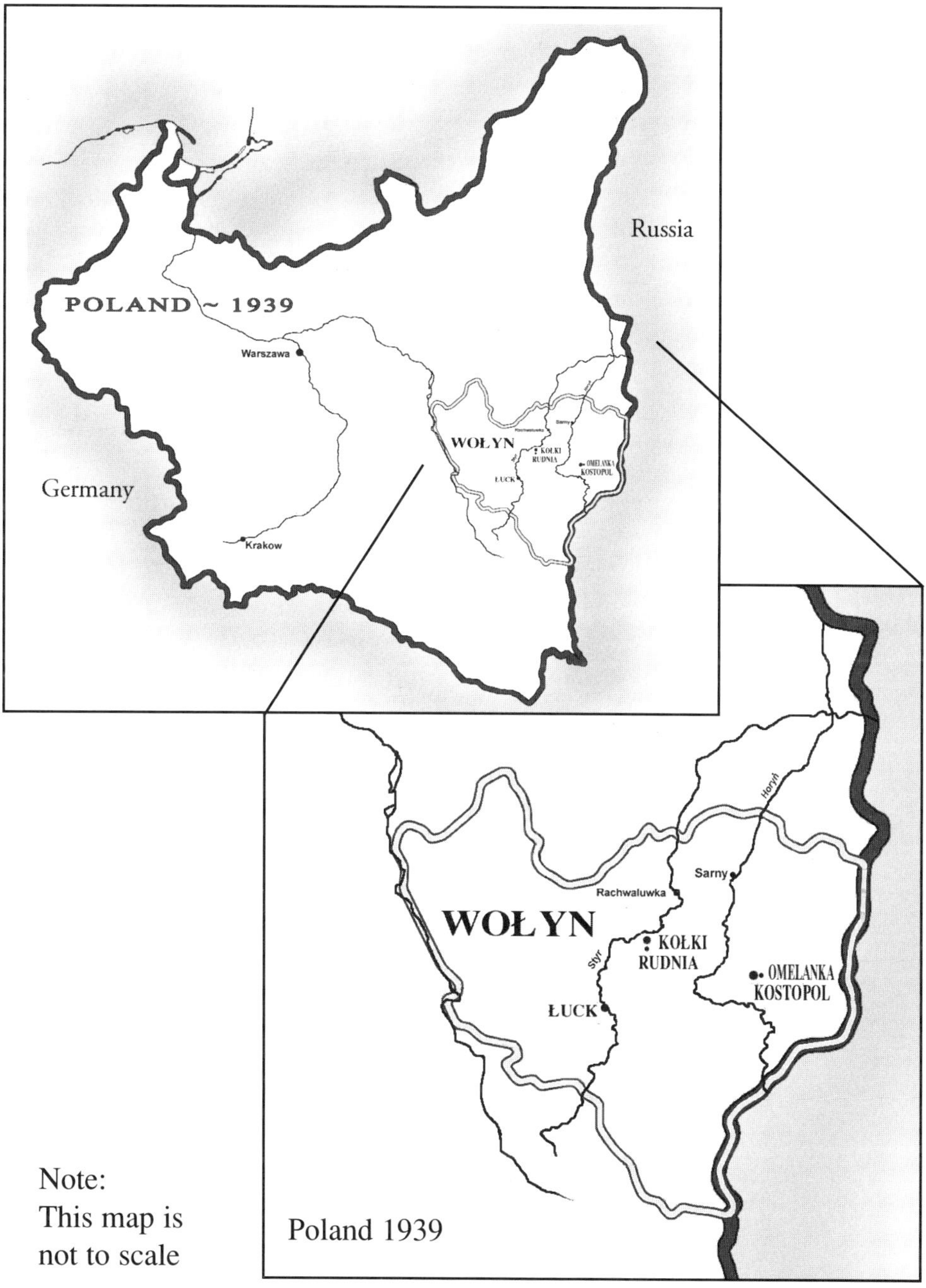

Note:
This map is
not to scale

Born and Raised Under a Straw Roof

A True Legacy of the Human Spirit

Mary A. Drzewiecki

Part 1

Rudnia, Eastern Poland

"You Don't Have To Be A Baby To Cry"

- Sylwester Drzewiecki, 2000

Sylwester Drzewiecki
Mój Ojciec - My Father

Cry, laugh, and celebrate with my parents as you follow their many journeys, both perilous and joyous, that brought them to Canada, freedom, and peace....I certainly did.

- Mary Drzewiecki, 2000

*Painting of Sylwester Drzewiecki's home in Rudnia,
as per his photographic memory.*

Painted by Mary Drzewiecki - 1979

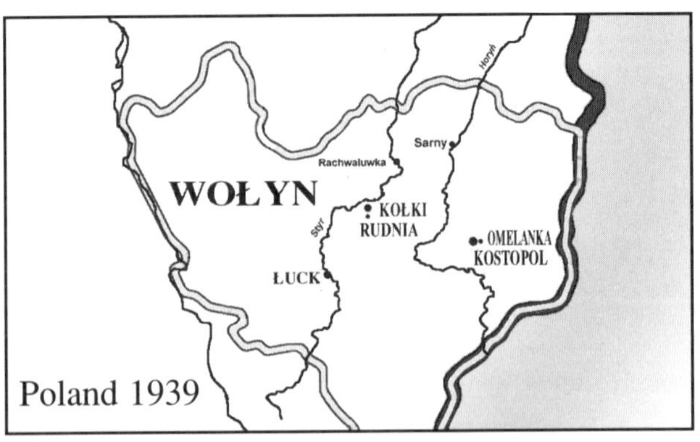

Part 1 Introduction

Growing Up In Rudnia
1925 - 1942

Part I takes place in Sylwester's home village of Rudnia in Eastern Poland, where he was *Born and Raised Under a Straw Roof*. The Introduction tells of his impoverished home life, some of his childhood experiences, and introduces family members, before moving on to Chapter 1 when Rudnia is under Russian occupation. Chapter 2 describes how he was taken from his home by the Germans and Ukrainians to work in the German forced labour camps.

The village of Rudnia was south of the Styr River, in:

Gmina Kołki - Municipality of Kołki
Powiat Łuck - Region of Łuck
Województwo Wołyńskie - Province of Wołyn
Wschodnia Polska - Eastern Poland

It is helpful to know the following events in Rudnia as they directly affected Sylwester's life:

1933: Sylwester's mother dies at the age of forty-two. Sylwester is seven. There are six children at home.

1935: Jan Drzewiecki marries Aniela Dawidowicz. They have three children together.

1939: The Second World War begins. Western Poland is claimed by Germany. Eastern Poland is claimed by Russia.

1939-1941: Rudnia is under Russian occupation.

1941: Germany attacks its Russian allies. Eastern Poland is under German occupation.

1942: Sixteen-year-old Sylwester is taken by the Germans to work in their forced labour camps in Germany.

Sylwester Drzewiecki:

Birth date:	December 31, 1925
Birthplace:	Wioska Rudnia - Village of Rudnia
	Wschodnia Polska - Eastern Poland
Nicknames:	His family called him Solek or Sylwek.
	The Russians called him Slavka.
	In Canada he was called Sylwester or Sylver.
Pronunciations:	Sylwek - Sylvek
	Sylwester - Sylvester
	Drzewiecki - Jev-yet-ski
Height:	Five feet, ten inches
Immigrated to Canada:	July 25, 1949

Sylwester was born into dire poverty. His parents were peasant farmers with little education and no money, who demanded obedience and hard work from their children. Everyone had to pitch in in order to put food on the table.

Sylwester's grandfather, his parents, and six children lived in a tiny one room house, with a thatched roof and a clay floor; a clay floor was common in many homes in the small villages. The clay was very hard and swept clean. There were no luxuries of any kind, not even a clock. The sparse furnishings consisted of beds that were arranged against the outer walls, and two wooden tables in the centre of the room; one table was used for meals and the other was used for prayer on Sunday. The family attended the Roman Catholic church in Kołki.

The impoverished home situation worsened when Sylwester's mother died in November of 1933. He was only seven years old and cried himself to sleep night after night. The struggle to keep food on the table, and keep everyone clean and clothed, deepened. His father remarried in the fall of 1935, and three more children were soon born into the family.

The tiny house was cramped. It was especially demanding in the winter months when the nights were long and everyone had to stay

inside. So many children under foot made tempers short and punishments quick. Humiliation was the worst kind of punishment to Sylwester; he'd rather get a smack than be ridiculed in front of others. Unfortunately, he usually got both.

Supplies were purchased at the market in Kołki, 5 kilometers from Rudnia. Only the simplest basics, such as salt for preserving food and kerosene for the lamps, were purchased. Sylwester loved to go with his father on the horse-drawn wagon to market, for he desperately yearned for his father's affection and acceptance. There were two bridges about 200 yards long that crossed the Styr River on the way. There was no need to cross the river because both Kołki and Rudnia were on the south side. Sylwester wanted to explore the bridges and see what was on the other side, but his father had no time to waste on such foolishness, and never once stopped to let his inquisitive son run and have a look.

There was no money for warm clothing or proper footwear, and Rudnia had extremely cold winters. Sylwester wore baggy denim pants that had no pockets and were held up with a draw string, most boys in Rudnia wore the same. He liked collecting things and having no pockets was a nuisance. He swore he would never buy denim pants when he grew up and he never did; even in Canada he never bought a pair of blue jeans. Sylwester and his siblings sometimes had to stay home from school when the temperatures plummeted below zero, for they would freeze on their way to school. They had no thermometer to tell them the temperature but they knew it was too cold to go out when they went out the door. There was a big difference in the bite between -20⁰ C and -40⁰ C. In 1940, one warm winter jacket was purchased from the market in Kołki. Sylwester and his three brothers, Marian, Roman, and Piotr shared the coat and took turns going to school in the winter.

The school house had one room and was one kilometer from home; Sylwester attended it from age seven to fourteen. He was very bright and interested in his studies, but his schooling was halted due to poverty and war. In 1939, when Rudnia was under Russian occupation, the children had to learn to speak Russian in school. Sylwester had a gift for languages and picked it up effortlessly. In his seven years of formal educa-

tion, even though his attendance was radically irregular, Sylwester successfully completed the required levels with flying colors.

Shoes called postoli, were woven from willow bark. Each spring a stockpile of bark was collected to last the winter; the bark was called łyka. Sylwester's father would cut willow branches and carry them home where he would strip them, but Sylwester was too small to carry such a bulky load. He did his work in the forest, and carried home only the bark. The postoli were woven during the long winter evenings by the light of the kerosene lamp. The bark turned brittle over time, and the łyka strips had to be soaked in water before they could be woven. Postoli didn't last long. They could possibly endure one week of wear, but usually they fell apart in a couple of days, it depended upon how much walking one did. Sylwester became very adept at weaving shoes. He not only made postoli for himself, he also wove them for his younger brothers, Roman and Piotr, when they were too little to make their own. He made hundreds of shoes in his childhood years.

A certain grass, called *osoka*, was also collected in the spring and stored for winter. It was used to protect the feet from freezing. Sylwester would put on a pair of postoli, wrap the dry grass around his foot and calf, and bind it together with rags. The straw boots barely insulated his feet from the cold, and they most certainly were not waterproof. In summer, he ran barefoot.

After breakfast in early spring of 1938, twelve-year-old Sylwester, set off towards the forest with his sharp axe to collect willow bark. He was supposed to stay on his property but he didn't. The willow trees were thicker on the neighbor's side.

Sylwester carefully hid his stockpile of valuable bark strips, making sure no one saw him. By the end of the morning he had peeled at least a hundred trees. It was hard work. He was tired and hungry and ready to go home. He returned to his hiding place, and found his pile of bark gone. He swung around looking in all directions, darting from tree to tree. It was nowhere in sight.

Sylwester cried as he headed home. He wiped his tears on his sleeve and tried to figure out who the culprit could have been. Someone had obviously seen him and waited until he was nearly done, but.... and then it dawned on him....Antek! He had no proof of Antek's guilt, but Antek was big and pushed around the smaller boys. He had stolen things from Sylwester before. Sylwester was angry. It just had to have been Antek.

His anger turned to tears once again when he reached home and explained to his father what had happened. He omitted that he had stripped the bark from the neighbor's trees. Jan said there was nothing they could do. They could not point a finger at Antek without proof, and even if Antek had a fresh bundle of łyka at home, one pile of bark strips looked like the next. Everyone was collecting at this time of year. Sylwester had to let go of his anger. He never did find out who took the bark, but for the rest of his life he convinced himself it was Antek...whether it was true or not.

Sylwester's first pair of store-bought shoes were purchased when he was fifteen years old. They were made entirely of rubber, salvaged from old tires. They were purchased during the time of Russian occupation when the market shelves in Kołki were virtually bare. Shoes were hard to come by. Although Jan did not take Sylwester to market that day, he bought the shoes before someone else grabbed them. Sylwester was so excited when he saw his shoes that he put them on right away, but they pinched his toes. He traded them for an old pair from a fellow in the village. He cherished those old shoes and wore them all the way to Germany.

Life in Rudnia was grim, but in spite of his impoverished and harsh home life, Sylwester managed to keep his cheerful disposition. His beautiful singing voice could be heard across the fields as he pastured the cows. He was inherently good and obeyed his parents, but sometimes curiosity got the best of him. His favorite pastimes were fishing and exploring, and he was intrigued by mechanical inventions. Growing up with horses and wagons, he would run full speed to the road whenever he heard the sound of an automobile just to get a glimpse of it, for no one had a car in Rudnia. He wished he could sit in one, just once. He loved seeing the wójt - mayor of Kołki drive by, looking so important with his burly chest and head held high behind the wheel of his car.

Sylwester had secret dreams of a better life somewhere away from Rudnia. He wondered what it was like elsewhere in the world. Surely not everyone lived a dismal life of hard work and dire poverty. He wanted to drive a car and be a big-shot like the wójt of Kołki. It seemed senseless to work as his father did from sun up to sun down and not have enough food on the table or clothes on his back. He hated being poor.

One day, when he was twelve, he was supposed to be working with his father in the granary, but it was cold and he buried himself in the straw. Shivering he said to his father, "Tato, ja nigdy nie będę gospodarz. Jak urosnę, to zbuduję dwa domy, sprzedam, kupię samochód, i będę jeździł jak wójt Kołkowski .... Dad, I never will be a farmer. When I grow up I am going to build two houses, sell them, buy a car, and drive like the mayor of Kołki."

Sylwester did not give up his dreams; he was going to get out of this desolate place. A bus from Łuck, a town 50 kilometers away, drove by the farm en route to Kołki. He looked at the bus and thought, "Ja kiedyś wsiądę na ten autobus i nigdy nie wrócę z powrotem .... I'm going to get on that bus one day and never come back."

In June of 1942, Sylwester was taken from his home by the Germans and never saw Rudnia again.

———

Jan Drzewiecki:
Sylwester's Father

Birthdate:	1891
Birthplace:	Wioska Rudnia - Village of Rudnia
	Wschodnia Polska - Eastern Poland
Died:	1943 in Kiwerce, Eastern Poland
	52 years old
	Buried in Kiwerce
Pronunciations:	Jan - Yun - short u sound
	Drzewiecki - Jev-yet-ski

Jan was a harsh man. He was head of the household, controlled the money, and made the decisions. Women played a subservient role, and his sons were held in higher regard than his daughters. Marian was his favorite, and he openly showed his favoritism of Marian in front of Sylwester, which hurt him deeply.

The farm belonged to the Hulkewicz family. Jan married into the land when he married Michalina Hulkewicz. In the spring when there was a severe shortage of food, Sylwester remembered his father sitting at the table eating *czarny chleb* - black bread, salt, and water, for lunch each day. Jan liked to drink and to play cards which added to his depression and his poverty. He gambled in his card games and often lost what little he had.

The stress of extreme poverty, hard work, and many children, sparked Jan's quick temper into lashings with the strap and the tongue. He did not take time for explanations when there was conflict. He abused Sylwester physically, emotionally and verbally. Sylwester desperately yearned for his father's love and approval. He tried so hard to be good, and worked diligently, but his efforts were not praised.

During the summer, Jan liked to sleep in the hayloft of the barn. Sylwester wanted so much to sleep outside with him but was never allowed. Every time he climbed up into the loft, his father sent him back into the house. In 1932, when Sylwester was six years old, he decided to climb the ladder early in the evening and wait for his father to come to bed. He was sure his father would let him stay when he saw him sleeping in the hay.

Night was beginning to fall but still no Jan. His vivid imagination began to conjure up all kinds of scary images as he sat waiting. The shadows grew and looked like demons. He had heard many spooky ghost stories and he believed them. He remembered when Dziadziuś - Grandpa Hulkewicz died two years earlier, and the old man's body was in their home for several days before he was buried. Sylwester frightened himself so much thinking of spirits and monsters that he started screaming. He ran towards the ladder to escape the ghosts that were surely in the loft. He grabbed the top rung of the ladder and flew down, shrieking all the way.

Jan was slowly climbing up as Sylwester, wild with fright and yelling at the top of his lungs, was flying down. Jan's temper instantly flared. He grabbed Sylwester by the arm, walloped his behind for making so much noise, and shooed him into the house. Sylwester ran into the house crying, scared, and rejected. He never did sleep with his father at any time during his life.

After church one Sunday Jan wanted to go into a Jewish store in Kołki; the other market was closed on Sunday. He did not want to take Sylwester inside the store and asked a friend to watch his young son. Sylwester was bored standing and waiting and wanted to go home. He saw Pan Hermann walking home from church; the Hermann's were neighbors and cousins. Without telling anyone, Sylwester followed Pan Hermann and joined up with him. Pan Hermann asked if his father knew he was with him, but by then Sylwester was too far away to turn back alone. He was afraid he'd get lost so he carried on home with Pan Hermann.

In the meantime Jan Drzewiecki emerged from the store. Finding no Sylwester he anticipated the worst. He knew his son had an adventurous spirit and feared he had gone to explore the bridges over the Styr river. A day long search ensued that carried well into the night. Jan was certain his son had drowned.

Sylwester went directly home. His step-mother, Aniela, told him his father would be angry when he got home. Everyone waited at the window for Jan. It was pitch black when he arrived. Sylwester ran to his father saying, "Tato czy mnie szukaleś? .... Daddy were you looking for me?" Jan was relieved to see his son alive, but he did not show his joy. He swore at him, grabbed a cane and began whipping him. Aniela intervened and saved him from the beating.

In 1937, when Sylwester was twelve, a widow in Rudnia, Pani Gluska, came to the Drzewiecki household and asked if Jan would let one of his boys live with her and tend the cows. In return for the work, the boy would receive room and board, a hat, and two Polish złoty. At that time, two Polish złoty could buy a pair of pants.

Jan sent Sylwester, even though he did not want to go. He felt sold by his father. Sylwester lived with the Gluskas for the summer and fall months, and was only allowed to go to school one day a week. One terribly rainy day, he sat forlornly under a tree with a sack over his head, tending the cows. He was drenched and miserable. He missed home and school, and to add to his sorrows, he had tremendous pain in his big toe. A splinter had deeply lodged itself and had festered into a bulbous mass. He walked barefoot during the warm months, so getting splinters was inevitable. The old belief was to leave the sliver, and let it fester and burst out on its own.

He couldn't tend the cows properly limping on one foot. Hopelessly he sat in the rain and cried. He became angry and used the worst profanity he could think of. He wasn't allowed to swear but he didn't care. There was no one around and he had had enough. He let the

obscenities fly, until he realized his father was walking towards him. If his father had heard him he would surely get a whack, but luckily he hadn't. Sylwester stood up and greeted Jan. They slowly walked, Sylwester showing his father his infection. A man going by in his horse and buggy saw Sylwester limping, and stopped. When he saw the infection he told Sylwester to sit down, tightly held his foot, and before Sylwester knew what was happening, he quickly punctured the infection with a pocket knife. The pain was instantly relieved as the puss oozed out and the pressure released.

There were no medicines except home remedies. To help his toe heal, Sylwester chewed a piece of bread, plastered it onto his big toe and wrapped his toe in a rag. In two days he could walk again. He discarded the myth of leaving splinters to fester and burst out on their own.

The following year, Jan once again gave Sylwester away to work for the same type of arrangement. He was 13 years old and stayed for several months with another widow, Pani Tereszkowa. She had been a good friend of Sylwester's mother. In the spring he seeded her potatoes, and when they were plowing, he lead the oxen while another man controlled the plow. He harvested and hayed, but most of the time he looked after the cows. Sylwester was fed very well at Pani Tereszkowa's. He loved the good food and the luxury of eating meat once or twice a week, but was hurt again that his father had given him away.

Jan's sister, Regina, had immigrated to France before Sylwester was born. Regina sent Jan a letter and a picture of her family sitting around their dinner table. The photograph showed a beautiful spread of food with wine and white bread. The family was overwhelmed to see such wealth. Jan asked Sylwester to write a letter to Regina as he dictated. He never forgot what his father said. "Życie jest lżejsze na zachodzie. Ja mam trudności przynieść wystarczająco czarnego chleba aby nakarmić moje dzieci, a wy macie biały chleb i butelkę wina .... Life is much easier in the West. I have a difficult time bringing enough black bread to the table to feed my children, and you have white bread and a bottle of wine."

His father's words of a better life in the West, stayed with Sylwester. Even though he was a boy, he began thinking of moving West.

———

Michalina Hulkewicz-Drzewiecki:
Sylwester's Mother

Birth date:	1891
Birthplace:	Wioska Rudnia - Village of Rudnia
	Wschodnia Polska - Eastern Poland
Died:	Nov. 30, 1933 in Rudnia
	42 years old
	Buried in Rudnia
Pronunciations:	Michalina - Mee-hu-lee-na
	Hulkewicz - Hool-ke-veech
	Drzewiecki - Jev-yet-ski

Michalina was old before her time. Multiple births and constant work stole her youth. She had eleven children, all born at home with the assistance of a midwife. During this era, five percent of mothers died during childbirth and twenty percent of children died in infancy or childhood. Sadly, five of Michalina's and Jan's children died. The eleven children were:

Stanisław - Male	1913	Died: 1919 - 6 years old
Bolesława - Female	Jan. 1	1915
Józef - Male	1917	Died: 1924 - 7 years old
Władysław - Male	1919	Died: Stillborn
Konstancja - Female	Apr. 6, 1921	
Marian - Male	July 7, 1923	
Sylwester - Male	Dec 31, 1925	
Włodzimierz - Male	1927	Died: Lived one hour
Elżbieta - Female	1928	Died: Stillborn
Roman - Male	Feb. 2, 1929	
Piotr - Male	May 19,1931	

The six who survived to adulthood were:

Bolesława - Bolka
Konstancja - Kostka
Marian
Sylwester
Roman
Piotr

Michalina showed affection to her children but disciplined them as well. Sylwester loved being cradled on her lap but knew if his mother told him to do something, he had to listen.

One day, Michalina told Solek - Sylwester to tend the geese, but Solek went with his father into the fields instead, and the geese went everywhere. Their favorite spot was the garden, and they made a mess uprooting the vegetables. Sylwester returned to the house with his father, unaware of what happened. Michalina spanked him, as he cried and yelled. To his surprise his father intervened. It was the first and only time Jan ever saved him from a punishment.

Michalina was very religious. She told her children that if they ever thought they were near death to pray aloud, "Jezus, Maria, Józefie Święty, Ratuj Duszę Moją .... Jesus, Mary, Joseph Holy, Save My Soul." Death was a visible part of life in Rudnia, especially infant death. All families lost loved ones. Sylwester remembered his mother's words and prayed them when he was mortally ill in the German slave camp in 1943, in Brandenburg Havel.

There was no money for doctors or hospitals in distant towns, and Michalina suffered for years from varicose veins. The villagers relied on a local man who doctored the farm animals to doctor them as well. Jan asked the man if he could help his wife. He stripped Michalina's varicose veins in her home. There were no antiseptic or sterile devices, nor any antibiotics to fight infection, only home brews and prayers. The pain was

intolerable. Infection spread. Michalina became critically ill with pneumonia and died at the young age of forty-two on November 30th, 1933.

Jan, Bolka and Kostka were at Michalina's bedside when she died. Kostka was sent to tell Stryjek - Uncle Bolek and Stryjenka - Aunt Pawlina. She wept all the way. En route she told their neighbors, Pan and Pani Czajkowski. They immediately went to help.

Sylwester was walking home from school when he met Kostka. Crying, she hugged her little brother and said, "Nasza Mama zmarła .... Our Mama died." They sobbed in each other's arms. She left her seven-year-old brother and continued on her way to Stryjek and Stryjenka's. He cried all the way home.

When Sylwester entered the house he saw Pani Czajkowska washing his mother's lifeless body and wept uncontrollably. His father and sister hugged him. Stryjek and Stryjenka arrived with Kostka. Stryjenka stayed overnight to help with the preparation of the body, and to help care for the children. The following morning, Jan, broken with grief, sent Kostka to get Ciocia Antonina; she was Michalina's sister.

Ciocia entered the house crying. When she saw her sister's body on the bench, with a candle burning above her head, she wailed. She kissed her hands and feet. She became faint and Jan and Sylwester held her.

Michalina's body lay in the house for three days as people came and went. Older women stayed overnight to help in whatever way they could. Pan Czajkowski was a carpenter and built a casket for Michalina, and Sylwester helped him. The job of sweeping the shavings was given to Roman and Piotr, who were preschoolers. Marian, the eldest son, worked the farm during this horribly depressing time.

When three days had passed, Michalina's body was lain in the coffin. Her children walked to her one at a time, from the eldest to the youngest. Each hugged her and kissed her hand to say goodbye. Then the neighbors said their goodbyes. The coffin was nailed shut, carried out to the wagon, and taken to the church in Kołki. Pani Czajkowska stayed behind with Sylwester, Roman and Piotr. The young boys could not go

because they did not have any warm clothes and the ground was already frozen with winter.

Wigilia - Christmas Eve 1933, the family broke and shared the opłatek....holy bread without their mother for the first time. Jan sadly said to his children, "Mama chciała podzielić się opłatkiem z rodziną ale Pan Bóg ją zabrał do Królestwa Niebieskiego, a my musimy pomagać sobie sami w naszym życiu .... Mama would have wanted to share the holy bread with her family but God took her to the Kingdom of Heaven, and we have to help ourselves in our lives." They all cried and continued their grieving for Michalina that Christmas Eve.

Sylwester saw his father crying often after the death of his mother, mostly when he was alone in the barn. Life was bitter without her. Their impoverished lives were even more so, and bad luck on the farm in 1934 added to their depression. In that year the pig, that Jan was raising, died. Then Bolka, the eldest daughter, announced that she and Bronek Kownacki would wed at the end of 1934. Jan went into debt for the wedding and their bleak situation deepened.

Jan took Kostka, Marian, Sylwester, Roman and Piotr to the church in Kołki for a holy celebration in the summer of 1934. After mass, he took his children to their mother's grave. On her grave site stood a wooden cross with a holy picture on it. They knelt beside her grave and said the Ojcze Nasz i Zdrowaś Maria .... Our Father and Hail Mary, as well as other prayers. Jan spoke to his wife, saying that she left him with such small children, and she left forever. The family cried the whole time and all the way home.

Sylwester never forgot the day he visited his mother's grave. He wrote in his memoirs in 1998, "Na grobie Mamy stał drewniany krzyż a na krzyżu wisiał malutki obrazek którego jeszcze dziśiaj mam w oczach. I te ojcowskie słowa co ojciec mówił klęcząc przy grobie Mamy jak długo żyć będę nie zapomnę. Nie znaczy gdzie ja byłem i co robiłem, gdy mam te słowa na myśli stale płaczę. A to mi się przypomiało i przypomina bardzo często. I dzisiaj piszę te nasze tradycje rok 1998 i płaczę co już przeszło 64 lata .... On Mama's grave stood a wooden cross, and on the cross a holy picture that I still see today in my eyes. And I hear my

father's words that he said as we knelt around Mama's grave. As long as I live I will never forget. It doesn't matter where I have been, or what I have, when I have these words and memories in my thoughts I always cry. And this I remember and relive very often, and I am writing this in 1998. I am crying over this and over 64 years have passed."

My father could not bring himself to speak to me of his mother's tragic death, instead he had to write the story. It was so emotional for him to recall, that it took four full days to complete. He was grief stricken, and could not read his memoirs to me. My mother read them, and we both wept.

———

Aniela Dawidowicz:
Sylwester's Step-Mother

Birthplace: Wioska Lade - Village of Lade
                Wschodnia Polska - Eastern Poland

Jan was a widower until 1935. Marriage was a necessary partnership; families depended on the men and women working together. Michalina's older sister, Antonina, was a widow with children. Her parcel of the Hulkewicz land was adjacent to Michalina's. Antonina thought a marriage partnership between her and Jan would benefit both of them. She asked Jan to marry her. It would have been a good financial arrangement but Jan did not get along with Antonina, and refused her proposal.

In 1935 Jan travelled to Omelanka, forty kilometers from Rudnia, to visit his cousin, Kazik Myszakowski. His cousin told him about a twenty-three year old widow with a four year old son, who lived in the village of Lade just two kilometers away. Jan went to Lade, met Aniela Dawidowicz, and married her two weeks later. He was twenty years her senior. She left her son to be raised by her first husband's parents, and moved to Rudnia to be Jan's wife and a step-mother to his six children, aged seven to seventeen. She was not much older than her step-daughters. Her workload was immense. Aniela not only had to take care of the

existing household, she and Jan had three children of their own: Zofia, Helena, and Wincenty.

The one room house was packed. Aniela was stressed to the limit and gave her share of lickings too. Bolka and Kostka eventually married and moved away, but there were still seven children at home.

———

Aniela told Sylwester to weed the garden one hot summer day. He decided to take a break, and snuck away to the river for a swim. He was having so much fun swimming and splashing in the cool water that he completely forgot about the garden until he neared home.

He quietly crept towards the house so as not to be caught. He was hungry and wanted a piece of bread. Aniela and his eldest brother Marian were in the house watching Sylwester creep closer and closer. Aniela had a plan to catch him, but she needed Marian's help. For whatever reason, Marian was happy to oblige. Aniela told Marian to stand inside the porch and cough as Sylwester approached. Sylwester would recognize his brother's cough and feel safe. She would be waiting inside and would grab him before he knew what hit him. Her plan worked perfectly.

Aniela nabbed Sylwester as soon as he walked through the door with Marian following close behind. She hit him any way she could and shooed him back out the door to weed the garden.

It was stifling hot but Sylwester stayed put doing his work. He was still hungry, and angry at Marian for helping his step-mother. He was finally given a piece of bread but Marian was given a slice with butter on it. Sylwester looked at the two pieces. He wanted butter too, but there was none for him. Sylwester was hurt by the favoritism, and the conspiracy, as he ate his unbuttered bread.

Later that evening Sylwester confronted Marian. "Sprzedałeś mnie za kawałek masła tak jak Judasz sprzedał Pana Jezusa za parę kawałków srebra .... You sold me for a little piece of butter like Judas sold Christ for a few pieces of silver." Marian ignored the ranting and walked away.

———

Aniela and Jan had a fourth child, Wiesława, after Sylwester was taken by the Germans in 1942. The baby died the following year.

Dziadziuś Ludwig Hulkewicz:
Michalina's Father
Sylwester's Grandfather

Birth date:	1819
Birthplace:	Wioska Rudnia - Village of Rudnia
	Wschodnia Polska - Eastern Poland
Died:	1930 in Rudnia
	111 years old
	Buried in Rudnia
Pronunciations:	Dziadziuś - Ja-joosh - grandfather
	Hulkewicz - Hool-ke-veech

Dziadziuś Hulkewicz always wore a long, white shirt tied with a sash, and baggy pants tucked into knee-high boots. He had lived 99 of his 111 years under Russian rule, when Poland was not recognized as a country. He was a small, slightly built man, about five feet six inches tall. Sylwester's earliest memory was in 1929, when he was only four years old. He had done something to spark his Dziadziuś's temper, and the old man gave him a wallop he never forgot. The belt landed right on top of a festering abscess on his bottom. The crime was forgotten, but the thrashing was remembered the rest of his life. It hurt immensely.

Ludwig Hulkewicz died in 1930 when Sylwester was four and a half. There were no funeral parlors. The body was prepared for viewing and burial by the family at home. Ludwig's body was lain on one of the tables in the house. Sylwester watched his mother and Ciocia Antonina wash their father's body, dress him in clean clothes, and lay him on a bench in the house. He lay there for three days as family and friends came to pay their last respects. Dziadziuś's body was then lain in a wooden coffin, nailed shut, and carried by horse-drawn wagon to the church, where the priest gave Ludwig Hulkewicz his last blessing.

The priest only travelled to the grave site if he was paid, and the Drzewieckis were too poor to pay the priest. When the church ceremony ended the family followed the coffin to the cemetery and buried Dziadziuś without the priest.

———

Bolesława and Konstancja Drzewiecki:
Sylwester's Older Sisters

Bolesława - Bolka
    Birth date: January 1, 1915
    Birthplace: Wioska Rudnia - Village of Rudnia
                Wschodnia Polska - Eastern Poland
    Died: March 21, 1986

Bolka

Sylwester's two older sisters took on motherly duties. They looked after their younger siblings and worked in the home and in the fields. Sylwester's memory of Bolka is uneventful, but Kostka was a different story. She was a strikingly beautiful young woman, and her beauty caused her much grief.

———

Konstancja - Kostka
>   Birth date: April 6, 1921
>   Birth place: Wioska Rudnia - Village of Rudnia
>   Wschodnia Polska - Eastern Poland
>   Died: March 6, 1986

Kostka

Kostka was working alone in a field near the river, while her parents were haying in an adjacent field, with six-year-old Sylwester beside them. Michalina was on top of a hay stack, and Jan was on the ground passing hay up to her. Michalina could clearly see her daughter from her high vantage point. The hay had to be layered properly so the rain would run off and not ruin the stack. Michalina skillfully arranged the hay in a dome shape for drying.

They were immersed in their work when suddenly they heard Kostka screaming. The girl was hysterical. Michalina saw her daughter on the ground, frantically fighting off two naked men. She hollered to Jan that two men were trying to rape Kostka! Jan took off like a raging bull, yelling at the top of his lungs. Little Sylwester was frightened by all the yelling and commotion. He didn't understand what was going on. Michalina sharply told Solek to run into the house as she jumped off the hay stack and ran towards Kostka. Sylwester bolted for the house.

Jan's yelling scared off the rapists, who ran into the bushes and hid. He ran to Kostka with Michalina not far behind. The poor girl was wailing hysterically. Michalina held her and took her into the house, while

Jan scouted for the two. He saw their clothing on a bush near the river and grabbed everything. The two had been swimming in the nude when they saw Kostka and went after her. Jan went back to the house with their shirts and pants and left the naked boys in the bush. They had to come out at some point to get their clothes. Several hours passed.

Jan returned to haying. As he worked, he spotted the two naked men in a sitting position, dragging their bare bottoms along the ground. With their hands on the ground, they lifted themselves and slowly edged their way towards him. They would not walk nude, just as Jan had anticipated. They would be humiliated to be seen naked in the village. Jan had them right where he wanted them. Enough time had elapsed for him to calm down; in his wild outrage he would have lost complete control. He watched without mercy as they inched forward. They dared not come too close. The rest of the family watched anxiously from the house, for they knew Jan's fury well.

They were not from Rudnia; they were hired farmhands for someone in the village. The young men sat helplessly begging for their pants. Jan let them grovel, and then refused. He shooed them away and told them to go and get their employer. The humiliated boys returned to their hiding place in the woods the way they had come, dragging their bottoms along the ground.

It was getting late and their employer came looking for them. He knew the boys had gone swimming and feared they may have drowned. Jan told him the story of the attempted rape. The man was livid. He apologized profusely, and assured Jan that their actions would be punished. Jan handed him their clothes and pointed in the direction where the boys were hiding.

Sylwester did not know the extent of their punishment, but the two were never seen again.

Step-mother Aniela and step-daughter Kostka did not get along. Aniela was not much older than Kostka, and Kostka did not appreciate a

stranger taking her mother's place. Because of the discord, Kostka left Rudnia to look for work in the town of Łuck. She returned several months later, pregnant, and her head shaved completely bald. She avoided talking about what happened to her in Łuck. There was speculation that she had wandered too close to the Russian encampment and the soldiers raped her, but Kostka shared her secret with no-one.

Jan flew into a rage at the news of his daughter's pregnancy. She had dishonored the family and he wanted to beat her. An unwed mother in the 1930s was looked upon with disgrace, as was her family. It was difficult living in the cramped conditions for Jan did not hide his rejection and scorn for his daughter.

Aniela was pregnant at the same time as Kostka, but Kostka was due first. Kostka went into labour the first week of March 1941, and Pani Słodkowska, the midwife, was called. As Kostka laboured, Jan fumed that his daughter was delivering an illegitimate child. Pani Słodkowska shoved him out the door, and told him to cool down. It was difficult enough for the mother to deliver her child without having someone ranting in the room. Jan stayed outside.

Kostka gave birth to Mirosław - Mirek Drzewiecki on a very cold March 6, 1941. Mirek was a very quiet baby and Jan eventually accepted his grandson.

Poor Kostka had another arch rival in Rudnia: Sylwester's godmother, Pani Sabina Fyszer. Sabina and Kostka couldn't stand each other. They couldn't even look one another in the eye.

Sabina and her husband Albert had no children. When Kostka was 20 years old, Sabina became ill and died. Albert Fyszer was 55 years old when his wife passed away. Shortly after her death, he asked his wife's enemy to marry him and she did! Perhaps Sabina suspected her husband's attraction to Kostka all along, but that will never be known. Albert and Kostka did not have any children, but the man was very good to Mirek. They were only married one year when Albert died. He left his

land, house and possessions to Kostka, which were all lost during the war.

After the war Kostka married Stanisław Mróz. She had two more children, but they died in infancy. Kostka never shared her secret of what happened to her in Łuck with anyone. She took her tragic tale with her to her grave. Mirek became a priest and visited his Wujek - Uncle Sylwester in Canada in 1998.

Marian Drzewiecki:
Sylwester's Eldest Brother

Pronunciations:	Marian - Mar-yun
	Drzewiecki - Jev-yet-ski
Birthdate:	July 7, 1923
Birthplace:	Wioska Rudnia - Village of Rudnia
	Wschodnia Polska - Eastern Poland
Died:	1943 in Przebraże, Eastern Poland
	20 years old

At a very young age Sylwester recognized that his father favoured his eldest brother Marian. Marian was pampered and given reprieves where the others were not. He never endured the severe beatings from his father, as Sylwester did. Perhaps it was because Jan's first two sons died when they were six and seven, before Marian was born, and maybe Jan feared losing Marian too. Whatever the true reason for his favoritism, Marian could do little wrong in his father's eyes, although in reality he did plenty. When the children had a cold or a flu, they had to fend for themselves. Minor sniffles and coughs were ignored. However when it was Marian who was sick, Jan nursed him back to health.

Marian was much bigger and he bullied Sylwester. He often flipped, punched and kicked his little brother and got away with it. One day the two boys were having a heated argument in the granary. Their tempers flared. They were kicking and punching, with Marian winning, when Jan walked in. They broke up the fight immediately. Jan disci-

plined violence with violence, except when it involved Marian. He explained why it was so wrong for two brothers to fight. Sylwester couldn't believe his father's preaching, and never forgot what he said, "Jesteście bracia. Byliście przy jednym sercu, u jednej matki. Nie wolno się bić .... You are brothers. You both were carried in the same mother, by the same heart. You must not fight." They were beautiful and truthful words, but years of resentment from inequality and bullying was not so easily erased.

Marian was given special privileges which Sylwester was denied. Occasionally on weekends, sports activities were organized or musicians played at the school, and Marian was allowed to go. Sylwester desperately wanted to join in the fun, but he had to stay home and work while his brother played. He could hear the fun going on at the school as he begrudgingly weeded the garden or tended the cows. He seethed with envy when he heard music coming from the school; Marian had every privilege for which Sylwester hoped.

———

There were several tough boys in Rudnia and Sylwester hated being bullied by any of them. He vowed he would never be a bully when he got older. However, one day in the fall of 1933 when he and Marian were walking to school, Sylwester bent his promise.

The trees were ripe with juicy plums. The two brothers picked as much fruit as they could eat, but without any pockets or hats, they had no way of carrying extra plums to school. As they continued on their way, they met two smaller boys who had just finished picking plums at their Babcia - Grandma's house. The young boys had filled their hats full of plums and were merrily eating, when Marian stopped them. Marian helped himself to one of the plum-filled hats, and called his thievery sharing. Sylwester watched and then shamefully, the sworn detester of bullies, helped his older brother. The smaller boys cried in protest. The two bullies continued on their way to school with the stolen hat full of stolen plums. The two crying boys stayed far behind the thieves, in case they came back for more. Afterwards, Sylwester felt terrible that he had taken the plums. He gave up bullying that day, at the age of seven.

———

Germany attacked its Russian ally in June 1941, pushing the Russian army back and taking over Eastern Poland. Nazis now were visible where the Russians had been for the past two years. The rounding-up of the Jewish people was evident. The Jews were selling anything they could for next to nothing; clothing and furnishings went for groszy - pennies. With the right connections, money could hopefully buy passage and forged documents. The market shelves were bare so people bought what they could from the desperate Jews, but poverty prevailed in Rudnia.

Jan learned that a Jewish man had come to Rudnia selling a suit for a few złoty - dollars. It was beyond imagination to own such a garment, for no one had one in the small village. The Drzewieckis worked day to day, year to year, just to eat. Jan inspected the suit. It would be just right for Marian. Sadly, the suit proved to be the beginning of Marian's brutal and tragic end.

Sylwester was very jealous. His clothes were tattered and he stewed over the favoritism. He tried to understand that his father did not have enough money for two suits but it did not make him feel any better. To make matters worse, Marian strutted around in his new clothes, showing himself off.

Marian took dangerous and foolish risks and was often in fist fights. In 1943, everyone in Rudnia knew of the Ukrainian uprisings in Eastern Poland. Horror stories from survivors who fled their burning homes put fear into everyone. But Marian felt arrogant and invincible. He ignored the warnings and foolishly went off one evening to the village of Szitnica. He wanted to show off his new suit to his friends and maybe impress some of the village girls.

Ukrainian rebels were in Szitnica that tragic night. They grabbed Marian and his friends, stripped the boys naked, tied them up, and brutally beat them. Somehow Marian escaped, but his friends did not. Marian was critically injured, and stumbled his way back to Rudnia, naked . He had to get home for help. He didn't want to die alone in the dark.

Marian had internal injuries and was dying, but there was no medical help; modern medicine could have saved him today. He was in terri-

ble pain. During his last month of life in mid 1943, Ukrainian rebels attacked Rudnia in full force. With their village ablaze, and murderers on their heels, the Drzewieckis fled to Przebraże, where Jan watched his beloved Marian die.

Shortly after Marian's death, Jan became very ill with appendicitis and was admitted to the hospital in Kiwerca eleven kilometers from Przebraże. He died in hospital from a ruptured appendix, and was buried in Kiwerca. Aniela, Kostka, Roman, Piotr, and Stryjek Bolek and Stryjenka Pawlina attended his funeral.

After Marian's and Jan's deaths, the Ukrainian revolutionaries attacked Przebraże. Eight year old Piotr was separated from his family as they fled. He witnessed outrageous horrors, alone and terrified. When all was quiet, priests from a nearby monastery cautiously entered the ruins. They found Piotr, frightened and crying, standing beside a well. They raised him.

Sylwester was in the German slave camps during the Ukrainian uprisings in Eastern Poland. He did not know the fate of his family until after the war in December 1947, four years later.

Roman and Piotr:
Sylwester's Younger Brothers

Piotr: Birth date: May 19, 1931
Birthplace: Wioska Rudnia - Village of Rudnia
                          Wschodnia Polska - Eastern Poland

Piotr

Sylwester had few memories of his youngest brother Piotr. Sylwester had to look after him but he didn't mind. He was quiet and bothered no one. However, Sylwester did not like having to watch Roman. Roman tattled on him and tried to get him into trouble. Sylwester was unjustly disciplined for things that weren't his fault. Roman was his mother's favorite and learned that crying and pointing the finger at Sylwester worked. Sylwester was no one's favorite. He was stuck in the middle between Marian and Roman.

Pronunciations: Roman - Ro-mun
                          Piotr - Pee-otr - Peter

Roman: Birth date: Feb. 2, 1929
                         Birthplace: Wioska Rudnia - Village of Rudnia
                                         Wschodnia Polska - Eastern Poland

Roman 1950

In early spring of 1932, Roman got a new puppy. He loved the little dog, and was having fun playing with it and showing it to Sylwester, when it wriggled out of his arms and ran straight into the cow pasture. Their cow, Berlina, was with her newborn calf and when she spotted the puppy running forward, she lowered her horns and aimed for the dog. Roman ran into the pasture to rescue his puppy, oblivious to the impending danger. Sylwester could see a horrible disaster was about to happen. He screamed at Roman to get out of the field, but Roman ignored Sylwester's desperate pleas. Both Roman and Berlina were heading for the dog and straight towards each other. Sylwester kept hollering at his little brother to get out, when Berlina charged. He watched in horror as the cow's sharp horn hooked the inside of Roman's mouth. She tossed him over her head like a rag doll. Roman's cheek was horribly ripped.

He was a bloody mess, and he was flat on the ground. Seven-year-old Sylwester risked his own safety as he ran into the field to chase the cow away from his brother. Sylwester helped him up and hurriedly took him into the house for help.

His father's temper instantly flared when he saw Roman's gouged and bloody face. He came after Sylwester, blaming him for the incident; he was older and should have been watching Roman. Jan grabbed Sylwester and thrashed him with the strap.

Sylwester cried and cried. No one acknowledged his bravery in risking his life chasing away Berlina to save Roman. No one thanked him either. He felt horrible.

The boys went fishing and were to check the garden from time to time to make sure the cows and the geese did not get into it. Sylwester was eleven and Roman seven, and the oldest was always in charge. He told Roman to check the garden, which he did.

Sylwester loved fishing. He would fish every day if he was allowed. A half hour went by and Sylwester again told Roman to check the garden, but Roman refused. Sylwester grabbed a twig and gave Roman one quick smack on his backside, telling him to go; that's how Marian dealt with Sylwester. Roman knew how to get Sylwester into trouble, and started screaming at the top of his lungs. It sounded like someone was killing him. Sylwester desperately begged him to stop. He was terrified of his father's temper and continued his pleading, but Roman screamed on.

Jan was working in the field when he heard Roman's screams and ran to save his son. Sylwester saw his father's fury as he approached, and knew Jan would beat him. Jan lost his senses. He did not ask what happened; he figured Sylwester did something terrible to Roman. He violently grabbed Sylwester and beat him as Roman watched.

Sylwester was covered in bruises and ached all over. He forlornly sat in the field the following day, looking at his bruised legs and arms. He wept alone but weeping didn't erase the physical and emotional abuse. Jan walked by his son sitting on the grass. Sylwester quietly said, "Zobacz Tatuś. Patrz na moje nogi jakie ja mam siniaki .... Look Dad. Look at the bruises on my legs." Jan did not look at his son. He walked right by.

Part 1 - Chapter 1

Rudnia Under Russian Occupation
September 1939 to June 1941

Introduction:

Life was even more bitter and cruel under Russian occupation. The market in Kołki had become virtually empty of any supplies; sugar disappeared altogether. Now on Jan's trip to the market he was lucky if he could buy kerosene for the lamps or the salt needed for bread and preserves. The shelves were bare.

One of the cruelest tragedies during Russian occupation was for the families who had any wealth, land or education. They were considered a threat to the state. Human rights were ignored. Freedom of speech and private ownership were abolished. Given twenty minutes to pack and leave their homes, these families were rounded up as criminals and deported by train to Siberia. February 1940 was the coldest winter Sylwester ever remembered, and it was in that bleak month, he witnessed 30 people from his village being rooted from their homes in the night. The wind howled and the snow blew, as he watched the desperate families trudge through the snow. Armed Russian soldiers were in front and behind the dismal procession of prisoners who had committed no crime. There was nothing anyone could do but helplessly watch and pray.

Sylwester knew every one of the people taken that horrid night. It was a nightmare watching the Tolsczyk, Waszyleski, Brzezinski, Augastewicz, Omelny, and Gryzand families forced to go with the soldiers. The children were taken too. They were Sylwester's school mates. They shuffled along beside their parents, frightened, confused, and freezing cold. Where were they going? Why were they leaving? They had committed no crime yet they were sentenced to a life of hard labour in the harshness of Siberia where few people survived.

Sylwester's heart wept when he saw Wala Tolsczyk walk beside her parents and her brother. Sylwester had a school boy crush on her, even though he knew his chances of catching her attention were slim. She came from a more fortunate home, so different from his own. She wore nice dresses and store-bought shoes, and always looked so clean. Sylwester only dreamt about the kind of life Wala had, and now it was costing her everything. He remembered picking an apple for her and giving it to her at school. Fresh fruit was a luxury, and it was a generous gift of his affection. Wala turned around and promptly gave the apple to her little brother. Sylwester was deeply hurt, especially because he didn't like her brother. He would have eaten it himself had he known she'd give it away, but he still cared for her. That frigid February night in 1940, Wala was taken from her home. She and the others were never seen again.

All the families in the village were drying bread and storing the crusts in sacks, just in case they were next to be called in the middle of the night with twenty minutes to pack. The fear of Siberia was in everyone. Life as they knew it was turned upside down.

All families were required to give a portion of their farm produce to the Russian authorities. The Drzewieckis had barely enough food for themselves. Their main diet in this dismal time consisted of black bread, salt, and potatoes. They harvested what they could from their land and the forest, and now the Russians took part of it. Each family was also required to give a specified quota of manual labour. The amount of work demanded from each family was in relation to how many people lived in the house. Jan would not allow his daughters, Bolka and Kostka, to work near the Russian soldiers. He sent his sons to do the family's work quota and kept his daughters safely at home. This he was allowed, for the primary concern was the free labour, not who did it.

It was strenuous working for the Russians when there was so much work to do on the farm, but Siberia was not an option. The work that was demanded, varied. One time Sylwester spent two weeks repairing roads and bridges. On another occasion, when they had a deep snowfall, he worked for two weeks shoveling snow off the main road for the army vehicles. The Russians wanted to make a runway for an airport in

Szitnica on the north side of the Styr River, so Sylwester sweated for two weeks shoveling dirt and loading it onto a horse-drawn wagon. Any family who owned a horse had to use it to drag timber and take it to the railroad. Sylwester guided their old family horse day after day as it hauled the required number of cubic meters. He was doing man sized labour when he was only a youth. The Russians swore profusely on the job, and Sylwester learned more Russian profanity in those two years, than he had in his whole life. Swearing was absolutely forbidden at home. His ears rang.

At age fourteen, he no longer went to school. He worked full-time for six months at the Russian Machine and Tractor Station - MTS, built in Rudnia. He learned to heat a barrel of water by placing empty artillery cartridges into a fire and then dropping the huge shells into the water. In this way the mechanics had warm water in which to wash their grease covered hands. At the MTS he helped lay bricks for a chimney, laid a floor with wooden blocks, moved sand, and did many other manual tasks. A coupon was issued after working the six months, and could be used to purchase a jacket and a pair of cotton pants from the co-op. Sylwester earned his coupon and went to buy the clothes, but the co-op did not have his size. He took what they had, and generously gave the pants and jacket to his father.

These were the depressing conditions under which Sylwester lived during the Russian occupation of Eastern Poland from September 1939 to June 1941. In spite of his impoverished youth and strenuous workload, he somehow kept his cheerful disposition and fostered his love for exploration and adventure, which sometimes resulted in getting himself into trouble.

Summer 1940
Sylwester Drzewiecki - 14 years old
The Emergency Landing in Szitnica

By the fall of 1940, Rudnia was overrun with Russians. Russian army vehicles of all shapes and sizes rolled in one after another. The novelty of running to get a glimpse of a passing vehicle wore off as truck after truck came into the village. Aeroplanes however, were still uncommon and to see a machine flying in the sky was the cause of great excitement. Sylwester looked up whenever he heard the drone of a plane's engine. He desperately wanted to inspect an aeroplane up close and to learn what it was all about. The airport on the north side of the Styr River in Szitnica was so close to home, but he was not permitted to go.

His luck changed one summer day. As he was pulling weeds, he heard the sound of an aeroplane. He squinted, looking up into the blue sky, and followed its path. The engine was choking. He watched as it sputtered, and came down for an emergency landing.

Sylwester took off like a flash in the direction of the plane. He'd suffer the consequences when he got back home, but right now he didn't care. All he could think about was the plane. Crossing the bridges over the Styr River, he ran through the field to the emergency landing site. He could not believe his eyes nor his luck; the plane was right in front of him. A few curious people from another village had come out to see too, but Sylwester could not understand why his entire village hadn't come running. How often did a plane come down near Rudnia?

It was a one prop, two-seater Russian plane; pilot in the front, co-pilot in the back. The pilots were dressed in leather caps complete with ear flaps, goggles, and leather bomber jackets. They were a fantastic sight. When Sylwester arrived the co-pilot was standing on the ground in front of the propeller, and the pilot was in the cockpit. The co-pilot ordered everyone to stay back and not touch the plane, as he tried to get it started. Sylwester memorized the scene and every word spoken. He remembered word for word what the pilots said to each other in Russian. The co-pilot at the prop said, "Выключить .... Disconnect."

The pilot replied, "Єсть выключено ....Yes disconnect"

The co-pilot called, "Контакт .... Contact."

The pilot answered, "Єсть контакт ....Yes contact."

The co-pilot spun the prop to start the engine. "Rrrrrrrr"...Nothing. It took several tries to get the engine going, and each time the same words were repeated. Sylwester watched the co-pilot pull down hard on the propeller, as it finally spun to life with a great roar. As the blades whipped around and the engine rumbled, the co-pilot shouted and motioned for the spectators to help push the plane, then he climbed into the back seat. This was a dream come true. Sylwester felt so important and so proud pushing the aeroplane, helping it taxi over the field for take off. What a grand spectacle it made as it started to climb. The pilots waved their thanks, and Sylwester and the other spectators waved back.

Sylwester couldn't wait to tell everyone his exciting news. He ran home, bursting with the story of his adventure. The news spread through the village like wildfire. No one in Rudnia had ever touched a plane or even seen one up close; he was celebrated like a hero. Everyone was so taken by his importance, that his disobedience for abandoning the garden was momentarily dismissed. He couldn't believe the reaction, or the fuss made over him. He thought they were all ridiculously foolish admiring him for something they could have so easily done themselves. Sylwester ignored the simplicity of their ignorance, and decided to bask in his moment of glory. However, this quickly died as his punishment set in. Not only did he have to pull the weeds, but he had to feed the cows and the geese, and was not allowed to go swimming that day, but seeing and touching the plane was worth it.

Autumn 1940
Selling Apples to the Russians

Russian soldiers patrolled the village, and thousands more were camped in the forest one and a half kilometers from Sylwester's home.

He was intrigued by the army hidden in the woods and was compelled to see the soldiers. He didn't tell anyone for he knew no one was allowed to go into the Russian camps.

He couldn't believe the number of soldiers in the forest. He was being a friendly, curious boy and no threat whatsoever, so the soldiers let him wander through the camps. Sylwester had learned to speak Russian in school, and he liked their company. He visited the forest regularly, but it was his secret.

In the fall, when the apples were ripe, an orchardist near Rudnia heaped a huge pile of apples onto his wagon and headed for the encampments in the forest. He planned to sell each apple for one Russian rubel. The true owners of the orchard, Pan and Pani Omelny, had been deported to Siberia that horrible February night as Sylwester watched from his window. The villagers did not look highly upon the new farmer who moved into Pan Omelny's place. No one in the village could afford such an exorbitant price for one apple, and the new orchardist knew it. The greedy farmer decided to sell his crop for more money to the Russians, and disregard his hungry neighbours.

Sylwester was visiting a camp when the soldiers heard fresh fruit was coming. They hurriedly queued up, anxious to buy and feared there would not be enough. Very quickly, fifteen long lines of men were formed side by side.

The farmer had taken his son along to help, but selling the apples was time consuming. There were too many buyers, and not enough sellers. The farmer needed help. Sylwester asked if he could assist. The farmer looked skeptically at him. He did not want to be tricked by a young thief. "Czy chowasz pieniądze do kieszeni? .... Will you hide the money in your pockets?" Sylwester sincerely had no intention of stealing any money. He showed the farmer that his baggy pants and loose pull-over shirt had no pockets. Seeing that there was nowhere for Sylwester to hide any money, the farmer agreed to let him help, but he made Sylwester promise to hand over every rubel. Sylwester agreed. The farmer hauled him up onto the wagon and the selling continued. It went much faster with three, and Sylwester handed over every rubel as promised.

He had no need for money for he was not permitted to travel to the market in Kołki alone, but when the soldiers filled their helmets with ten apples and started handing him ten rubel notes, the temptation to steal the money was too hard to resist. He was aware of the financial duress of his family, but his family's poverty was not the motivating factor; it was the thrill of not getting caught.

Sylwester had no idea his loose, scoop-neck shirt would come in handy for a swift deposit of Russian money. His quick hand was undetected by the farmer. He had hidden quite a cache around his middle when the farmer's son spotted him stealing. "Tato, on chowa pieniądze w jego koszuli!....Dad, he's hiding money inside his shirt!" The farmer instantly grabbed Sylwester and threw him off the wagon, right on top of the soldiers! Villagers who had been watching the apple sale from the sidelines, saw Sylwester being hurtled. His father's brother was there, but did not come to his aid. Instead, he shouted to the farmer, "Zbij go po dubie bo on na to zasłużył .... Hit him on his backside and give him what he deserves!" Sylwester was publicly humiliated and he wanted to run and hide. The soldiers picked him up and told him in Russian, "Маленький мальчик идёт домой .... Little boy go home."

Sylwester was ashamed and ran clutching his baggy shirt with the rubels still tucked inside. He was afraid of being robbed so he stayed off the main road and took a short cut through the bush. He stopped and cautiously looked around as he counted the money. His jaw dropped when he counted 80 rubels! It was a tremendous amount of money.

He decided to confess what he had done to his father and give him the 80 rubels; his uncle would tell him anyway. He entered the house and found his father having his sparse lunch of water, czarny chleb - black bread, and salt. Sylwester was afraid. He apprehensively walked up to Jan and said, "Tatuś ja mam coś dla Ciebie ale boję że mnie uderzysz .... Dad, I have something for you but I am afraid you will hit me."

"Co Ty zrobil? Ty .... What have you done? You ...."

Sylwester lowered his head and fearfully told his father what he had done, how he had hidden 80 rubels in his shirt and had brought the money home for him. In the long silence that followed Sylwester expected the

worst, but Jan looked at his son and solemnly said, "Zrobiłeś dobrze .... You did a good job." These were the first words of praise Sylwester had ever heard from his father. He was fourteen years old.

Jan knew the apples didn't belong to the orchardist who sold them. His reaction would have been very different before the time of Russian occupation. He made a trip to the market in Kołki with the eighty rubels. There was a boy's winter jacket in the store. It was made of heavy wool, and although it was a short design, it was more than his children had. He purchased the jacket for his sons. The four brothers Marian, Sylwester, Roman and Piotr took turns wearing the jacket and going to school in the winter. Sylwester was given the honor of wearing the jacket first for it was he who brought the good fortune into their home.

———

Sylwester Drzewiecki - 15 years old
The Stolen Christmas Tree

The Russian Machine and Tractor Station - MTS, where Sylwester worked, was built when the Russians took over in 1939; before that time there were no vehicles to repair. Villagers were in awe of the size of the building. They were amazed that a horse-drawn wagon could completely turn around inside. Rudnia had never seen anything like it.

The head foreman, Pan Mychałowski, worked out of his office. Sylwester's immediate supervisor was Pan Nizynski. Mychałowski asked all the workers to come to his office at quitting time, just before Christmas 1940, for an announcement. "Ja szukam choinkę co ma krótkie igły. Ja dam dziesięć rubli kto dla mnie dostani .... I am looking for a short-needle Christmas tree. I am offering ten rubels to anyone who can get me one."

Short-needle evergreens were very uncommon in the area, but Sylwester knew where one was growing. The ten rubels would come in very handy for his family. "Ja dostane Panu tą choinkę .... I'll get you a Christmas tree," volunteered Sylwester. Pan Mychałowski was very pleased, and it was agreed that Sylwester would be paid ten rubels upon

the delivery of the tree. What Sylwester neglected to say, was that the short-needle evergreen that he had in mind, was growing in Pan Fedor's garden, right below his front window.

That evening Sylwester carefully sharpened his axe. He believed he could get away with his plan with a razor sharp axe and the cover of darkness. He had to be quick and quiet. In the wee hours of the morning, he crept out of the house. He thought he had left everyone unaware and sleeping. He had no idea his father hadn't yet returned from an all night game of cards, and was anxious when he met him on the road. "Gdzie idziesz? .... Where are you going?" Sylwester left out the details. "Ja idę zrąbać choinkę dla Pana Mychałowskiego .... I am going to chop a Christmas tree for Pan Mychałowski." His father gave a low grunt and continued home.

Sylwester crept into Fedor's front garden and carefully bent the tree. He quietly sliced through the trunk in a sawing motion with his razor-sharp axe. He was zealous in his work and didn't notice the snow starting to fall. He was pleased, for the fresh snow would cover his tracks.

He tried to hoist the tree over his shoulder but couldn't. He grabbed the trunk and dragged the tree to Mychałowski's house. The bushy branches left a wide track, but just as he had hoped, the heavy snowfall was covering them. However, the snow stopped falling, and a very visible path lead to Mychałowski's front door.

A great commotion arose in Fedor's house at the discovery of their missing tree. Fedor was fuming when he saw the bare stump in his garden. He would catch the culprit and make him pay. It didn't take him long to find the thief's trail and follow it directly to Mychałowski's house. There was no way Mychałowski would have stolen his tree, and he didn't have any children who would have done it either. He didn't even knock on his door. He knew there were plenty of teenage boys nearby who could have chopped down his tree. The thief would be easy to find.

Pan Nizynski, who lived next door to Fedor, had five teenaged boys. He headed over there for his first interrogation, but Nizynski told him he was talking to the wrong man. He told Fedor to speak to Jan Drzewiecki. Jan had plenty of boys who could have done such a thing. Fedor started toward's Jan's house.

While Fedor was carrying out his investigation, Sylwester had returned home, given the ten rubels to his father, and started his chores. He fed and watered the horse and cows, and hauled heavy buckets of water out of the well with the kluczka - a long pole with a hook on one end. It was hard work lifting bucket after bucket out of the well. It was still early morning, but he felt like he had already done a day's work. He needed a break, and decided to go skating on the pond. His homemade skates were made of a piece of wood with a wire pulled tightly across the length of the bottom. Two straps were attached to the sides of the wooden slats so that the skates could be tied onto his foot. Sylwester was enjoying himself on the ice when he saw his brother Roman coming towards him with a smirk on his face. Roman wasn't dressed to be outdoors and Sylwester knew there was going to be trouble. Roman sang, "Sylwek idź do domu. Tam Fedor przyszedł .... Sylwek go into the house. Fedor has come."

He slowly walked into the house, dreading the humiliation of facing Pan Fedor and his father. He shamefully lowered his head and told them the truth. Jan was ashamed of what his son had done and gave the ten rubels to Fedor. It helped appease the man's anger but Fedor wasn't going to let Sylwester get away so easily. He told the fifteen-year-old he would report him to the Russian authorities and he would be sent to Siberia.

Terrified by the word Siberia, he cried beside his father. He had seen the reality of the deportation; it was happening all over the country. Poles from his village had been deported to Siberia for committing no crime, and Sylwester had committed a crime. He would be sent for sure. He wept in misery at his fate.

Fedor had only wanted to scare Sylwester. He hadn't meant to terrorize him. He said he would forgive him, but as punishment he had to cut hay in his fields for two days the following summer. Sylwester didn't care about the hard work, but he dreaded the humiliation of having to face the entire Fedor family.

Summer 1941 came too quickly. The hayfield was ready for cutting and Fedor did not forget the debt Sylwester owed him. Jan was notified. Sylwester was up with the sun, hard at work with his scythe before any

of Fedor's family arrived. He desperately wanted to avoid facing them. Fedor's two sons were strapping big men in their mid-twenties, who towered over Sylwester. The three worked side-by-side swooshing down the tall grass with their scythes. Sylwester dreaded being teased or ridiculed for what he had done, but the brothers did not mention a thing.

Mid-morning, Fedor's daughter came to the field and told the three that her mother had made a big breakfast and they were to come to the house. Sylwester immediately declined. There was no way he wanted to go into their house, walk past the tree stump, and face the whole family. Seeing that Sylwester was not going to join them, one of the sons effortlessly picked him up and swung him over his shoulder like a sack of potatoes. As he headed towards the house he said, "Czy pójdziesz sam, czy muszę Cię nieść? .... Are you going to walk or do I have to carry you?"

Sylwester walked but his feet were heavy. He humbly lowered his head, as he entered the house. He ate in silence with the family, but it was painful to share their bread when he had done them wrong; his conscience was punishing him.

Fedor's sons were friendly and Sylwester became more relaxed as the day progressed. He found it much easier to join the family for lunch. He obediently worked his two days. There was never any mention of the tree, for which he was thankful. He had learned his lesson.

Sylwester's memory was so vivid of this entire scene that he relived his embarrassment when retelling the story fifty-nine years later.

Pan Michałowski's life ended tragically in 1943. He was murdered in Rudnia by Ukrainian dissidents during the uprising in Eastern Poland. Sylwester learned about Pan Michałowski's death after the Second World War. Miraculously, the entire Nizynski family survived the Ukrainian uprising in Eastern Poland, and the Second World War. In the year 2000, Sylwester wrote them and jokingly asked which one of the five boys had told on him about chopping down Pan Fedor's tree in 1940.

Part 1 - Chapter 2

Goodbye Rudnia
1942

Introduction:

Although Europe was completely immersed in the Second World War during the time of Russian occupation from 1939 to 1941, the war as the world knew it was still unknown to Sylwester. That changed in 1941 when the family awoke to an alarming noise. Jan immediately thought their horse and cows were fighting, and kicking the walls in the barn. They had done it before. Sylwester and his father hurriedly ran outside before the animals could damage the building, but the animals, although agitated, were not fighting. As they stood in the barn, a gigantic blast, followed by another, thundered. They ran for cover as the pounding continued.

Germany was attacking its Russian allies. The Germans pushed the Russians back and took over Eastern Poland. Sylwester's life changed forever.

Sylwester Drzewiecki - 16 years old
Sylwester is Taken to Germany

In June of 1942 the Germans came to Rudnia to take one member from each family to work in the forced labour camps in Germany. They wanted the father or the eldest son, but a daughter was taken if no male was available. Children had to be at least fifteen years old. The families had to choose who would go, and be ready when the German soldiers returned to collect their workers. The dilemma of who must go to Germany agonized the Drzewiecki household. It could easily be a death

sentence for anyone who went. Sylwester would not let his father go. Jan was ailing, and Sylwester believed the ordeal would kill him. His older brother Marian was eighteen and much bigger, but Marian was needed to work on the farm and help his father. Seven children were still at home, five of them under the age of twelve. His 29 year old step-mother, Aniela, could not manage the farm and take care of all the children without Jan and Marian.

Sacrificing himself for his family, sixteen-year-old Sylwester volunteered to go to Germany. The family could fend without him, and he believed he could fend for himself. It was a tragic but realistic choice.

Jan embraced his son and they both cried. Tears streamed down their cheeks. Jan gave Sylwester advice that hopefully would help him wherever his journey lead. "Bądź cicho i rób to co Ci każą. Bądź sprawiedliwy i dumny z tego że jesteś gospodarzem. Dadzą Ci pracę na gospodarce i dostaniesz dosyć jedzenia. Jak potrzebują ochotnika to idź i będziesz za to wynagrodzony....Be quiet and do as they tell you. Be honest and proud to say you are a farmer. You will be placed on a farm and have enough to eat. If they need a volunteer, go and you will be rewarded." Jan gave his counsel as a parting gift; it was all he had to give. A fretful night preceded the dreaded day.

One armed German soldier accompanied by a Ukrainian militiaman, entered the Drzewiecki household to get Sylwester, while a wagonload of local slave labour waited outside the house. He hugged his family, and everyone wept. He took bread, the clothes he was wearing, and nothing else; he had nothing else. He was wearing the old shoes he had traded for his rubber ones the year before. The family helplessly watched and grieved, as Sylwester climbed into the wagon with the other villagers. As the horses slowly pulled the wagon along the dirt road, Sylwester waved his hand high in the air until he was out of sight.

They were taken to the school house in Rudnia, to wait until all the workers had been assembled. En route Sylwester saw his first true love, Jadzia Czajkowska, in the distance. It was her wedding day. She was walking with the groom and the wedding guests to the church. She was only sixteen and her parents had arranged the marriage with a thirty year old man from another village. She looked neither happy nor in love.

Sylwester's heart went out to her. Sylwester and Jadzia were only ten years old when their love blossomed. She had knit him a beautiful pair of mittens that year, which he wore as he shoveled snow to make a path for her from her house to her well. Jadzia made pancakes for him on one of his visits, and Sylwester brought her a piece of fresh bread with butter on another visit; butter was a special treat. It was wonderful having Jadzia in his life. She was his sunshine and his best friend. He would go to her house in the evening and ask her to walk down to the river with him to listen to the frogs and the ducks. They would sit by the water listening to the chorus echoing all around them. One evening after walking Jadzia home from the river, Sylwester kissed her good night at her front door. He had a skip in his step and a song in his heart all the way home. How innocent their lives had been, and now Jadzia was getting married, and Sylwester was being taken to Germany. It added to his misery and the realization that things were changing forever.

When they arrived, Sylwester recognized some of the others. There were a few adult men, but most were boys and girls his age. They had a common bond of fear and helplessness. He saw his school friend, Stefan Słodkowski, and they immediately hugged each other. The two boys stayed together. Everyone was crammed into the tiny school until the quota of one person per household was delivered.

Only one German soldier was in charge, the rest of the guards were Ukrainian and there were many of them. They menacingly displayed their clubs and guns. Anyone trying to escape would be beaten or shot. Some of the boys planned to run as soon as they got a chance. They were oblivious to the danger, and consumed with the thought of getting away.

Once all the prisoners had been collected, they were ordered back into the wagons for transport to the school in Kołki. There were six to a wagon, five prisoners and one driver. Sylwester and Stefan made sure they rode in the same cart. Families came running out of their homes as the wagons took their loved ones away. They stood by the roadside crying and waving. The entire village wept for its sons, daughters and husbands.

Sylwester's father and step-mother were standing by the road waiting for him. They were holding his little step-siblings. The prisoners were

permitted to say one last goodbye to their parents as the wagons moved passed their homes. Sylwester jumped off the cart and firmly embraced his father. Tears were in their eyes. "Synu, ja myślę że ja już cię nigdy nie zobaczę .... Son, I don't think I will ever see you again." Sorrowfully it was true, for Jan died the following year. Sylwester then hugged his step-mother. She gave him a loaf of bread, some sliced cheese, and told him to be careful. He was quickly back on the wagon waving goodbye, his bread and cheese carefully tucked inside his shirt. His desperate parents stood waving at the roadside until he disappeared.

Kostka lived a short distance down the road. When she heard the wagons coming she ran outside to get one last glimpse of her brother. She was crying. Little Roman and Piotr were holding hands, standing beside her at the edge of the road. Sylwester wasn't permitted to jump off for his sister and brothers, but he called to them and waved goodbye. They waved and stared at each other until they were out of sight. He closed his eyes to remember them all.

His long journey to Germany had begun. He had never been farther than the village market in Kołki, five kilometers away, in his entire life. He never saw his father, his step-mother, Marian, his three step-siblings, or Rudnia ever again.

———————

Three days later
From Kołki to Kiwerca, Poland

They stayed under armed guard in the Kołki schoolhouse for three days while more frightened boys and girls were delivered from nearby villages. They were not fed and they slept on the floor. Sylwester was so hungry but carefully rationed his cheese and bread which Aniela had given him. The timing of the next meal was unknown.

Once all the workers were rounded up from the surrounding villages, the farmers who had driven the horse-drawn wagons were ordered to return to the Kołki schoolhouse, and the workers were ordered to get on board. Sylwester and Stefan climbed into one wagon and sat down on the hard planks. They were being taken to the railroad station in Kiwerca for transport to Germany.

The German soldier who was in charge meant business. It was an all day journey to Kiwerca and he had to deliver his cargo to the train on time. He demanded obedience from everyone, and everyone obeyed. Sylwester knew to be quiet and to do as he was told, just as his father had told him. He and Stefan sat silently in the back of the wagon as it jostled its way to the train station.

The teams of horses had been pulling all morning. At noon the farmers stopped to feed and water their tired animals without asking permission. The German officer angrily marched over to the Ukrainian militiamen and demanded an explanation. His hands were flying as he bellowed in German, "Was ist los?! Wer gab Erlaubnis stehen zu bleiben?! .... What is going on?! Who gave you permission to stop?!"

The militiamen answered in Ukrainian, pointing at the horses, "Коні є змучені і треба їм дати пити .... The horses are tired and need to be watered and fed." The German soldier went wild. "Ich muss den Zug erwischen. Lass das füttern. Mach schnell! .... I've got to meet the train on time! Never mind feeding the horses! Get moving!" He took out his bull whip and furiously started whipping the Ukrainian guards and the farmers. Sylwester and Stefan were terrified as they watched him whip the men. The farmers scrambled and frantically took the food away

from the horses. The poor animals barely had time to wet their mouths before they were back at work. The two friends nudged closer together.

The convoy of wagons was approaching a forest. Some of the boys were desperate to flee, and disregarded their safety. When the forest drew nearer, they frantically jumped from the wagons and bolted for the trees. The armed Ukrainians immediately pursued them, hollering as they ran. The wagons never stopped moving during the dreadful scene. Sylwester and Stefan were paralyzed with fear, and wept as they heard shots being fired.

The guards returned but did not tell the prisoners anything about the boys. Sylwester never knew of their fate. He was terrified and wanted desperately to go home, but the wagon carried him towards Kiwerca and far away from his simple life in Rudnia, forever.

June 1942
From Kiwerca to Germany

Every sight and sound was new. They had left Kołki only that morning but it already felt like a lifetime ago. The train station in Kiwerca was swarming with armed German soldiers who controlled the hundreds of prisoners brought in from the surrounding areas, and kept their eyes open for anyone trying to escape. Rows of boxcars stood waiting with their doors wide open. Sylwester was overwhelmed by the sight of the massive train. He had never seen one before. The wooden wagons and the horses looked pathetically obsolete beside the black steel.

They were each given half a loaf of bread and herded directly into the boxcars. When there was room for no more, more were shoved in. They were packed like sardines. Thankfully the doors were left slightly open for ventilation, for they surely would have suffocated in the summer heat. The train left Kiwerca for Frankfurt Oder, Germany. Its destination was four days away, and Sylwester had half a loaf of bread to get him there.

Just before Warszawa - Warsaw the train stopped in the town of Rembertów. Heads peered out trying to see what was happening. Armed German guards were everywhere. The doors slid wide open and the guards hollered, "Desinfeckion und Dusche. Aus steigen. Eine Reie zum Desinfektion und Dusche...Disinfection and showers! Get out! Line up for disinfection and showers!" The prisoners obeyed. As Sylwester climbed down from the boxcar he noticed that the heel of his shoe was missing. It had fallen off somewhere along the way. He limped as he followed the others towards the big shower houses.

Men and women were separated. The men stripped together and filed in naked. No one had running water in Rudnia so Sylwester did not know what to expect. Bathing at home was a laborious and uncomfortable chore. The water had to be carried, heated on the stove, then poured into a small galvanized tub. His knees touched his chin when he sat in it. One tub of water was used for many people; he felt privileged if he was the first.

There were many shower heads in the shower house, to accommodate the mass numbers. Sylwester liked the feel of his first shower as the warm water pelted down his back and the soap washed away the dirt. It was the only good thing about this horrible nightmare.

The Germans checked for head lice. Those who were lice-free had an 'X' marked on their forehead. No 'X' meant the person had lice and needed a buzz shave. Sylwester understood it in reverse. He and the fellow next to him were marked with an 'X'. He figured they were going to be shaved. It was taking a long time to shear so many heads. The Germans asked for volunteers to help and Sylwester stepped forward. He and the boy standing beside him agreed they would shave each other. Sylwester took a pair of clippers and cropped off his neighbor's hair. He was about to have his turn when a German guard hurried over saying, "Nein, nein, nein! .... No, no, no!" He made the boys understand that an 'X' meant not to cut. Sylwester still had his hair, but his poor neighbor was bald.

They stood naked in line waiting for disinfection. The Germans held puffers filled with a white powder, and liberally doused the prisoners from head to toe. Sylwester did not know what the disinfectant was.

Breathing in the fine dust was unavoidable, for it flew everywhere. The guards liberally used the disinfectant on themselves as well. Everyone had to turn over their shoes and were given wooden ones. They were each issued one blanket. They dressed in their same clothes and were pushed back into the boxcars, crammed again like sardines.

The train finally came to a halt in Frankfurt Oder, Germany, amidst squeals and billowing steam. They were ordered out of the cars and Sylwester, a naive sixteen-year-old farm boy from Rudnia, stepped into a foreign world.

The massive job of sorting the prisoners and placing them according to their abilities began as soon as they disembarked. Skilled tradesmen, professionals, and manual labourers were all needed in the many factories and mills supporting Germany's war operations. Some of the prisoners lied hoping that they would be sent somewhere where they could perhaps learn a trade or have a little more to eat. "Какая ваша робота? .... What is your occupation?", the interpreter asked the boy just ahead of Sylwester. The interpreter spoke Russian, not Polish. "Я пекарь .... I'm a baker," he replied in Russian. He was no more a baker than Sylwester.

Jan Drzewiecki did not know farmers were sentenced to backbreaking work with a pick and shovel, when he told his son to be proud to say he was a farmer. Sylwester knew a little blacksmithing and barbering, but heeded his father's advice. When it was his turn to answer he replied, "Я роботал на ферме .... I worked on a farm." Sylwester regretted that moment of naive honesty for the next three years as he slaved and starved in Germany's forced labour camps.

Part 1 - Epilogue

Epilogue:

Sylwester did not return to Poland until May 1979, 37 years later. The trip was his first flight, and I was pleased to accompany my father on this momentous occasion. As the plane landed in Frankfurt, Germany he said to me in English, "The last time I was here I was a prisoner. I was sixteen years old."

Watching the reunion of the brothers and sisters was heartwarming. There were many tears, and much reminiscing during our five week stay. My father learned, as he mellowed into adulthood, that the power of love and forgiveness are greater than the power of force. He tried to understand the injustices and the violence he suffered as a child. His generous heart let go of his hurtful beginnings, and he found peace in forgiveness. He invited his siblings to visit him in Canada. Roman and his daughter visited in 1980, and Piotr and his wife in 1981. Sadly, Kostka and Bolka passed away before their opportunity arose.

A Joyous Family Reunion, Poland 1979
Above: Bolka, Sylwester, Kostka
Below: Sylwester, Roman, Piotr

Neither distance nor time, can separate
what the heart has truly joined.
Mary Drzewiecki, 1994

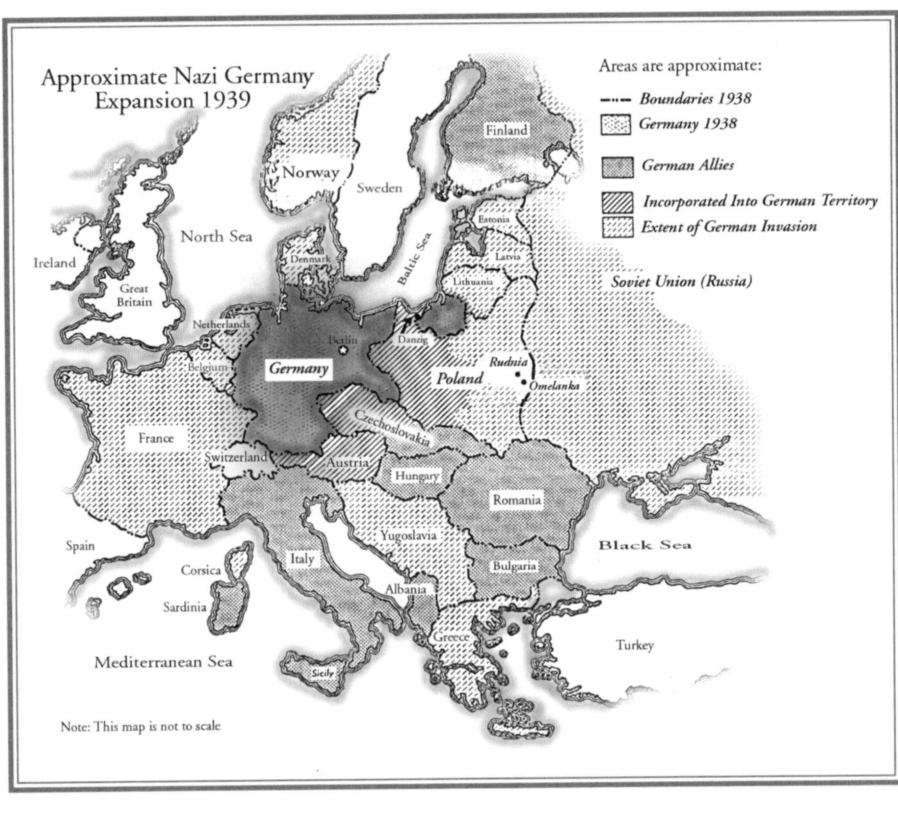

Approximate Nazi Germany
Expansion 1939
Areas are approximate:
Boundaries 1938
Germany 1938
German Allies
Incorporated Into German Territory
Extent of German Invasion
Soviet Union (Russia)
Finland
Norway
Sweden
Estonia
Latvia
Lithuania
North Sea
Ireland
Denmark
Great
Britain
Netherlands
Berlin
Danzig
Rudnia
Belgium
Germany
Poland
Omelanka
Czechoslovakia
France
Switzerland
Austria
Hungary
Romania
Italy
Yugoslavia
Black Sea
Spain
Corsica
Bulgaria
Sardinia
Albania
Greece
Turkey
Mediterranean Sea
Sicily
Baltic Sea
Note: This map is not to scale

Part 2

The German Forced Labour Camps
Germany 1942 - 1945

Sylwester Drzewiecki
Mój Ojciec - My Father

Waste not your sorrows,
For from hardships
Come your greatest strengths.

-Mary Drzewiecki, 2000

Part 2

German Forced Labour Camps
Germany 1942 - 1945

Introduction:

Sylwester entered the German labour camps an innocent, naive 16 year old boy, and emerged a cunning, shrewd 19 year old man. His quick wit and agility saved his life many times. He lied when he had to, and pilfered whatever he could. The training of his harsh childhood, and his faith in God, helped him endure the grueling years he spent in the German slave camps from 1942 to 1945.

There were thousands of men in the camps. The Polish prisoners from Eastern Poland were classified as Russian. Sylwester was given Russian identification papers. He wore the German word OST - East on his shirt, identifying him as Russian. He was stationed in Russian work camps, called Russisches Arbeits Lager, and worked with Russian prisoners. His Polish identity was taken from him, and although he became friends with his Russian comrades, he hated wearing the OST badge. The Russians were good men and considered Sylwester one of their own. They called him Slavka. As the years passed, Slavka seldom had the opportunity to speak Polish. He learned to speak the Russian language as fluently as his own. He learned many Russian songs from the men. They sang as they worked which lightened their depression. Each morning and night Sylwester prayed, just as his parents had taught him. The Russians with whom he worked were atheists and teased him about his senseless praying, but the day they were all trapped in a cellar, facing death during a bombing attack, the Russians prayed too.

The camp commandant, guards, and work foremen were all German. Sylwester became fluent in German as well. The men worked seven days a week with a half day rest on Sunday. Their shifts were twelve hours long, either 6 a.m. to 6 p.m., or 6 p.m. to 6 a.m. Even though

Sunday was a half day, they still worked six hard hours. They had a one hour break for lunch, but sometimes there was nothing for the men to eat. On those days their lunch and dinner portions were served together when they returned to camp. They were rationed three bowls of soup and one piece of bread per day. The soup was mostly broth with a little cabbage and potato in it. Sylwester was literally starving.

The prisoners salvaged anything they could from around the camps and the work sites. String, pieces of wood, rags, and buttons were valuable. Absolutely nothing was wasted. Sylwester would hide things in his shirt or in his baggy pants. He tied the bottom of his pant legs to keep things from falling out. He would stash his treasures in his locker or under his mattress. The most valuable possession of all were stolen potatoes. Without them Sylwester would surely have died from starvation long before the end of the war.

Sylwester worked in three different Russisches Arbeits Lager - Russian Work Camps, in Germany:

Camp #1:   Küstrin Neue Stadt, Germany
            June 1942 to January 1943
            Labourer in a large Pulp Mill

The first camp, in Küstrin Neue Stadt, was surrounded by a barbed wire fence. The men had to walk a long distance through the city to reach the pulp mill. No one could leave the camp without a guard.

Camp #2:   Brandenburg Havel, Germany
            January 1943 to April 1944
            Labourer in a Steel Plant

The second camp, in Brandenburg Havel, was also surrounded by barbed wire. Many camps housing thousands of men from different countries were side-by-side. Each camp had a different colored pass. The steel plant was a short distance away and the men could leave the camp on their own, but they had to show their pass at the gate.

Camp # 3:   Meseritz, Germany
April 1944 to December 1944
Building a tunnel built for German military operations.

The third camp, in Meseritz, was not surrounded by a barbed wire fence. Trees skirted the perimeter. There was a German military rest camp next to Sylwester's compound that was surrounded by a barbed wire fence. The military would allow its soldiers to rest a few days in that camp, before going to the Russian front.

Sylwester was moved to the following cities after Camp #3:

Dec. 1944   Meseritz to Andernach to Berlin
Dec. 1944   Berlin to Mainz
Jan. 1945   Mainz to Düsseldorf
1945   Düsseldorf to Bielefeld to Bad Oeynhausen
Apr. 1945   Bad Oeynhausen - Liberation

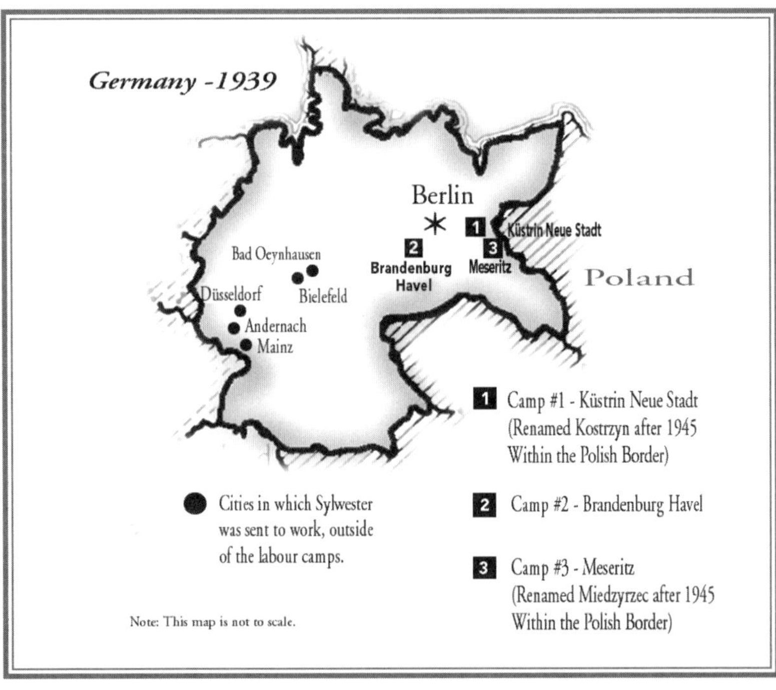

Part 2 - Chapter 1

Camp #1
Küstrin Neue Stadt, Germany
June 1942 - January 1943

Work Assignment: Pulp Mill and Railroad Work
Sylwester Drzewiecki - 16 years old

Sylwester's first months at Küstrin Neue Stadt were hell. He was only 16 years old and dreadfully homesick. He had never been away from his home or his family, and he had never been so hungry. It seemed that he cried non-stop for the first six months. He worked twelve hour shifts on one piece of bread and three bowls of watery soup. He rapidly lost weight and could see every bone in his rib cage.

Sylwester's naivete and open honesty almost cost him his life in Küstrin Neue Stadt. His farm-boy innocence resulted in getting himself and his Russian co-workers into serious trouble. The threat of being sent to Auschwitz, a notorious Nazi extermination camp, hung over all their heads because of his novice truthfulness. They were all jailed and whipped because of him. His Russian comrades wanted to kill him. An older Polish prisoner in his barrack, Józef Dubitski, protected Sylwester from the others in those first months. His first German foreman was a Volksdeutsche - a Pole of German parentage, who also took him under his wing. Sylwester became a survivor and learned not to trust. He learned to lie and to steal. There was no place for an innocent in camp.

The men had to walk a long distance through the city to reach the pulp mill where they worked. No one could leave the camp without a guard. When they left the mill to return to the camp, they had to be counted by the guard at the gate. They lined up in threes and the guard quickly counted in German drei, sechs, neun....three, six, nine, and so on. If one man was missing the entire group had to stand and wait at the gate until the missing man was found. This happened many times in Küstrin

Neue Stadt. The missing worker was usually found sleeping somewhere. The workers were exhausted and hungry after their twelve hour shift. Sometimes they had to stand and wait at the gate for an hour or more. Camp life was brutal.

Sylwester and Stefan Słodkowski worked side-by-side in the same work crew the whole time they were in Küstrin Neue Stadt.

June 1942
The First Day

Wagon loads of wood were brought by train, and the prisoners were ordered to unload and stack the wood in the Holzplatz - wood place. Sylwester and Stefan wanted to make a good impression by showing that they were hard workers. They quickly threw the wood from their wagon and stacked it. The other men had been working before Sylwester and Stefan had arrived, but the youngsters worked hard and fast and were done before anyone else. They sat down in their empty wagon, feeling proud of doing a good job, and waited for the others to finish. What the two new recruits didn't realize was that the other men were making an easy job last.

Sylwester and Stefan were sure they would be praised for their hard work, but the opposite happened. When the foreman saw the two boys relaxing, he furiously got after them. They tried to explain in Polish what they had accomplished, but the foreman paid no attention. He angrily hit them and shooed them like dogs to help the others. They immediately set to work.

An important lesson was learned that day. They would never again work harder than necessary, and they would prolong the easier jobs. Sylwester lived by that rule for the next three years.

1942 - A few weeks later
The Russian Prisoner and the Bowl of Soup

Sylwester and the Russians with whom he worked, were installing a turbine for an electric generator in the pulp mill. It was an ominous task, for the turbine was awkward and massively heavy. The twelve men took turns, with six men at a time hoisting up the huge load.

At the noon lunch break the German foreman told them they could not all go at once and leave the turbine hanging. They would have to go in two shifts. Sylwester had learned that sometimes there was a little soup left over at the end of lunch. "Jak pójdę później to dostanę repetę .... If I eat on the second serving, I might get some extra soup," he thought. He volunteered to keep working and eat later.

Just as he had hoped, there was some soup left over, and all six of them had an extra portion. The six workers were seated at the table in the canteen, finishing their soup when a Russian prisoner-of-war ran up to the open window and called, "Товарищи могу ли я иметь суп если что-то осталось? .... Friends may I have a bowl of soup if some is left over?" Sylwester's heart went out to the starving man. He turned to the others and asked, "Могу ли я дать ему суп? .... Is it okay to give him some soup?" The more experienced workers knew that no one was to give any Russian prisoner-of-war food. Prisoners-of-war, P.O.W.s, were captured soldiers. Workers like themselves were not classified in the same way. Even though they knew better, they all agreed.

Sylwester stuck his head through the window and passed him a bowl. As the prisoner ravenously gulped the soup, a sadistic foreman came running around the corner. He was after the Russian and Sylwester knew this meant trouble. Sylwester quickly side-stepped and flattened his back against the wall. The foreman's ruthless beatings, especially of the Jewish prisoners, were well known. The Russian P.O.W. could see what was about to happen, but he desperately kept drinking as the foreman began beating him. The P.O.W. put the empty bowl back on the window ledge and ran. Why he didn't just throw it down, Sylwester would never know.

Sylwester was afraid. He knew he would be beaten if he was recognized. The foreman stuck his head through the window and only saw

the five men seated at the table. He did not see Sylwester against the wall. He was fuming and quickly ran around the building to get inside. Sylwester had to flee. He dashed to the table, grabbed his hat, and headed for the door, but came to an abrupt halt in the doorway. He was face to face with the furious foreman.

He carefully studied Sylwester's face, but did not recognize him and let him go. Sylwester did not dare run until he was safely around the corner. While he was walking away he heard the German confront the older Russian who sat closest to the doorway. He demanded in German, "Warum hast du dem Gefangenen die Suppe gegeben? Er ist nicht erlaubt! .... Why did you give soup to the prisoner? He's not allowed to have any!" The Russian did not understand German but understood the accusation. He defended himself saying, "Это был не я. Это был мальчик который проходил через дверь. Ты его видел .... It was not me. It was the boy that just went through the door. You met him." The German did not understand Russian. The Russian kept trying to explain that it was not him, but the sadist slapped his face left and right, again and again. Sylwester ran, terrified.

Sylwester needed protection and went to his foreman, who spoke Polish and German, and watched over him. The foreman knew he was just a scared sixteen-year-old boy. Sylwester said, "Ja jestem w kłopocie. Ja jestem w dużym kłopocie .... I am in trouble. I am in big trouble."

"A co ty robiłeś? .... What did you do?", he asked in Polish.

"Ja dałem miskę zupy dla Ruskiego więźnia .... I gave a bowl of soup to a Russian prisoner-of-war."

The foreman then spoke sharply in German, "Schnell, gehe zur Arbeit! Zie! .... Fast, go to work! Pull!" He knew Sylwester was in trouble. Sylwester started pulling the chains. If the sadist didn't get him, for sure the Russian would. The Russian had been working side-by-side with Sylwester, and they would be working side-by-side when he returned. He figured he was lost no matter what.

The Russian worker furiously marched towards Sylwester. All five

men had told him to give the soup, yet Sylwester was blamed. Shaking his fist he shouted, "Я перережу тебе горло. Я тебя убью! .... I'll cut your throat! I'll kill you!" Sylwester was terrified. He had no doubt the man meant it, and the foreman had no doubt he meant it either. The foreman grabbed the Russian worker and set him to work on the other side of the turbine. The men pulled for another hour. Glares of hatred stabbed across at Sylwester.

Once the turbine was in place the foreman took the men to work in the fields. He placed the angry Russian a good distance away from Sylwester, and kept Sylwester close to him. The sadist arrived, marched up to Sylwester's foreman and pointed his finger at the accused Russian. "Der Mann gab dem Gefangenen Suppe das ist nicht erlaubt! .... That man gave soup to a Russian prisoner-of-war and that's not allowed!" He wanted the Russian to be turned over to him for punishment. Sylwester's foreman was not about to turn anyone over to this evil man. He simply replied, "Ich weiss. Ein Mann hat mir schon darüber berichted .... I already know. One of the men told me what happened." The accused Russian wasn't about to get another beating because of Sylwester. He walked up to the two foremen and pointed at Sylwester, saying in Russian that he was the one who gave the soup away.

Sylwester's foreman protected all of his men and kept everyone working where they were. Disgruntled, the sadist left empty handed. The rest of the day the foreman continued to place the angry Russian well away from Sylwester, and kept a careful watch over him. Sylwester had learned not to share anything with prisoners-of-war.

June 1942 - One week later
The Ripped Fingernail

Sylwester's group was sent to remove a pile of huge boulders off to the side of a road near the pulp mill. The labour was long and tedious. He was pushing a boulder with all his might when a second boulder smashed into his hand. It split his fingernail down the middle. The pain was excruciating.

Cupping his bloody hand, the foreman lead him to the First Aid station. Two German First Aid attendants were on duty. Sylwester's hand was throbbing. It was agony at the slightest touch. The First Aid attendants quickly examined the nail and picked up a pair of small pliers. One of the attendants clamped the split nail with the pliers and yanked. The pain seared through him and he automatically pulled away. The heartless attendant slapped Sylwester across the face, roughly grabbed his finger, and violently yanked out the nail. He cried in pain. He taped on a bandage and shouted, "Raus! Zurück zur Arbeit! .... Out! Get to work!" He kicked Sylwester out the door.

Sylwester wiped the tears from his face as he walked back to work. With his finger throbbing, and his heart aching, he continued moving boulders. This was an awful place.

Mid-August 1942 - Two Months After Arrival
The Rubber Pipe

Sylwester and seven Russian men were again working at the Holzplatz near the Oder River. The wood was brought in by barge to the edge of the canal. Wagons from the small train were hoisted onto the barge one at a time, and workers on board loaded wood into them. The wagons were set back on the train track when they were full, and a small locomotive pulled them up to the Holzplatz where Sylwester and the others unloaded and stacked the wood.

As they worked, the Russians spotted a rubber connecting pipe. The Germans transported tons of sand by barge via the Oder River. The

sand was pumped through pipes with water, and spewn over a large area to make the land level. The big pipes were connected with smaller rubber connectors. The rubber pipe they found was about three feet long and one foot wide. The men felt the quarter inch rubber and found it was flexible. It would be perfect for the soles of their wooden shoes.

They did not waste any time. One of the men had a knife, and cut the pipe into pieces. Some fastened their piece of rubber securely to their waist by cinching the draw string that held up their pants. Others tucked it inside their shirt and carried it under their arm. The older more experienced workers neglected to tell their newest and youngest recruit, Sylwester, to keep it a secret.

They carried the rubber back to their barracks and hid the pieces under their mattresses. When it was dark, the older men buried their rubber in the sand under their barrack. Sylwester did not know, and left his where it was. A week or so later, a worker experienced in shoemaking nailed the rubber to the soles of their wooden shoes. There was still some rubber left. The Russians hid their remaining pieces back in the sand, but Sylwester tucked his under his mattress.

The Germans again transported a huge pile of sand by barge. When they were connecting the pipes, they discovered one of the rubber connectors was missing. They knew a Russian crew had been assigned to work in that area of the Holzplatz, and immediately guessed where their pipe had disappeared.

After supper the Germans searched room to room and questioned those who had worked at the Holzplatz. They took each man aside and asked, "Hast Du dort gearbeited? Hast du ein Rohr dort gesehen? .... Did you work over there? Did you see a pipe?" Each man answered, "Nein...No."

Sylwester had the end room in the barrack and was questioned last. The Germans had a Polish interpreter with them. They asked, "Czy Ty wydziałeś rure? .... Did you see the pipe?" He had only been in the camp two months and naively answered, "Tak .... Yes."

"Co się stalo z rurkom? .... What happened to the pipe?"

"My utnielym .... We cut it."

"Czy Ty masz kawalek? .... Have you got a piece?"

"Tak .... Yes."

"Gdzie Ty masz? .... Where do you have it?"

"Tu, pod matracem .... Here, underneath the mattress." Sylwester showed them what was left of the rubber pipe and gave it to them. "I kto był stobo? .... And who was with you?" Sylwester gave the names of every man who was with him. He did not realize that he had betrayed everyone.

The Germans had already questioned the other men, and had searched their rooms. They went back and demanded the return of the rest of the rubber or they would be severely punished. "Wir wissen ihr habt es .... We know you took it." The men had no option but to dig their pieces of rubber out of the sand and return them to the Germans. The workers knew it had to have been Sylwester who betrayed them for he was the last one to be questioned.

That night the Germans left them alone, however, the Russians threatened to cut Sylwester's throat. Sylwester was fearful of the others and cried. One of the workers was an older Pole from the town of Łuck, not far from Kołki. His name was Józef Dubitski and he bunked in the same room as Sylwester. Dubitski was a kind man and he took it upon himself to protect Sylwester from the others. He knew how to box, and how to defend himself and the boy. The workers weren't allowed to go from room to room in the barrack after supper, but Sylwester still did not feel safe, even with Dubitski protecting him, he could not sleep.

The following morning the Germans rousted the men for their twelve hour shift that started at 6 a.m. They lined up for breakfast, drank their soup, and then lined up for work. Nothing was different. The eight men were ready to be lead to the pulp mill by two German guards, when a policeman from the city of Küstrin rode into the camp on his bicycle. He walked up to the line and pointed to the men who had stolen the pipe, "Du und Du und Du und Du, rauss! .... You and you and you and you, out!" All eight men stepped aside.

They were locked in the camp prison in one tiny room until 9 a.m. Everyone, especially the Russian named Husiew, was enraged. They were there because of Sylwester, and threatened to kill him. He was terrified. The Russians were full grown men, and he was a scrawny sixteen-year-old boy. Józef Dubitski grabbed Sylwester. He had no doubt the men would hurt him. He shoved Sylwester against the wall and braced himself in front of him. Dubitski's hands were on his hips and his elbows were fanned out to cover Sylwester's body. He turned on the angry mob, "Mieliście dziecko z wamy. Dla czego nie kopneliś cie dziecko w dupe zie by nie wydzial co wy robicie? Dziecko jest dzieckiem i nic nie muwiliście zie by był ćicho! On nie wiedźial! .... You had a child with you. Why didn't you give the child a boot in the ass so he didn't see what you were doing? A child is a child and you didn't tell him to keep quiet! He didn't know!" Dubitski did not let down his guard and Sylwester didn't dare leave his side.

The city policeman returned from the commandant's office. He took the eight men outside and lined them up. The policeman mounted his bike and lead the men to the city prison in Küstrin. He looked down at their feet and said, "Soo, Ihr habt den Gummi schon auf eueren Schuhen .... So, you already have the rubber on your shoes."

The men had to empty their pockets and hand over their belt strings, sharp buttons, and anything else. They were locked in one cell for three days and were given a jug of water and one slice of bread each per day. Everyone drank from the same jug. They had no cups. There was one chamber pot in the cell.

Dubitski watched Sylwester like a hawk. He put Sylwester in his bunk, placed him against the wall, and laid down in front of him. The men had to get past Dubitski to get to Sylwester. Husiew threatened Sylwester while he hid, "Попробуй пёрднуть и увидешь что случится. Я сижу здесь через твой длинный язык, а ты пойдёшь туда и будешь загрязнять воздух для меня. Попробуй .... You just try to fart and see what will happen. I'm sitting over here because of your big mouth and you're going to go over there and pollute the air for me. Just try it." Sylwester didn't dare pass gas.

When he used the chamber pot he only urinated.

Husiew had already been in the Küstrin jail for three days on a different offense. He told everyone in Russian, "Через три дня если они отдадут наши вещи, мы пойдём назад в наш лагерь. Если они не отдадут наши вещи мы пойдём в Авшвиц .... In three days if they give us back our belongings, we will return to our camp. If they keep everything, we are going to Auschwitz."

Sylwester was so afraid, and thought of home. It was mid-August. In Rudnia that very day, it was a religious celebration for the Holy Virgin Mary, called Matky Bosky Szkapleźnej. People from other parishes travelled to the church in Kołki to worship. Sylwester thought of everyone going to church on this holy day as he sat in jail, with a hateful mob, and the threat of going to Auschwitz. He was homesick and he was scared.

Two days later they were infested with lice. The itching was enough to drive Sylwester crazy. He put his hand in his collar and pulled out all sizes of lice: big ones, small ones, fat ones. He threw them on the floor and stomped on them. It seemed that there were thousands of the wretched things. On the third day, the men and their lice were rousted from the cell and stood in the hallway that lead to the office of the chief of police. Sylwester was first in line. Husiew was second.

As the German guards opened the door, Sylwester saw their belongings heaped on a table. He was relieved knowing they would not be sent to Auschwitz. He started passing the word down the line, "Наши вещи на столе. Мы идём назад в наш лагерь .... Our belongings are on the table. We are going back to our camp." Sylwester was ushered in alone and the door was closed.

The chief of police was sitting behind his desk. A huge, bald man came into the office from an adjoining room. He wore a short sleeved T-shirt which stretched tightly across his chest and biceps. He was so massive, he looked like a weight-lifter. He said in German, "Komm her .... Come here." Sylwester thought he was to gather his belongings and leave. He said to the chief of police, "Das ist mein Hut .... This is my hat."

He replied, "Nein, nein, nein. Folge diesen Mann .... No, no, no. You go with that man." He motioned him towards the doorway that lead to the other room. The bald man took him inside and closed the door. Sylwester looked around. He had no idea what was going to happen. There was an odd looking bed in the room. It was a whipping bed, but Sylwester did not know. The prisoner was to bend over the bed with his buttocks protruding, his ankles would be secured to the floor and his arms to the sides of the bed.

The bald man held a whip in his hand and said, " Lege Dich hin .... Lie down", and then started laughing. Sylwester thought the man was joking when he laughed, so he did not lie down. He started smiling and laughing too.

The bald man cracked his whip on Sylwester. It felt like a knife cutting him in two. Sylwester quickly laid down on the whipping bed. His legs and arms were not secured. "Und eins...And one"...SNAP! "Und zwei...And two"...CRACK! "Und drei...And three"...SNAP! The whip hit his back, his buttocks, wherever. There was no meat on him and the whips felt like razors slicing him. The burning pain was excruciating. He couldn't hang on much longer without being strapped down. "Und Vier...And four"...SNAP! Sylwester thought the fourth one would do him in. He was crying and wanted to run. CRACK!..."Und fünf...And Five!" It was over. Sylwester got five lashes, plus the extra one for not lying down right away. He left the whipping room crying, and stood in front of the chief of police. The chief smiled and mockingly said, "War das gut? .... Was that good?"

Sylwester was gone a long time. The rest of the men were waiting for him to come out so they would know what to expect. When Sylwester entered the hallway, they all could see he was crying. They started asking, "Что случилось ? Что они сделали с тобой ? .... What happened? What did they do to you?" Husiew, the biggest bully, was next in line and desperately wanted to know what they had done to Sylwester. He asked, "Они били тебя? .... Did they beat you?" There was no time to tell him. He was already being called into the chief's office. Sylwester replied, "Ты увидеш .... You'll find out." He told the rest of the men that

he had been whipped. He was glad he had been first. He thought the rest of the men had it worse knowing what was awaiting them.

The men were lead back to the camp. Dubitski still kept a protective eye on Sylwester but the whipping had cooled down the group. They left Sylwester alone. He had learned a valuable lesson in survival. He would never again be so honest as to put others in danger. Stealing was part of survival in the camps, and he vowed if he ever was caught breaking the rules again, he would never divulge names. He would suffer alone.

September 1942 - One Month Later
Locomotive Off The Track

It was the night shift at the Holzplatz, when the small locomotive that hauled the wagon loads of wood up from the barge had derailed. The men had to set it back on its track. They found a long beam to act as a lever, and shoved one end under the engine. They lined up on either side of the beam and held on. Sylwester was squeezed out of the sidelines and took the place at the far end of the beam. He was looking straight down at the train with his chin resting on the end of the board, and his hands holding both sides.

It took several attempts to set the engine back on its tracks. "Один два три .... One....Two....Three." They pushed down with all their might, and as soon as it was set back, quickly let go. WHACK! The beam hit Sylwester square under the jaw. His neck snapped back and he went flying. He was out cold.

Sylwester awoke in the dark, on a bed of sand. He looked up and saw a bright light overhead and a circle of heads staring down at him. He was disoriented and did not know where he was and what had happened. He thought, "Dla czego ja to usnoł? .... Why did I go to sleep over here?" He began to cry. He was very fortunate that he did not break his neck or sever his spinal cord. He could easily have been killed or become a quad-

riplegic. The foreman let Sylwester rest, but he couldn't leave the Holzplatz. His head pounded, and his jaw and neck ached. He wanted to lay down in his bunk and go to sleep. Instead he sat on a pile of wood waiting for the night shift to end.

When they returned to camp, the foreman notified the camp commandant that Sylwester had been hit unconscious at the Holzplatz. Explanations were given, papers were filled, and the commandant excused Sylwester from work for three days.

During his convalescence, a school mate from Rudnia, Antek Markowski, was working on the wharf near the barge. A few days earlier Antek had been violently kicked in his testicles by his camp commandant. His testicles were immensely swollen and the boy was in agony, but he still had to work. His movement was greatly impeded by his injury. Tragically, Antek fell into the river, was unable to swim, and drowned. Sylwester wept and wept when he heard the news. Men were needed to dig his grave. The camp commandant asked Sylwester and two Russians, who were also recuperating in the camp, to take on the job. Sylwester had never dug a grave, and the thought of digging a grave for his friend was too much for him to bear. He was afraid to go to the cemetery. He could not bring himself to do it and stayed behind. While the two Russians dug Antek's grave and buried him, Sylwester prayed and cried for his friend. He wrote a letter to the boy's family. *It is unknown if the Markowski family received Sylwester's letter.*

Sylwester was wretched and wanted to go home. He was abused and hungry. His body ached. His school mate was dead. Each day felt like one month; and each year would feel like ten.

Four days after the accident, and being knocked unconscious, Sylwester returned to the Holzplatz for another twelve hour shift.

October 1942 - One Month Later
Hiding in the Outhouse

A new German foreman was assigned. The first foreman had been compassionate, and had taken Sylwester under his wing. The new man was the absolute opposite. He was rude, drove the men relentlessly, and didn't allow them to rest. Sylwester was tired and needed a break, but the foreman drove the men on, so he asked permission to use the washroom. He headed for the outhouse, and could hardly wait to relax. He sat and sat and lost track of time. He wanted to sleep. The foreman wondered what was taking Sylwester so long, and went looking for him. Sylwester jumped when the door flung open. The man was furious to find Sylwester resting. He grabbed him, kicked him, and shoved him out the door. He would make Sylwester pay for this. The foreman phoned the camp commandant.

The men dragged themselves back to camp after their twelve hour shift, tired and hungry. Sylwester could hardly wait to eat. He lined up with the others for his bowl of soup, as the line trudged forward. He held out his bowl. "Raus! Kein Essen für dich! .... Out! No food for you!" Tears stung his eyes as he left the line. He was desperate. He had to eat. Sylwester knew there was a pile of potatoes beside the soup barrack. He had stolen some from there before. He glanced over at the heap and his mouth watered. It was night and the potatoes were hidden in the night shadows. His barrack was only twenty feet away.

He ran to his room and grabbed a small sack that he had salvaged and had hidden away. He quickly skirted the outer perimeter of the camp along the barbed wire fence, stopping and hiding in the shadows before sneaking off again. He reached the soup barrack and hugged his body against the wall. His heart was pounding. He was only a few feet away from the staff and the workers. He could not let anyone see him, not even the workers, for they would swipe the potatoes from him. Sylwester had to be quick and quiet. Bending over the potato heap, he held the bottom corners of his sack with his feet, and the opening with his teeth. He rapidly scooped potatoes into the bag. Whoosh! Whoosh! Whoosh! The sack was full in a matter of seconds. He hugged his precious potatoes, and swiftly ran back the way he had come.

In his barrack, he took out one potato and hid the rest in his locker. He could have eaten the whole sack but there was still tomorrow, and another day after that. Dismal and alone Sylwester sat with his potato and cried. He wanted his bowl of soup. Tears ran down his face as he ate his raw potato.

There was a small heater in Sylwester's room. Near the end of the following work day, he collected wood scraps. He tied the ankles of his baggy pants and carried bits of wood back to camp. After his evening soup, he lit a small fire, sliced one of his stolen potatoes and having no pan, placed the pieces directly on the metal. He was famished. He watched as they slowly cooked, but he could not wait. He devoured them raw.

Some Time Later
The 'Flush Toilet'

Rumor spread that there was an indoor toilet in the mill that flushed everything away with the flick of a lever. Sylwester had only seen and used outhouses. Who would ever have thought to put a toilet inside a building? This was something he had to see.

No worker was permitted to walk alone in the plant, but Sylwester's curiosity to see the toilet compelled him. He wanted to see it flush. When he found it, he was impressed. It was made of white porcelain, had a comfortable seat, a bowl full of clean water, and a shiny lever. He was amazed that it was without unpleasant odor. He was about to press the lever, when a guard spotted him and spoiled his fun. He grabbed Sylwester, and kicked him out the door. Rubbing his sore behind, he returned to work.

It was quite some time before Sylwester saw another flush toilet, and actually flushed it. It was quite remarkable, but like all things the novelty soon wore off. When you've seen one flush you've seen them all.

December 1942 - Two months later
Trapped on Barbed Wire

It was now winter. Days were short and nights were long. Temperatures plummeted. Sylwester was working the night shift, trying to keep warm and trying not to think about his stomach. He was cold and hungry, and it made the twelve hour shifts seem even longer. Wagon load after wagon load of wood were relentlessly hauled to the Holzplatz by train.

Beside the Holzplatz was a compound for Russian prisoners-of-war. It was surrounded by a double row of high barbed-wire fence. Sylwester had seen heaps of potatoes covered by straw and sand, on the other side of that fence, and couldn't stop thinking about them. His small stockpile of stolen potatoes was nearly gone and he needed more.

He would perish on the soup rations alone.

It would be terribly dangerous to try to dig his way into the compound, for these prisoners were captured enemy soldiers and were guarded by armed German military. Civilians, like himself, were overseen by German civilians. He would have to dig under the first and the second fences, run over to the potato pile, fill his sack, run back, crawl under the two fences and stash his loot. He was hungry enough to risk it.

The armed guards walked around the perimeter of the double fence all night, except during the changing of the guards. Sylwester had watched the changing of the guards take place many times. The new and the old guards would stand facing each other in front of a building on the far side of the compound. They were clearly visible from the Holzplatz for they stood under a lamp post. They would salute, exchange words, and the old guards would leave. They followed the same ritual, at the same time every night, and Sylwester knew exactly at what time. The changing of the guards took about three minutes. It was all the time he needed.

Sylwester needed accomplices to help him look out for the guards, and easily found them amongst the workers. The potatoes would be shared by the three of them, even though Sylwester was the one risking his life to get them. It was agreed the accomplices would stand watch on either end of the wood pile nearest the double fence. Sylwester had his sack tucked inside his shirt ready to run to the fence when the time was just right. The Holzplatz was covered with sand, and so was the ground under the two rows of barbed-wire fencing. Sylvester whipped over to the first fence and started digging the sand with his hands. He was fast. When the hole was just big enough he crawled on his belly and wriggled himself under. The guards were walking towards each other, going through their procedures. He scrambled to the second barbed-wire fence and did the same. He didn't have a moment to spare. His hands flung the dirt left and right. Again he went under on his belly. He hastily looked around and was off to the potato heap. Swiftly removing some of the straw and sand from the pile, he held the two bottom corners of his sack with his feet and the opening with his teeth, and quickly scooped in the potatoes.

Swoosh! Swoosh! Swoosh! The sack was full. The guards were still saluting and talking. Back to the fence he went. He pushed the potatoes under the first wire and then wriggled himself under. Another quick check and off he went to the second fence. The sack was through and Sylwester froze. A guard bringing a group of Jewish prisoners was approaching. They were walking beside the fence.

The Jews had finished their shift and were being lead back to their barracks. Sylwester dared not move. If he was spotted by the German guard he would be shot. They were walking so close to him, he could almost touch them. He was on his belly and his back was strained in a severe arch. He had to hold still. His discomfort soon turned to pain but he dared not move. Slowly the prisoners walked by him. Several of the Jews spotted Sylwester but said nothing. They never turned their heads, as they walked in silence.

They were gone. Sylwester had to get out, now. He had taken far too long. The changing of the guards was nearly complete, and the new guards would start patrolling the fence. He tried to move, but he was stuck. The back of his shirt was caught on the barbs! He couldn't get himself free.

He was in a serious predicament. He couldn't stay where he was, and to move would make noise and alert the guards. His two useless accomplices had left at the first sign of danger. Sylwester was desperate. He'd be dead if he stayed where he was. He might have a chance if he ran. He wriggled with all his might and ripped his shirt free. With a grunt he pushed the sack out of his way. The commotion alerted the guards. The search lights went on, and the guards started shouting and running. Sylwester grabbed his potatoes and ran. He hid in the wood piles while the guards scrambled and searched. He was afraid to even breathe.

Finding no one and no prisoners missing, the guards gave up. Sylwester was safe, and so were his potatoes. He stayed absolutely still until the coast was clear. He found his accomplices hiding in the wood piles and was furious. He could have been killed. They did not warn him that the guard and prisoners were approaching. They had abandoned him when he was stuck on the barbs of the fence. His accomplices didn't

deserve even one potato. The potatoes were his and that was final. "Nie podziele się z wamy to kartoflo bo byliscie tchurze, a ja byłbym złapany przez wasze strachy!! .... I am not sharing the potatoes with you because you were cowards, and I could have been caught from your fear!!"

The three were starving and hungrily eyed the sack of potatoes. Sylwester couldn't bring himself to deny them food, even though they abandoned him. All three took a few potatoes and tucked them inside their shirts. Sylwester stuck his sack inside his shirt too. They buried the rest of the potatoes in the sand by one of the wood piles, and scratched a piece of wood to mark the spot. The following night, Sylwester found himself in a crisis once again.

The Following Night
The Lime Pond

They had already unloaded one train load of wood and were expecting another, but no train arrived and it was almost quitting time. Sylwester went around the wood piles and dug up some of the potatoes he had stolen the night before. He tucked them in his shirt, ready to go back to the barrack. It was 6 a.m. He would have his potatoes after his soup ration. But the foreman did not let the men go at quitting time. They had to wait for the train. Sylwester wondered what the problem was. Foolishly he and another young fellow decided to go down to the docks to find out.

No one was allowed to walk alone in the mill. There were watchmen patrolling everywhere. Sylwester, his potatoes, and his friend carefully made their way down to the canal to see what was up. It was still dark at 6 a.m., so they crept in the night shadows and stayed out of the lamp lights. When they reached the canal the boys stopped and watched. There was nothing unusual going on. The men were unloading the wood from the barge onto the wagons. They could see no reason for the delay. Sylwester wanted a closer look, but ventured out a little too far. The light caught him, and so did the foreman.

The foreman was a Pole of German decent. He recognized Sylwester and asked in Polish, "Co ty tu robisz? .... What are you doing here?"

"Ja przyszed zobaczycz dlaczego pociąg nie przyszet. Juź godzina do domu .... I came to see why the train is not coming. It is time for us to go home."

The foreman looked suspiciously at Sylwester and his bulging shirt. It was obvious Sylwester was hiding something. Maybe he stole something from the mill, or maybe he stole potatoes. The foreman was hungry too. "Chocz zemno do Moje budy .... Come with me to my shed," he ordered. Sylwester followed. Once inside the foreman asked, "Co ty masz podspodem ubior? .... What do you have underneath your clothes?"

"Ja mam kartofle .... I have potatoes."

"Wysyp kartofle tu .... Unload the potatoes here," he ordered.

Sylwester would have shared some of his potatoes, for he would help a hungry Pole, but the foreman rudely ordered him. Sylwester had risked his life for his potatoes the night before, and would not give them up. When Sylwester refused to obey, the foreman hit him as hard as he could across the head. Out of spite, he yanked his shirt out of his pants, letting the potatoes fly. The foreman was furious and profusely beat him. He ordered Sylwester to pick up every potato and put them beside his desk. Then grabbing him, he threw him out the shed, and ordered him to get back to work.

Wiping the tears from his face, Sylwester returned to his friend who had been hiding the whole time. Bitter and defeated, Sylwester explained what had happened as they headed back. Losing his potatoes hurt more than being hit.

Since he had been ordered to return to work, Sylwester assumed there was no need to sneak back. The two walked through the pulp mill on the main roads. The night watchman's job was to ensure no one was wandering about. "Halt! Hände hoch! .... Halt! Hands up!" The boys stopped in their tracks and raised their hands. The armed guard approached. He was a tall, older German of Latvian decent. Sylwester

was intrigued by the guard's hat, for it was different. It looked like a cowboy hat. "Was macht Ihr hier? .... What are you doing here?" The boys told him they were ordered to go back to their work site, but the guard ignored their excuses. He had his own orders to follow. If he caught anyone walking in the mill he had to turn them in to his superior at the guard house. "Folgt mir! .... Follow me!"

The guard walked briskly in front of the boys who obediently followed. Sylwester didn't want to go to the guardhouse and get another beating. He knew there was a side road coming up between the next two buildings. The side road was not well lit, and if they were quick enough, they could get away. They were much younger than the guard, and figured they could outrun him. Sylwester signaled his friend. They slowed their pace. When they reached the side road they took off as fast as they could. The guard yelled out, "Halt! oder ich schisse! Halt! oder ich schisse! .... Halt! I'll shoot! Halt! I'll shoot!" The boys kept running.

The guard lost sight of them in the darkness and did not shoot, but the boys didn't know if he was chasing them or not. They could still hear him yelling, "Halt! Halt!", so they kept running. As long as they were in the dark he wouldn't know where to aim.

There were three big lime ponds in the field near the Holzplatz. The lime was used in the pulp processing in the mill. The lime settled in the ponds and turned to a thick gumbo. Over time it hardened and could be walked upon. During the day Sylwester knew exactly where the ponds were, and which of the ponds were safe to cross and which were not. The soft ponds were like quicksand, and extremely dangerous. They offered no escape. In his panic to get away, Sylwester was confused as to which ponds were safe. He couldn't tell if he was at the first, the second, or the third pond. If he ran around the perimeter of a hard pond, the guard would take a short cut across and catch him. Sylwester bent down and checked the lime by rubbing it with his hand. It was hard. He took off as fast as he could. He ran out a few yards and down he went, into the gumbo. The lime was only hard around the edges and gumbo farther out. The more he wriggled, the deeper he sank. He was up to his chest and sinking farther. His arms were above the goo. He tried to reach the solid edge to pull him-

self out, but he couldn't. He was stuck. He would drown in the muck if he didn't get help in time. "Pomoc mnie! Choć nazat! .... Help! Turn back!" Sylwester pleaded to his friend. "Choć nazat! .... Turn back!"

His friend was running around the perimeter of the pond, and was almost on the other side, when he heard Sylwester's pleas for help. He didn't know that Sylwester had tried to run across. He stopped. If he kept going he was sure to get away. If he went back to help Sylwester he might get caught. He ran back, wondering how he was going to rescue Sylwester without both of them drowning.

Sylwester always wore a shawl around his neck in winter. He unwrapped the shawl, grabbed one end and tossed the other end to his friend. His friend pulled with all his might but the muck clung to Sylwester like concrete. The suction would not break. "Ciąg! Ciąg mocno! .... Pull! Pull hard!", Sylwester urgently pleaded. He was finished if his friend couldn't pull him out. They both held on as tightly as they could to the shawl. "Ciąg! Ciąg mocno! .... Pull! Pull hard!" The guard was still yelling somewhere in the distance. Sylwester didn't care now if he was caught. It would be merciful to be beaten compared to drowning slowly in the lime. His friend pulled and pulled. Sylwester clung for dear life. Slowly he inched forward. His friend heaved. The edge was getting closer. Finally his friend was close enough to grab his arm. He was free. Sylwester wanted to laugh and cry at the same time, but there was no time to waste. They didn't know where the guard was. The two took off like bullets to the Holzplatz.

Sylwester was covered in white muck. He dropped to the ground and rolled in the sand. The sand stuck to the lime and the men scraped it off with sticks. He rolled again and again, with more coming off each time. The Latvian watchman would probably be waiting at the gate at the end of their shift. The guard did not get a good look at the two in the dark, but Sylwester was concerned his clothes would give him away. After he was cleaned up he looked as dirty as the others. If he was lucky he might not get spotted in the dark. The men thought up a plan to save Sylwester. They lined up in threes to be counted, and stuck Sylwester in the middle. The Latvian guard, with his cowboy hat, was at the gate, just as Sylwester had dreaded. The guard slowly walked between the rows looking care-

fully at each man's face. The men contorted their faces into bizarre con-figurations. Some yawned, some squinted, others puckered their mouths. Sylwester tilted his hat down on his face, screwed up his features and yawned. The guard passed him by.

When Sylwester returned to his barrack that morning, he did not go to bed. The clothes he wore were the only clothes he had. There was a wash basin in the barrack. He took off his clothes and began to scrub off the grime. He had to scrub and rewash several times. His clothes were not clean but they were better than before. He rung them out as hard as he could and took them back to his room to dry. He hoped they would not be too damp by 6 p.m. when it was time to go back to work outside in the cold. He started to think of the potatoes he still had buried in the sand at the Holzplatz, and fell asleep.

Part 2 - Chapter 1 - Epilogue

Camp #1
Küstrin Neue Stadt, Germany

Küstrin Neue Stadt came under Polish territory when the Polish border shifted west after the Second World War, and was renamed Koszczyn. In 1992, Sylwester travelled a second time to Poland since his immigration to Canada in 1949. His eldest daughter, Krystyna, accompanied him. Sylwester visited the pulp mill in Koszczyn where, at age sixteen and seventeen, he had worked as a German slave. He walked down the same roads that he had fled escaping the Latvian guard, fifty years earlier. The three lime ponds were still there.

In 1992 Sylwester also visited Auschwitz, the death camp where he could have been so easily sent. He walked through the rooms and gas chambers and saw remnants of the holocaust that took place. Auschwitz resumed its original Polish name after the war, Oswiencim.

Part 2 - Chapter 2

Camp #2
Brandenburg Havel, Germany
January 1943 to April 1944

Work Assignment: Smelting Plant - Steel Mill

In January 1943, Sylwester was again crammed into the boxcar of a train. He and Stefan left Küstrin Neue Stadt and were transported to a camp in Brandenburg Havel, Germany, to work in a smelting plant. The plant sub-contracted work to different companies. Stefan and Sylwester did not work together in Brandenburg Havel. Sylwester worked for a construction firm at the mill by the name of Company Müst. Stefan worked on the railroad lines, changing tracks and disconnecting cars. Stefan was issued a good pair of boots for his new job. Sylwester needed footwear too, but was not issued any.

Sylwester was no longer the innocent and naive boy of sixteen years who had arrived from Rudnia only seven months earlier. He was an extremely alert and quick seventeen-year-old. His instinct to survive was sharp. He became an expert at stealing potatoes and hiding things in his clothes. He was ingenious at making things from virtually nothing.

In Küstrin Neue Stadt he had acquired an old can that he used as a pot. He carried it with him to Brandenburg Havel. He collected small pieces of wood for fuel and carried them back to camp in his pants. He cooked his stolen potatoes on the heater in his barrack, when the other men were not there, just as he had done in Küstrin Neue Stadt. He devoured the food and scraped the can.

Whenever he had a stash of stolen potatoes, he would prepare them the night before and carry the pot to work the following morning. On his lunch break he would run to the mill to cook his pot of potatoes. He was

more hungry than scared to think of his potential punishment. His stomach overruled his caution. He had to be quick. In one hour he had to run to the mill, access the boiler room, cook and eat his potatoes, wash his pot, and run back in time to start work. He knew how to sneak into the boiler room, and how to access the top of the boilers. He'd climb up, open a little peep hole on the boiler, and place his pot over the hole. He had to watch carefully for the boiler was so hot it would melt his worn out pot in no time. In a matter of minutes the water boiled.

Brandenburg had many industries, and near the smelting plant was an aeroplane manufacturing plant. Its workers came from another huge Russisches Arbeits Lager - Russian Work Camp, separate from Sylwester's. Three kilometers from the aeroplane manufacturing plant was an automobile manufacturing plant. Each plant had its own slave camps of free workers.

The Germans brought in tens of thousands of men to work in Brandenburg Havel. Next to Sylwester's Russisches Arbeits Lager - Russian Work Camp, was a Polish camp, and then a Dutch camp. There were French, Belgium and Czechoslovakian camps as well, all side-by-side. Each camp housed thousands of men. The compounds were surrounded and separated by high barbed-wire fences. There was one gate in each compound and a guard at each gate. The men had to show a colored pass each time they left or entered their compound. Entrance was only permitted with the correct color. Sylwester carried his pass in his shirt pocket. They could travel on their own, unlike Küstrin Neue Stadt where they had to be led everywhere by a guard.

Sylwester arrived in Brandenburg Havel in the dead of winter. He froze working outside. He wrapped his thin, issued blanket around himself, and tucked the front into his pants. He cut off a piece of the blanket and sewed himself a hat. The chill went right to his bones. He wrote his father, asking if there was anything he could send to keep him warm. He received no reply. Sylwester did not know until 1979, 37 years later when visiting his brother Roman in Poland, that his father had mailed him a pair of pants and a jacket. They were the ones which Sylwester had bought with his Russian work coupon, and had given to Jan. The family

assumed the parcel had reached Sylwester, while Sylwester assumed his letter had not reached home. Sylwester was comforted by the thought that his father had indeed cared and sent him clothes to keep him warm.

The barracks were long with a narrow corridor running down the centre. Rooms were on either side of the hallway. Each room had double or triple bunk beds. Some rooms slept nine men, others slept sixteen. Sylwester slept in a room with nine men. The men did not necessarily bunk in the same room with their co-workers. No one was allowed to visit other rooms after the evening meal.

Showers were assigned by barrack once a week. After showering, each man had to rub himself down with a liquid disinfectant. The disinfectant was in a large barrel near the showers. Every week Sylwester dipped his hand in the liquid and smeared it all over his body. It burned his skin. He had no idea what chemicals he was using.

The outhouse in Brandenburg had a concrete floor and concrete walls. There was a row of holes on a long wooden plank where the men sat side-by-side. The urinals were separate holes off to the side. There was no privacy, but they no longer cared, for their lives had deteriorated to mere survival.

April 1943 - Four Months After Arrival
The Ambulance

Sylwester was deathly ill. He had a prolonged case of diarrhea and his stool was full of blood. He was in severe pain and terribly weak. A German doctor came to the camp once a week. He postponed seeing the doctor as long as he could, but his condition worsened. He thought he was going to die. The doctor came to the camp by ambulance. After he examined the sick, he transported the very ill to hospital in his ambulance. The hospital was close by. Sylwester noted that the men who were taken to the hospital by ambulance never returned. He became very suspicious of the doctor and had a terrible fear of the ambulance. These were young men who were taken away. It just didn't add up. How long could

a young man be sick, and why were they never seen again?

The night before Sylwester was to see the doctor, he could hardly walk, and was dizzy and faint. When Sylwester was a young child in Rudnia, his mother, Michalina, had taught him the words to pray when he was in the face of death. Sylwester remembered his mother's words and prayed aloud, "Jezus, Maria, Józefie Święty, Ratu Dusze Moje .... Jesus, Mary, Joseph Holy, Save my Soul," and wept.

The following day he went to the doctor. The physician examined him and could see Sylwester was gravely ill. He told him he must be hospitalized. Sylwester was scared beyond belief.

It just so happened that on that particular day, the doctor did not travel by ambulance. He asked Sylwester, "Soll ich den Krankenwagen holen, oder willst Du zu Fuss gehen zum Spital? .... Do you want me to call the ambulance or do you want to walk to the hospital?" Sylwester was too ill to walk, but his instinct told him not to trust the doctor, and not to go in the ambulance. "Nein. Ich will zu fuss gehen .... No. I will walk."

He was lead to the hospital by two Russian nurses. He had so much pressure and pain in his bowels, he had no control over them. He felt his eliminations and was embarrassed. He was sure he had soiled his pants, but discovered at the hospital that he had been passing blood, not stool.

Sylwester was taken to be examined by a Russian doctor. Whatever he had was extremely contagious, and he was immediately put into isolation. His windows and doors were sealed with tape, and he was left completely alone for three days. No one fed him. No one told him what was wrong with him. The doctor and nurses only looked in on him through the window in the corridor. He was drifting in and out of consciousness. He was in agony and the only relief he had was sleep.

At the end of the third day Sylwester awoke to the sound of tape ripping and the door opening. A Russian nurse wearing a surgical mask entered, carrying a tray. She spoke not a word to Sylwester. He feebly tried to speak but she gave no reply. He watched her quickly set down the

tray, with one slice of dry toast and half a glass of milk, beside him. She immediately left and again sealed the door securely with tape.

The following day the same nurse entered his room again. This time she was carrying a bed pan. The doctor needed a sample of Sylwester's stool. Sylwester sat on the pan, but was only able to urinate. The nurse returned to collect the stool sample and showed her disapproval. She scolded him. Sylwester said, "Это четвёртый день что я ничего не ел. Ты дал мне один кусок хлеба. Мне надо больше пищи .... This is the fourth day that I have had nothing to eat. You only gave me one slice of toast. I need more food."

The nurse haughtily left with the bed pan and took it to the doctor. The doctor authorized Sylwester be given soup and a slice of bread once a day. Sylwester was slowly starting to recover. Eventually the nurse got her stool sample.

Sylwester was exceedingly weak but deemed well enough to return to camp. No one at the hospital had expected him to survive. He asked for his clothes, but the day he had been admitted his clothes were given away. The medical staff believed he would only last a few days and got rid of his things! Sylwester had nothing to wear. On the same day he was being discharged from hospital, a Russian worker with the same illness was being admitted. Once the new patient was settled, they gave Sylwester the man's clothing and told him to go back to camp. Sylwester was never told what illness he had. All he wanted now was to get well and get out of there.

Sylwester walked back to his camp unescorted. When he arrived, he was supposed to report to work at the steel mill but he didn't. Instead he went to the kitchen and asked Makaro, the man in charge, if he could peel potatoes. Makaro would let the men peel potatoes if they worked the night shift. He did not allow them to peel potatoes if they worked the day shift. Sylwester was supposed to be working the day shift but did not tell Makaro. Nor did he mention that he had just been discharged from the hospital. He was too weak to work, and knew he could not endure hard labour for twelve hours day after day. His primary concern was food and rest, and he could get both by lying. It was worth the risk.

Sylwester worked day after day in the kitchen, peeling potatoes for Makaro. At night he slept. The extra food and the rest helped him recuperate. Each day he would sneak an extra bowl of soup or a potato. He swiped a few potatoes to take back to his barrack. No one seemed to miss him. Apparently the hospital did not notify the camp that he had been discharged. The men in Sylwester's barracks worked in different parts of the mill. They did not know where Sylwester was supposed to be. His Russian co-workers did not see him. Sylwester cleverly hid for two weeks.

After two weeks Sylwester's supervisor, Franz, wondered what had happened to him. He phoned the hospital to enquire and was told that Sylwester had been discharged two weeks ago! The supervisor phoned the camp commandant at once. Sylwester was missing.

The camp commandant went to Sylwester's room, and found him there. "Sylwester! Was machst Du hier? Du sollst doch bei der Arbeit sein! .... Sylwester! What are you doing here? You should be on the job!"

"Ja, Herr Kommandant. Ich arbeite in der Küche. Ich schäle Kartoffeln für alle Männer in der Fabrick .... Yes, Camp Commandant," Sylwester replied in German, "I am working in the kitchen. I am peeling potatoes for all the people who are working in the mill."

"Das ist nicht deine Arbeit! Deine Arbeit ist in der Fabrick! .... That is not your job! Your job is in the mill! Out! Quick!" Sylwester immediately did as he was told.

Franz was a short, mean, and ugly man. He was literally the ugliest man Sylwester had ever seen. Franz had already been notified that Sylwester had been hiding for two weeks. He had an extra mean look in his eye when Sylwester returned. Sylwester knew Franz would heartlessly punish him. Franz scowled at him, shouting, "Du fauler Kerl! Du Schweine Hund! .... You Lazy Bum! You Pig Dog!"

Franz assigned him to extra hard labour. He sent him to join a work crew of French and Belgian military prisoners, all older and stronger than Sylwester. The Frenchmen and the Belgians had been unloading bags of cement from a ship all morning and had been carrying them up the hill to

the train. The dock was well below the train. Sylwester had to go down to the ship, heave the sack of cement over his shoulder, climb a stairway, a hill, another stairway and then load the bags into the boxcar. It was back breaking work. He hauled and lugged for six hours straight. His body was still dreadfully weak and he was ready to collapse. Sylwester was so relieved when the last of the bags was unloaded. He no sooner sat down when he saw another ship come into view.

The ship was full of cinder blocks. They could not be packed like the bags of cement. They had to be passed from hand to hand. The following day the Germans brought in more men to work alongside the French and Belgian prisoners-of-war. Hundreds of men, including Sylwester, were queued from the dock all the way up to the train. Two stacked blocks were passed at a time. A non-stop procession was passed from one man to the next. The men had to keep up with the flow or the next two blocks would land on their feet. The cinder blocks were passed left to right, all the way up the long line to the train. Sylwester passed to his right and missed a pass from his left. Down the blocks went on his feet. Oh how it hurt! Each man had to relentlessly push to spare his own feet from getting smashed.

Sylwester was still not fully recovered from his illness. He was exhausted from hauling cement the day before, and now his feet were injured, and his hands, fingers and wrists were raw and bleeding. No one had gloves. He pulled the ends of his shirt sleeves down over his hands, but the thin cloth was useless against the rough cement. By the end of the twelve hour shift Sylwester's hands were painfully swollen. In camp he found any rag he could and wrapped them. He slept with his hands bandaged in rags. They throbbed all night.

His hands were literally useless. He could not bend them or grasp anything, and yet he had to return for two more grueling twelve-hour days of the same work. Sylwester was sure Franz was trying to work him to death for the two weeks he convalesced hiding in the kitchen. The only reprieve about his ordeal was that he had potatoes from Makaro's kitchen waiting for him in his barrack.

July 1943 - Four Months Later
The Frenchman

It was Sunday and the men worked six hours instead of twelve. Sylwester had been carefully following orders since he last hid in the kitchen, and was in the camp commandant's good books. He gave Sylwester and two other fellows a pass to go into town. On their way, they were met by three older French prisoners walking back to their camp. The Frenchmen were extremely friendly with the three young boys. They stopped and said in German, "Willst Du Schokolade haben?.... Do you want some chocolate?" Sylwester and his friends looked at each other. They knew the French received parcels with chocolate. The temptation of sweets, after a daily diet of soup and bread, was hard to resist. "Komme zu unserem Lager. Wir haben Schokolade und andere Sachen .... Come to our camp. We have chocolate and other good things."

The three boys decided to follow the Frenchmen to their camp, but as the Frenchmen neared their camp they veered off onto a path that went over a bridge and into the forest. Sylwester's two partners were a few years older and were suspicious. They took off, leaving Sylwester behind. He wondered why they left.

Sylwester vividly remembered the day his father rescued his sister Kostka from two men who tried to rape her, but he knew nothing of men raping boys. Sylwester hadn't heard of such things. He kept walking with the Frenchmen oblivious to any danger. Two were walking ahead of him and one close beside him. The Frenchman, who was walking beside Sylwester, steered him into the bushes.

Sylwester's instincts told him something was terribly wrong. He looked around to orientate himself in case he needed to run. There was a hill to one side. Trees surrounded them. He felt very uneasy. Sylwester quickly sat down on a stump at the base of the hill to give himself time. He didn't want to go any further into the bush. The Frenchman approached, leaned over, and put his hands on Sylwester's knees. He leaned in closer. Sylwester was scared but angry, and ready to defend himself. The man was right in his face and wiggling his behind. "Hey!

Ich bin doch kein Mädchen. Ich bin ein Bursche .... Hey!" Sylwester yelled, "I'm not a girl! I'm a boy!" Sylwester tried to shove him away. The Frenchman leaned over him even farther, saying something in French. Sylwester pushed and wriggled from beneath him. The Frenchman tried to grab him, but Sylwester scrambled up the hill and ran as fast he could. He escaped the potential rapist.

October 1943 - Three Months Later
The New Cooking Pot

The Germans were bringing the American and British planes that they had shot down, to the smelting plant in Brandenburg Havel to be melted for their own use. Sylwester had an hour for lunch but nothing to eat. He was out of potatoes. The men had to wait until after 6 p.m. for their meal. They would get two bowls of soup when they returned to camp after their shift. A hungry Sylwester went exploring. He walked around the plant and spotted a plane near the canal. He approached and examined the wings and the rest of the body. It was built of aluminum sheeting.

"Ja moge zrobić garnek ztego aluminium! .... I can make a pot out of this aluminum!", he said to himself. This was a stroke of luck. His old pot that he had carried with him from Küstrin Neue Stadt, was completely worn out. Sylwester pulled off a strip of aluminum and bent it gently around his body. He hid it under his coat so the Germans would not detect it and went back to his work site. He knew he was putting himself at tremendous risk. He remembered well his imprisonment and his whippings for stealing a piece of rubber pipe in Küstrin Neue Stadt just a few months before.

Over his next two lunch hours, Sylwester hid and carefully molded his cooking pot. It had a lid and a wire handle and held about two litres of water. It was ingenious and Sylwester felt proud. All he needed now was an opportunity to steal potatoes.

Some Time Later
Sylwester - 18 years old
The Explosion

There was a huge explosion in the mill. Sylwester could hear the excitement and desperately wanted to find out what it was, but he had to stay put with the other workers at the Holzplatz. His curiosity got the best of him. He quietly crept away, and headed towards the pulp mill. He knew that walking alone in the mill was forbidden, but he just had to find out what exploded. When he came into the central core of the mill, men were scrambling. The explosion had caused a fire. There were no fire hoses and every man was needed to throw bucket after bucket of sand to dowse it. A German guard spotted Sylwester and assumed he belonged there. He ordered him to grab two buckets of sand and follow him. Sylwester quickly tried to pick up the buckets, but their weight stopped him short. They were heavy, and difficult to carry. He tried to keep up to the guard but fell further and further behind.

Sylwester hadn't come to work. The guard was empty-handed and was well ahead of him. Sylwester slowed his pace more and more. When the guard was far enough away he put the buckets down, and ran back to the Holzplatz, well away from the commotion....and more work. He was no fool.

He never did find out what the explosion was all about.

January 1944 - Three Months Later
Sylwester's Potatoes are Stolen

Sylwester had had his evening bowl of soup but was still hungry. He knew where a huge stash of potatoes was hidden outside his compound. The potatoes for all the camps were stored in the basements of a new construction site nearby. Only the basements of the buildings were completed.

Sylwester grabbed his sack and hid it inside his shirt. He had sewn the sack long ago, from an old towel he had scavenged. He showed his colored pass at the gate and went out. It was a cold night, but he had potatoes on his mind and ignored the chill. He secretly moved along in the dark making sure no one saw him. The moon cast just enough light. Sylwester reached the construction site and quickly crawled through a small window into one of the basements.

It was pitch black inside. He couldn't see a thing. He outstretched his arms and inched forward, feeling for a heap of potatoes. He moved in every direction hoping to bump into a mound, but there was none. He got on all fours and felt the ground. It was dirt. He rubbed his hands all over hoping to find potatoes, but found nothing. He wasn't about to give up. He shuffled his hands farther over the ground, moving them back and forth, and found them. Potatoes! They had been buried.

Sylwester dug with his bare hands pulling out one potato after another and sticking them into his sack. The ground was rough and hard to dig. After two hours his sack was only half full, but his hands were so sore he had to quit. He had enough potatoes for a few days. Sylwester lifted his sack to push it through the window but the sack wouldn't budge. He thrust with all his might but the sack just would not move. Something was blocking the way. He was baffled. Again he tried to shove the sack and again it stopped. He cautiously looked out. Snow! A foot of snow had fallen while he had been working.

It would be easy to track him. He had been tracked once before, in Rudnia in 1940, when he had chopped down a Christmas tree from his neighbor's yard. Sylwester had no time to waste. He must get out while

it was still snowing heavily. His trail would be covered. He dug the snow away from the window and heaved his potatoes onto the snow. He pulled himself up, crawled through, grabbed his sack, and quickly made his way back to his compound.

He could not rush past the guard at the gate with his sack of potatoes, and there was no way he could conceal it on himself. He heaved the sack over the barbed-wire, out of sight of the gate. The sack landed softly in the snow on the other side. He was anxious to get his potatoes but he had to calmly walk to the gate to avoid suspicion. He showed his pass and went in.

Quickly, he went to retrieve his loot. He was ravenously hungry and could hardly wait to eat. He stood exactly where his potatoes had landed, but they were not there. He felt around in the snow. He looked left and right, but his potatoes and his sack were gone. One of the men in the barrack had seen him sneak up to the fence and throw the sack over. By the time Sylwester walked around to the gate and back to the spot where the sack had landed, the other man had grabbed it and disappeared. He was furious. The thief had left a trail of footprints in the snow, and he followed them. They lead into a barrack that was close to his.

Sylwester opened the door and stood in the long hallway. His hopes of finding the thief were in vain. There were no more footprints to follow, and with hundreds of men living in the many rooms on either side of the corridor, it was hopeless. Sylwester knew his potatoes and his sack were in there somewhere, but he left the barrack and fumed back to his own sleeping quarters. It was past midnight. He would not get much sleep before he was awakened for the 6 a.m. shift.

The following day Sylwester was working outside the steel plant in the miserable, freezing cold. He was bitter about his stolen potatoes and his stolen sack. He had no potatoes to cook and no clothing to keep him warm. He was so cold he ached. On his lunch break, he headed straight for the heat of the boiler room. He had to warm up.

Huge metal sheets, three inches thick, had just been pulled from the ovens by French prisoners and were placed on saw horses to cool. No one was around. Instead of climbing up to the boilers, Sylwester curled up

under the warm metal. The heat from the metal was wonderful. He was warm and tired, and fell fast asleep.

The metal sheets were to be cut with welding torches to specified dimensions, once they were cool enough. The heavy steel was to be used in building tanks and ships. Sylwester was sound asleep when the Frenchmen returned. He continued to sleep as they set up their welding equipment. Whether or not the welders knew Sylwester was there, we will never know, but Sylwester awakened to a shower of sparks. He was panicked into immediate flight. He was being sprayed from every direction. He scrambled from under the metal sheet and took off like a bullet. The freezing cold and reality hit him. He was hungry and his stomach ached for food, but there was none. How he longed for his potatoes, but they were somewhere with his sack in the other barrack, perhaps already consumed by the thief. His misery continued.

A Short Time Later
Sylwester's First Bombing Raid

After almost a year in Brandenburg Havel, Sylwester experienced his first bombing raid. The air raid sirens screamed for everyone to run for the bunker, but Sylwester decided to head for the canteen and sneak some food instead. He never missed an opportunity to eat. He slipped into a storage shed while the rest of the men scrambled for cover. He was waiting for the coast to clear when the bombs whistled down and exploded all around him. The shack rattled and the floor shook. The blasts were so loud he couldn't hear his own screams. He was terrified. He huddled alone in a corner, screaming and crying as the bombs poured down.

When all was quiet, he emerged from the shed totally shaken. Small fire bombs had been dropped on the steel plant and fires were everywhere. These bombs did not have the fierce blasting power of the bombs Sylwester would experience before the end of the war, but his first experience was terrifying enough. The men scrambled to put out the flames and Sylwester was caught up with them. There was no time to

think about what had just happened. It was time to get back to work.

Sylwester was almost killed over a piece of bread that he never got. Thankfully no bombs were dropped on the barracks where the men lived.

Part 2 - Chapter 2 - Epilogue

Camp #2
Brandenburg Havel, Germany
January 1943 to April 1944

In 1961, when Sylwester had already been in Canada twelve years, he learned the truth about the ambulance. He was watching a documentary about Hitler's special ambulances on CBC television. The ambulance would take away the very sick and stop just outside the camp compound. The exhaust was reversed into the ambulance, killing those inside with carbon monoxide. Sylwester's astute observations and premonitions had saved his life eighteen years earlier.

Sylwester carried the aluminum pot that he had made from the downed plane with him until the end of the war. He lost track of how many stolen potatoes he had cooked in it over the years. He regretted throwing the pot away when the war ended, for it held many stories of his life, but at that time he was not thinking of memorabilia. He wanted to leave his memories of the hell he lived through far behind.

Stefan Słodkowski did not get transferred to Meseritz with Sylwester in April 1944. He stayed behind in Brandenburg Havel, and the two did not see each other again. Sylwester corresponded with Stefan over the years from Canada. He learned that his boyhood friend owned and operated a huge farm near Lublin. Sylwester last wrote his friend in 1994, but received no reply.

Part 2 - Chapter 3

Camp #3
Meseritz, Germany
April 1944 to December 1944

Work Assignment: Building a Tunnel

Sylwester had lived through the misery and abuse of the first two camps. He was now eighteen years old and shrewd to the ways of the war. He was not easily fooled, and knew how to look out for himself. The camp in Meseritz was different from the other two that Sylwester had endured. It was not surrounded by a barbed-wire fence, but by a forest. Guards patrolled the perimeter of the compound day and night, but without a fence, Sylwester was able to explore. The food was the same as it had been in Küstrin Neue Stadt and Brandenburg Havel: watery soup morning, noon and night. The foremen had separate canteens and kitchens from the workers, and ate far better.

There was a German military compound next to Sylwester's camp, about 100 yards away. It was surrounded by a high chain-link fence. The military would send its soldiers, who were fighting at the Russian front, to rest there for a few days before returning to the front. If the German soldiers wanted to leave their compound, they had to ask permission from their officer. Sylwester often visited the military compound asking for bread. Sometimes a piece was given.

In Meseritz, Sylwester was assigned to work in a tunnel which was being built for military maneuvers. He was excited when he discovered that the tunnel was directly under a potato field. Potatoes were more valuable than gold. In the fall, after the potatoes were harvested, many remained in the fields. Sylwester and the others would scoop them up whenever they worked there. Sylwester carried his potatoes home in his baggy shirt and stashed them in his locker. He could have eaten them all

in one sitting, but he carefully rationed his potatoes, for starvation faced him every day.

Sylwester's foreman in Meseritz was Herr Schlick, who was under Herr Schwartz. Sylwester really liked Herr Schlick. He found him to be a good and fair man. He enforced the work, but was helpful and protected the men when needed. Herr Schlick spoke both German and Polish, and was with Sylwester until the end of the war.

April 1944 - A few weeks after arrival
The Forlorn German Officer

Sylwester would quite often walk near the military compound when he wasn't working. Sometimes he would call to the soldiers and they would come to the fence with a piece of bread. Sometimes the soldiers invited him into the compound. Their lives at the front were different from life in the work camps. Sylwester was curious to know more about them.

The German soldiers were friendly, and Sylwester realized that they were somewhat like prisoners too. He could see a parallel between himself and these men. They were not free. They were caught in the war without a choice, like himself. Sylwester started to think about what really made a man friend or foe.

One day Sylwester approached the military compound and saw a lone German officer pacing back and forth beside the fence. His head was hanging low and his hands were clasped behind his back. He looked disheveled and forlorn, not at all like the officers Sylwester was accustomed to seeing. His buttons were undone and his jacket gaped open. He was the picture of gloom.

Sylwester did not know how to address an officer so he called, "Herr Meister .... Sir Master", which is what he called his foreman. The German officer slowly raised his head and somberly said, "Ja? .... Yes?" "Hast Du ein Stückchen Brot oder etwas fur mich? .... Would you happen

to have a piece of bread or something for me?", Sylwester asked. "Ich habe einen Hunger....I am hungry."

The German officer slowly walked towards Sylwester, his hands still behind his back, and said, "Du bist hungrig? .... You are hungry?"

"Ja. Wir arbeiten lange Stunden und sind schlecht ernehrt .... Yes. We work long hours and we are poorly fed."

"Young man, I have two loaves of bread. Bring a girl to me and I will give you both of them. I am only thirty kilometers away from my wife and family and I cannot go visit them. Tomorrow morning I go back to the Russian front."

When Sylwester heard the German officer say he had two loaves of bread and that tomorrow morning he was going to the Russian front, that was all he needed to know. He instantly started to think up a plan to get the bread. The officer even told Sylwester the time he was being sent out in the morning. Sylwester did not know any girls, and even if he did, he would never broach them with such a request. "Herr Meister," he said. "Give me one loaf of bread now. I know the girls over there. They are as hungry as the rest of us. A girl will not come over here unless I take something to her. Give me the loaf and I'll take it to her. I'll be back in about half an hour or maybe a bit longer. It will take some time to talk." The German officer left and went into his barrack. He returned. He did not change his stance or his walk. His hands were still clasped behind his back. The loaf of bread was tucked inside his jacket, under his arm. He moved his shoulder towards the opening in the fence. Sylwester reached inside his jacket, pulled the loaf out, and hid it underneath his shirt. "Halbe Stunde nicht mehr höchstens 45 Minuten, nicht laenger .... Half an hour or 45 minutes, no longer," Sylwester said.

With the bread tucked safely inside his shirt, Sylwester walked about 300 yards away from the compound, sat himself down in a thicket, and ate half the loaf right away. He was ravenous. He knew the officer was being sent to the front early the next morning. There was no way he would have a chance to come after him. Sylwester could have eaten the whole loaf, but saved the other half for the next day. He'd be starving again tomorrow. The following day on his way to work, he had to

walk right past the military compound. It was empty.

That same night a different regiment of German soldiers was brought in from the Russian front to rest for a few days. The soldiers were wearing German uniforms, but Sylwester heard them speaking Ukrainian. He thought this was interesting, German soldiers speaking Ukrainian. He opened the gate of the military compound and walked right up to the open window of the barrack. He called out in Ukrainian, "Приятелі, чи маєте кусок хліба для мене .... Hey friends do you have a piece of bread for me?" Two heads immediately poked out the window. "Якої націонйальности ти є .... What nationality are you?" they asked. "Я є поляк .... I'm Polish." The look of hatred from the two men told Sylwester to get out of there, and fast! The Ukrainians were filled with hate propaganda against the Poles. The Ukrainian uprising was full blown in Eastern Poland. Thousands of Poles were being slaughtered in their homes by Ukrainian dissidents. The enraged Ukrainians ran for the door. They'd kill him if they caught him. Sylwester was out the gate in no time, too scared to look back.

Sylwester never again walked through the gate of the military compound uninvited, but he still called from outside the fence, just in case an enemy soldier with a kind heart would give him a piece of bread.

June 1944 - two months later
Onions

Sylwester was desperately hungry. He needed potatoes. They were stored in the basement of new construction near the foremen's kitchen. A small window leading to the potatoes was open.

Sylwester had heard there was going to be a dance that night for the German guards and foremen. Many German Freulein - girls were brought in from town. The unfinished floor of the new construction would serve as the dance floor. No walls of the building were yet erected. It was a warm night, and perfect for an outdoor dance. Sylwester was too hungry to be rational. His stomach drove him to steal amidst a crowd of Germans.

Around 9 p.m., Sylwester took his sack and edged his way through the dark. He had to go right by the German barracks and kitchen before reaching the basement. The gaiety had already started. The orchestra played and there was much laughing and singing. Feet were stomping to the music. He inched along the wall of the barrack, sure that the men would be too preoccupied drinking and dancing, and wooing the women, to look for anyone sneaking into the basement. However, he had not counted on anyone leaving the dance with a pretty Freulein and trying to seduce her outside, right where he was creeping.

He stopped short when a German soldier with a Freulein came around the corner. Sylwester hugged the wall even closer. The couple drew into the shadows, not far from Sylwester. They were amorously fondling each other. Sylwester dared not move. He did not want to breathe. They were blocking his route to the cellar window. They were immersed in each other, oblivious to their terrified spectator. The orchestra played, the couple fondled, and Sylwester froze. He'd be dead if he was caught. The couple finally stopped, and walked back to the dance. As soon as they rounded the corner, Sylwester slipped past the barrack and wriggled himself through the window and into the basement.

As soon as he was in, he stopped and listened. It was pitch black. The dance floor above his head was shaking. The music pounded. Everyone was singing, dancing, and laughing. Sylwester carefully looked out the window. People were walking about, paying no mind to the goings on in the basement. He set to work. Sylwester quickly felt around. He had to be in and out as quickly as possible, for the situation could change in an instant. He couldn't see a thing in the unfamiliar black hole. He felt a pile of potatoes right beside him.

With unbelievable speed, he held the two corners of the sack with his feet, grabbed the open end with his teeth, and scooped the potatoes in with his hands in seconds. He checked out the window, tossed out his potatoes, crawled through, and crept safely back to his barrack.

He anxiously opened his sack in his room. His mouth was already watering for a potato. He looked inside and found onions! He risked his life to steal a sack of onions! What could he do with so many onions?

How many onions could a person eat? He certainly couldn't eat them like potatoes. Maybe he could trade them with some of the other men for something more palatable.

When Sylwester's friend, Sam (pseudonym) saw the onions he saw a wonderful thing. He was an older man. "Oj, Panie Drzewiecki, Panie Drzewiecki .... Oh, Mr. Drzewiecki, Mr. Drzewiecki," he said with excitement. "Jak dasz mnie twoją cebulę to ja wyszlem do Mojej żony .... If you would give me your onions I will send them to my wife." There were extreme shortages of food everywhere. His wife could put them to good use. Sylwester had no use for a sack of onions anyway. He kept a few for himself and freely gave the rest to his friend, without any kind of trade. Sam sent a few onions home to his wife every week. He had to declare to the authorities that there were onions in his parcel. The authorities approved his packages and let them go through.

July 1944
Assassination Attempt on Hitler's Life

An assassination attempt was made on Adolf Hitler in July of 1944. A bomb had been smuggled into the Führer's closely guarded headquarters. Sylwester's life in the camp was drastically affected by the assassination attempt. All the workers fell under military jurisdiction. Armed German soldiers took over the camps and the work sites. Civilian foremen no longer supervised the men. For more than one week, soldiers carrying bayoneted rifles stood guard over Sylwester and the other men as they laboured inside the tunnel. Speaking was absolutely forbidden. The men were to walk to and from work, labour twelve hours, eat their meals, and retire to bed in complete silence. It was near torture not being allowed to talk or sing while working. Talking and singing made the day pass much faster, but he didn't dare utter a sound with a bayoneted rifle ready and loaded beside him. He lived in mortal fear.

A small electric train was used to transport the men and equipment in and out of the long tunnel. It was time to leave the work site and

Sylwester and the others climbed on board. A young Czechoslovakian prisoner was operating the train. As they left the tunnel, the train stalled. The armed soldiers grabbed the innocent Czech in front of everyone, and accused him of sabotage. They took him away, and he was never seen again.

After one week, the armed German soldiers left, and camp life resumed as it had been. Sylwester was relieved to have Herr Schlick back.

Sometime later
Potato Pancakes

The potato field above the tunnel where Sylwester worked produced a good crop, and had been harvested. Sylwester and the other men took any upturned potatoes left in the field when the guards were not looking. Some of the potatoes were huge.

It was his afternoon off after six and a half long work days. Sylwester wanted to make some potato pancakes, just as he had seen them made many times at home in Rudnia. He prepared the potatoes in his barrack, grating them carefully on a primitive grate, which consisted of a can with nail holes punched through it. It was a slow process grating the potatoes on the rough surface, and his mouth salivated in anticipation.

Sylwester carefully collected his grated potatoes and asked Sam if he could borrow his frying pan. Sylwester took his prepared potatoes and the frying pan out the door. He would cook them in the blacksmith shop. He was on his way, thinking of his delicious pancakes, when he was met by a burly Russian who had just come out of his barrack. He made a straight line for Sylwester, and angrily grabbed the frying pan out of Sylwester's hands. "Это моя сковородка! .... That's my frying pan!", the Russian yelled.

"Нет. Это не твоя .... No! It's not yours," shouted Sylwester. Sylwester tried to grab it back from the giant man and a struggle ensued.

The Russian dwarfed Sylwester but Sylwester was not about to let go of the frying pan. Back and forth it went, curses flying. Sylwester saw Sam leaning on the window sill, watching the scuffle. Sylwester was furious! Sam never made a move to help him, nor did he say a word. "Jesteś Mojim kolego tylko wtedy gdy jesteś wynagrodzony! .... You are my friend only when you want to get something from me!", Sylwester thought. Sylwester won the tug-of-war. He kept the frying pan but lost all his grated potatoes. His dinner was spewn over the ground. He was outraged! Only God stopped him from hitting Sam with his own frying pan, and stuffing an onion down his throat!

1944 - A short time later
The Chisel

Sylwester did many different jobs inside the tunnel. One of his jobs was to pound a chisel into concrete, hour after hour, making holes into which steel pegs could be embedded. Huge electrical cables would be suspended on the pegs throughout the tunnel. Every few hours the blacksmith would come by with sharpened chisels so that the work would go faster. The men had to hand over their dull chisels. If the blacksmith found the chisel was not dull enough, it meant the worker was slacking off, and the worker would be in trouble.

Sylwester was slacking off. It was a horrible job pounding concrete hour after hour. The work he did do, did not make his chisel dull enough and the blacksmith was on his way. Sylwester looked at his chisel and his hammer. He knew how to blunt his chisel quickly. Holding it tightly, he gave it a tremendous blow on its sharp edge. The metal was so hard it split and a sharp piece flew off, cutting threw Sylwester's pant leg, and embedding itself in his thigh. Sylwester could feel he was bleeding. The blacksmith was down the tunnel exchanging chisels. Sylwester quickly jumped down from the platform where he had been working, and headed to the outhouse. He threw down his pants and tried to squeeze the metal out of his leg. He didn't know if he got it out or not. He cleaned himself up as best he could and was back in time to exchange chisels.

The blacksmith could see Sylwester had been working very hard, for his chisel was broken. He gave Sylwester a sharp chisel, and left. When he was out of sight, Sylwester went back to slacking off. He knew what to do when the blacksmith came back the next time. He really was an ingenious fellow.

He must have removed the metal chip that was lodged in his thigh, for it healed and caused him no further problems.

August 1944
The Stolen Military Jackets

After many months of working in the tunnel, Sylwester and his fellow Russian workers had explored as many aspects of it as possible. It was huge, and building it was a massive undertaking. There were many branches going left and right, and they had ventured through most of them. In the branches were storage compartments called Magazines.

The men were assigned to remove debris from the tunnel in preparation for pouring concrete. They would load the garbage into a wagon and push the wagon down the railroad tracks to the field outside, where everything was dumped. There were many empty cement bags to remove from the tunnel. The men would load the empty sacks with the other garbage, but would save the bags after dumping the garbage. Bags were valuable. They did not know how valuable they would be until the following day.

They had worked hard all morning and it was lunch time. They had an hour break but nothing to eat. They just had to sit in the tunnel and wait. Sometimes they were outside, dumping the cart at lunch time and they could sit and wait out on the field, but today they were all in the tunnel. The foreman had taken the electric train out to the field for his lunch. The men were alone inside. Balabon, a young Russian in Sylwester's group, and a couple of others, decided to explore the Magazines and find out what was in them. They weren't gone long when they returned with the exciting news that one of the compartments was stocked full of

German military jackets. This was very good news to the men who sat around in thin rags. They could use the lining for shirts.

There were about 150 coats, tied and bundled, and locked behind bars. They tried to pry apart the bars and found they would give enough to allow a small sized body to pass through. Sylwester and Balabon were the smallest and the youngest and volunteered to go in, but the men decided they needed a plan first. It was a serious offense to steal military uniforms. If they were caught, they all would die.

The next day they planned their work so that the buggy they used to take things in and out of the tunnel, would be in the tunnel at lunch time. They had saved many cement bags that morning for the coats. They deliberately worked slower than usual, leaving the trolley half empty. The foreman, Herr Schlick, was yelling at them to go faster but one had a stomach ache, another was not feeling well, and on the complaints went. The foreman took the electric train out to the field for lunch and the men stayed inside the tunnel with a half empty trolley just as they had planned. They had one hour.

The tunnel was curved. One man was posted under each of the lights leading to the Magazine where the coats were stored, just in case a German guard showed up. The lights were about 200 yards apart. One man could see another as he stood under the light. If there was danger the first sentry would call the code kapusta - cabbage, to the next man. Kapusta, kapusta, kapusta would go down the line from one man to the next until the code for danger reached the men in the storage bin.

Sylwester and Balabon squeezed into the storage compartment and started ripping the bundles apart. There were stacks of them, five to a bundle. "Сколько плащей ты хочеш? .... How many coats do you want? Two? Three?", they asked the men on the other side. They quickly passed the coats through the bars. Sylwester only took one for himself. Then they squeezed their way out and wasted no time in helping the others stuff the coats into the bags and into the trolley. The sentries still stood guard under each light down the long, curved corridor watching and listening for danger. The lunch hour was almost over. Everyone was panicking to finish. The foremen would soon be back.

Their password, Kapusta, was never used. They pushed the cart onto the potato field, dumped it, and buried the cement bags full of coats in the potato patch, and headed back to work.

At quitting time, they dug up the bags and took them back to camp. Since the camp was not surrounded by wire, there was no gate and no guard checking them in. Sylwester hid his coat under his mattress, thinking about his new shirt. Little did he know what awaited him.

August 1944 - two weeks later
The Interrogation

The horrible chiseling job was finished, and the big hooks were secured into the holes overhead. The tunnel was ready for the huge electrical cables that would be strung across the hooks, mile after mile. For the next four Sundays every man, no matter where he had been stationed, had to carry the cable. It was thick and immensely heavy, and was an enormous job. Thousands of men lined up, one behind the other, in a queue that seemed to go on forever. Each man stood very close to the next, front to back. On command, the men heaved the monstrous cable onto their shoulders. Each man supported about 2 feet of the line, and strained under the weight. The long train of men inched its way into the tunnel, hour after hour.

The first Sunday, Sylwester was standing between two taller men. The taller ones carried some of his weight on their shoulders. He was lucky that first Sunday, but the following two Sundays he was between two shorter men, and carried the brunt of their loads, plus his own. He felt like his shoulder would collapse. He tried to ease his load by stooping down and letting some of the weight fall on the man in front and behind, but the man behind him kicked him in the rear and shouted, "Встань и неси свою часть .... Straighten up and carry your share!" Sylwester carried the huge cables for three consecutive Sundays and hated the job. On the fourth Sunday, the last monster cable was to be carried. He did not want to go. After breakfast when all the men were heading out, Sylwester snuck into his barrack and hid.

The camp commandant walked through the barracks with his German Shepherd after breakfast, making sure everyone was out. He shouted, "Raus! Jeder raus! Zur Arbeit! .... Out! Everyone out! Get to work!" They went from room to room. Sylwester heard them coming and hid inside his tiny locker. Cramped, rigid, and petrified, he froze as the commandant and his dog walked around the room. He could hear the dog sniffing and his master's boots pounding the wooden floor. If the dog smelled him out, he would be finished. Deathly still, he prayed. Each second seemed an eternity. The door closed. They left.

Sylwester slowly began to relax, and prepare for his day off. He dug out a potato, cooked and ate it. He took out the military jacket from under his mattress, sat down on the bed closest to the window for light and started to unstitch the lining. No one could see him as he quietly worked, thinking of the shirt he would have. The shirt would be big, but he was wearing rags and did not care. Young Sylwester had overlooked one very crucial detail. Only a minimal number of German foremen went to supervise the cables on Sunday. The majority of the foremen remained in the camp.

A barber, whose service was sought by workers and foremen alike, shared Sylwester's room. One of the German foremen wanted a haircut on that particular Sunday. Why he thought the barber would be in, when every man had to be at the tunnel carrying the cable, is unknown. The foreman came to the window where Sylwester was so diligently working just out of view. The window was open and the foreman stuck his head in and asked, "Ist der Friseur hier? .... Is the barber in?" Sylwester was startled by his sudden appearance. He quickly hid the jacket behind his back. "Nein .... No." The foreman saw the coat before Sylwester concealed it, and immediately recognized it as a German military jacket. As the foreman ran around to the door, Sylwester hid the jacket under his mattress.

The guard entered the room and found Sylwester on his bunk. He demanded, "Zeig mir! Zeig mir! .... Show it to me! Show it to me!" He grabbed Sylwester by the neck of his shirt, and in one motion, pulled him off the bed and flipped the mattress. He held the jacket and glared at Sylwester. "Was ist das? Das ist eine Uniform Jacke! Von wo hast Du

das? .... What is this? This is a military jacket! Where did you get this?" He violently hit Sylwester. Sylwester took the hard blows without resistance, thinking, "Ja jestem skonczony ale ide samem. Nie odam nie kogo .... I am finished but I go alone. I will never give anyone away." He remembered well the rubber pipe incident, where every man involved was jailed and whipped. He would not betray anyone ever again.

"Komm mit mir! .... Come with me!" barked the guard. Sylwester obediently walked in front of him. There were so many men and so many barracks, that the camp was divided into sections. Each section had its own commandant. The guard was not from Sylwester's section. He bypassed Sylwester's commandant's office, and took him directly to his own. They entered the office.

Sylwester sat silently with the military jacket on his lap. His mind was racing. His situation was grave. It seemed impossible that he would be able to get out of this one. He needed a story that was believable and yet would not get the others arrested. "Proszę Boga pomiec mnie teras .... Please God help me now," he prayed. He swore to God he would not turn anyone in. He vowed to die alone. As Sylwester prayed, the foreman and the commandant looked at him and spoke very quickly. He understood most of what was said but not all. The commandant marched over to Sylwester and, looming over him, demanded, "Von wo hast Du diese Jacke? .... Where did you get this jacket?"

Sylwester was petrified. He could not tell the truth. He would be shot for stealing. He had to lie to try to save his life and not implicate the others. "Ich habe es gefunden im Tunnel in einem Haufen Zement Säcken .... I found it in the tunnel in a pile of cement bags," he replied. The commandant slapped him across his face with such force that his head swung left and right with the blows. The guard looked on. Sylwester had no defense except his lie. He started to cry. The commandant repeated the question. Sylwester repeated his answer word for word, and again the commandant slapped him across the face.

Sylwester would not change his story no matter what lay in store for him. He wept at the thought of his fate. He was powerless and knew execution was an imminent reality. Lying was the only defence he had.

The commandant walked over to his desk and dialed Sylwester's commandant. Sylwester silently cried and waited, with the jacket on his lap.

Sylwester's commandant strode in with authority. Everyone in the room jumped to attention and saluted, "Heil Hitler! .... Hail Hitler!" Sylwester did not know he was to jump up and salute as well. He sat quietly. The commandant marched over to Sylwester. He had no sympathy for the tears and the red, swollen face. He grabbed Sylwester and effortlessly lifted him to his feet. "Weisst Du nicht wie Du Dich zu benehmen hast, wenn Officiere kommen? Du muss stehen und Heil Hitler grüssen! .... Don't you know what to do when authority enters the room?", he shouted. "You must stand and say Hail Hitler!"

Sylwester did not know. He was so afraid. "Heil Hitler!" he desperately said, hoping that was what his commandant wanted. But as he was uttering the words "Heil Hitler", his commandant slapped him across the face, over and over. Again Sylwester tried to show respect and make him stop by repeating "Heil Hitler", but the hard blows continued.

The first commandant spoke. "Nimm den Kerl in dein Büro und mach mit ihm was Du willst. Ich will kein Blut hir haben. .... Take him to your office and do what you want with him there. I do not want to see blood in here."

"Nimm diese Jacke zu meinem Büro! .... Take this jacket and go to my office!", he ordered. Sylwester obediently left, wiping his bloody face on his sleeve, as tears streamed down. The door closed behind him and he was alone. He thought his commandant would follow him but no one followed. He looked around. There was no one. Why were they not following him? Were they waiting to see if he would try to escape? Were they watching to see if he would warn the others? Sylwester's mind raced. He looked at the trees surrounding the camp, and wanted to run. Should he or shouldn't he? But where would he go, what would he do, and where would he sleep? He was taunted by the temptation but decided running was not a choice. They would track him with their dogs and bullets. He'd be dead in no time.

Sylwester walked to his commandant's office and stood outside the door. He looked behind him and still there was no one. Sylwester knew

to run was futile but again he started to think, should he or shouldn't he run, when he heard the phone ringing inside. The commandant's wife answered and said, "Nein .... No." His commandant was phoning to see if he had arrived. When Sylwester realized they were checking up on him, he dismissed the thought of running. He immediately knocked on the door and heard the woman say, "Eine Minute, es klopft wer an der Tür .... Just a minute, someone is knocking at the door." She opened the door and let Sylwester in. She wiped his tears with her apron, sat him on a chair, and went through a door that led to the kitchen. He waited alone.

The commandant arrived a few minutes later, and Sylwester instantly jumped to attention saying, "Heil Hitler!" The camp commandant scoffed it off saying, "You don't need to do that. Over in the other section, there was a different authority. Here it's not necessary." Sylwester was baffled by his new attitude. The man had just beaten him in the other office. Now he was being nice. The commandant politely said, "Setze Dich hin .... Sit down." Sylwester sat down holding the coat on his lap. The commandant offered him a cigarette, but Sylwester declined saying he did not smoke. He did not trust the man at all.

Two guards with short rifles entered. They walked behind Sylwester's chair and stood in the back corners of the room. Sylwester was uncomfortably aware of his surroundings and predicament. His life, and the lives of the other men, depended on his wit and an unfaltering lie. He must not confuse his story. Even though he was only eighteen years old, he was prepared to die, but he would not take anyone else with him. He must not break, no matter what they did to him.

The commandant sat behind his desk, with Sylwester in a chair in front of him. The commandant leaned across his desk. "Drzewiecki sage uns wo Du diese Jacke geklaut hast .... Drzewiecki, tell us where you stole the jacket. Nothing will happen to you."

Sylwester was too experienced to fall for this lie. Once again his mind went back to Küstrin Neue Stadt when he naively told the truth about the rubber pipe. This was a bigger offense. He wasn't naive anymore. Sylwester spoke slowly. He had to remember every word he said.

He knew he would be interrogated again and again. "Herr Kommandant," he began. The commandant was writing everything down. "I was working in the tunnel under my foreman Herr Schlick. The master foreman was Herr Schwartz. Our job was to remove the railroad track, remove the cement tile, and remove the sand out of the tunnel. Another group of men were coming with concrete to pour and level. Another group were coming behind them setting the machinery. We had to clean whatever was on the ground out of the tunnel before the concrete could be poured. There was a pile of empty cement bags that we also had to remove. We put everything in the buggy and dumped it in the field. I found the coat in the pile of empty cement bags."

The commandant listened and wrote down everything that Sylwester said. "Und die Männer neben Dir? Haben Die nichts gesehen?.... What about the men that were beside you? Did they not see it?"

Sylwester had to be careful in his reply but he was able to think quickly on the spot. "If they would have seen it they would have grabbed it away from me. Some of them are much stronger than I am so I tried not to show it to them. I hid it in one of the cement bags. When everything was loaded in the buggy, we pushed it out to the field and dumped it. I took the bag that had the coat in it and I hid it in the potato patch. When it was quitting time I took it and I brought it home."

"Sylwester, das ist nicht wahr. Wir vermissen viele Jacken von diesem Magazine vom Tunnel. Du hast sie geklaut! .... Sylwester, this is not true. We are missing many coats from the Magazine in the tunnel. You stole them!" he shouted, pointing his finger.

Sylwester started again, "Herr Kommandant, I was working in the tunnel under my foreman Herr Schlick. The master foreman was Herr Schwartz".... and on he went telling exactly the same story, remembering in sequence and detail what he had just said, about cleaning the tunnel, the pile of empty cement bags, finding the coat, hiding it in one of the bags, loading the bags into the cart, dumping the cart onto the field, and hiding the bag with the coat in it in the potato patch.

The commandant was very quickly writing everything down. He tried coaxing Sylwester in artificial politeness, "Drzewiecki sage uns. Da

passiert Dir doch nichts .... Drzewiecki tell us. Nothing will happen." Again he tried to give Sylwester a cigarette and again Sylwester declined. The commandant was mad and yelled, "Drzewiecki, sage die Wahrheit. Wenn nicht, ruhfen wir die Gestapo und schicken Dich nach Auschwitz! .... Drzewiecki, tell the truth. If you don't we'll call in the Gestapo and ship you to Auschwitz!"

Sylwester repeated his story and the commandant continued to record what was said. The interrogation seemed endless. Over and over again Sylwester told the same story. The commandant compared his notes. Angrily he threatened, "I will give you five minutes. If you don't tell me in five minutes I will phone the Gestapo and they will take you to Auschwitz!"

As the commandant spoke the armed guards cocked their rifles. Sylwester was startled by the sudden noise. He turned and saw the guards handling their rifles, and couldn't breathe. He was gasping for air. He thought they were going to shoot him right then and there! But as they aimed, he could see the light go straight through the barrels. The chambers were empty! Sylwester turned back to the commandant and slowly repeated the same story. No matter what happened he would not change it. He would not let any other man go down with him. "Herr Kommandant, I was working in the tunnel under my foreman Herr Schlick. The master foreman was Herr Schwartz. I was cleaning the tunnel".... and on and on he went ending with, he hid the bag with the coat in it in the potato patch.

The commandant picked up the phone. Sylwester realized if the commandant phoned the Gestapo they would only be coming for him, but if he called the army, they would do a camp search. Nothing could stay hidden once the soldiers were brought in. Everything would be ripped upside down, every jacket would be found and every man with it.

As they waited, two high ranking officers entered. Sylwester was crying, sitting on the chair with the coat in his lap. The officers and the commandant talked amongst themselves. Sylwester had been stripped of his belongings which included the string that held up his pants. He held the over sized waist of his pants with one hand. Looking out the window, he saw one of the Russian men who had stolen the jackets with him,

walking from work. Soon everyone would be back from carrying the cable. He had to let the Russian know that he was caught so that he could warn the others.

"Herr Kommandant, would I be allowed to go to the outhouse, please?" The officers looked at one another and agreed. Again they let him go alone. Sylwester had to be quick. He knew he would be watched to see if he would run, or if he would try to notify the others. The outhouse was in full view of the commandant's office. Holding his pants, he headed straight for the outhouse. It was at the edge of the forest that perimetered the camp. There were trees and thickets behind it and around it. Sylwester went inside and closed the door. Risking his own life to warn the others, he quickly climbed up and wriggled himself through the tiny opening high up on the back wall. He dropped down into the bushes at the back. Staying low, and running as fast as he could, he circled around the back, through the thicket, and into the Russian's barrack. Short of breath, he spoke quickly and quietly, "Меня споймали. Ты скажи всем чтобы спрятали свои куртки. Я не выдам никого, они могут искать .... I got caught. Tell everyone to hide their jackets. I will not turn anyone in, but there could be a search."

The Russian worker knew that all of their lives were in danger. He was scared and angry. "Ты дурак! .... You stupid ....!" Profanities followed. Sylwester had no time to listen. He quickly left and ran like the wind. His life was on the line. He circled the thicket, crawled back through the tiny opening, and into the outhouse. Once inside he dropped his pants, and was pulling them up as he came out.

The outhouse was not far from the office and Sylwester could see the officers standing in the window watching him. He was gone no more than a few minutes. When he entered the office he saluted and said, "Heil Hitler!" No one said a thing. Sylwester picked the coat up off the chair, sat down and waited. A limousine pulled up.

Two members of the Gestapo had arrived. They were ominous in their size and authority. One had a huge belly. They were completely dressed in black and exuded power. When Sylwester saw them through the window, his entire body went numb and he felt faint. His fear was

immeasurable. He had heard horror stories of the Gestapo. He knew he was going to die a horrid death. When they entered, everyone, including Sylwester, jumped and shouted, "Heil Hitler!" The Gestapo gruffly ordered, "Setze Dich hin! .... Sit down!"

They asked the commandant and the two officers the details of Sylwester's detainment. There was much talking amongst them and then the Gestapo's voices began to rise. They were furious, especially the barrel-bellied fellow. Sylwester was sure that he was going to be killed.

Suddenly the bigger of the two, turned and slammed his fist down on the desk as hard as he could. The desk shook with the crash, and Sylwester jumped.

The Gestapo ordered the commandant to give Sylwester all of his belongings and to let him go! It was a miracle! The guards gave him his pant string, hat, and whatever else they had taken from him. Once he had his possessions, the bigger Gestapo waved his hand in dismissal and ordered, "Gehe! Du bist frei. .... Go! You are free." Sylwester held his pants with one hand, and his hat and belongings in the other. He humbly left the room bowing, walking backwards saying, "Danke. Danke .... Thank you. Thank you." The coat was left on the chair as he went out the door. Tears of joy ran down his face.

Sylwester's life, and the lives of the other men, had been spared because of his sharp wit, and because he did not break under pressure. The jackets were never found.

Part 2 - Chapter 4

Mainz, Germany
December 1944 - January 1945

Forced Labour
Outside the German Work Camps

Work Assignment: Rescue and Repair
Sylwester Drzewiecki - 19 years old

The German cities of Andernach, Koblenz, Koln, Düsseldorf, and Mainz, were in ruins. They had been mercilessly bombed. Workers were needed to rescue survivors trapped in the rubble, and to repair railroads, bridges, and transport routes.

Sylwester's foreman, Herr Schlick spoke well of his men. Their work in the tunnel in Meseritz was finished. They were selected to be sent to Berlin, where they would be dispatched by train to one of the demolished cities. Sylwester had never before seen the rampage and carnage of war. That was about to change.

On December 15th, 1944 Sylwester climbed into yet another boxcar. He left Meseritz at 4 p.m. and arrived in Berlin two hours later. As the train took them into Berlin, he saw the destructive power of the bombs. The demolition was formidable. Huge buildings were now heaps of rubble. Wreckage lay everywhere.

In Berlin they waited and rested for nine days, while more train loads of men arrived from different locations. They stayed in barracks, waiting to be sent to Andernach, Koblenz, Koln, Düsseldorf, and Mainz. There was one foreman for about twenty men. Sylwester and the workmen under Herr Schlick were sent to Mainz.

Berlin to Andernach to Mainz
Wigilia - Christmas Eve

On December 24th, 1944, the men were loaded into a boxcar and shipped west of Berlin. The train stopped in Andernach where it stayed overnight, before continuing on to Mainz. Sylwester spent Wigilia - Christmas Eve, in the boxcar of that train. He was cold and hungry, and thought of home. Wigilia was the holiest night of the year when he was growing up, but Rudnia was a lifetime ago.

Later that night, another train pulled up beside theirs. The second train was empty and Sylwester wanted to explore it. He took his sack, and went. The empty train had been transporting German soldiers. He climbed inside the different cars., going from one to the next, and couldn't believe his find. Pieces of half-eaten bread and crusts, that the soldiers had left, were scattered on the floor. Sylwester picked up every piece from every car, eating some as he went. He returned to his boxcar and shared the bread with his fellow workers. They devoured every crumb of their Wigilia feast.

He slept huddled together with the others, trying to stay warm. He was shivering with the cold. He awoke the next morning to Święta - Christmas Day, and a hearty bowl of soup from the kitchen. It was thick with barley, not the usual watery broth with a bit of cabbage and potato floating in it. The last time he had a bowl of soup like that was at home in Rudnia, two and half years ago. Sylwester scraped his bowl clean. He wanted more, but there were no seconds. As the men were finishing their morning meal and cleaning up, the air raid sirens screamed their warning that bombers were in the air. Everyone scattered and headed for any cover available. Sylwester could hear the planes but couldn't see them. He listened and prayed. All was quiet. The planes had come and gone without dropping a bomb. The men came out of hiding, scared and shaken.

They were transported that day from Andernach to Mainz. The train stopped three kilometers outside of the bombarded city. It was already evening, and very cold when they arrived. A light snow covered the ground. One of the cars had been converted into a kitchen, and the

menu returned to the same watery fare that Christmas night. There were no barracks, and the men slept huddled together in the boxcars. The train would be their sleeping and eating quarters while working in Mainz.

In Mainz
Trapped

They left the train on foot, on December 26th, to look for survivors in the rubble. Sylwester could not believe the destruction. The city was entirely leveled. Rubble lay everywhere, as far as the eye could see. Smashed buildings with partial walls and floors stood amidst the devastation. How many had died here? How many had been buried alive? He shuddered at the thought. The men began their gruesome task, but too many days had passed. They found no survivors. The entire scene was ghostly. There were a few nuns, and police walking through the ruins, but no one else. The workers were told to cease their search. There was no one left to save.

A vital bridge had been bombed, cutting off movement of supplies to the Germans. The workers were ordered to begin repair on the bridge that day. Huge beams were needed, which were salvaged from demolished buildings. They were hauled to the bridge site on a two-wheeled wooden cart. The men unloaded the timber and returned for more. A destroyed cathedral nearby was a source of many beams. As they worked in the cathedral's rubble, they noted that the cellar of the cathedral had not been destroyed in the bombing. It was still intact.

The men worked on the bridge for three days, December 26th, 27th, and 28th. The 28th of December, 1944, was the most beautiful, sunny day. The sky was so clear they could see for miles. It was 11 a.m., and they had just delivered another load of beams to the bridge site. Upon their return to the cathedral, they heard the dull drone of approaching bombers. There were no air raid sirens to warn them, for they had been destroyed, too. The American bombers were coming back. The men could see them clearly against the blue sky. They had to run for cover.

"Быстро. В кафедральный подвал .... Quick! Into the cellar of the cathedral!", one of the Russians shouted. They all scrambled into the tiny room. It was no more than eight feet by eight feet. They were squished together like sardines. Sylwester's curiosity pulled him towards the window. He wanted to watch the planes. Józef Dubitski saw Sylwester's impending danger. He urgently called him to stand by the post that was supporting the ceiling. "Panie, nigdy nie stuj po serotku pokoju i dźwi. Jak bomba spadnie sufit pierw załamujiesie. Stuj wrogu tego pokoju .... Sir, never stand in the middle of the room or by the door. If the bomb hits, the ceiling goes first. Stand in the corner of the room." Before Józef Dubitski finished speaking, the whistles of the falling bombs could be heard. The men helplessly waited.

The bombs came down like a thunderous downpour all around them. The noise was deafening. The impact was enormous. Everything shook. Kaboom! Kaboom! Kaboom! The blasts shattered everything in their paths, spewing debris of all sizes at lethal speed. How much could the walls and ceiling withstand? Thick, black soot from the cellar's chimney exploded and filled the tiny space, clogging their nostrils and the lining of their throats. They couldn't breathe! They couldn't see! They were choking and coughing. Sylwester removed his hat and covered his mouth and nose. Others did the same. It was impossible to escape the thick soot. It flew everywhere.

They listened. The planes left. All was quiet. They wanted to get out of the choking hellhole, but huge mortar blocks and giant timbers had fallen all around the cellar, blocking any escape. They were trapped.

One of the older Russians, Mashka, quietly spoke, "Сегодня здесь мы все умрём .... It is here today that we all shall die." Sylwester's terror became frenzied panic when he heard those words, for he realized Mashka spoke the truth. Their situation was hopeless. Sylwester dropped his hat, that protected him from the choking soot, and began screaming and pulling his hair uncontrollably. All the men were screaming and pulling their hair like madmen! They knew they would slowly suffocate.

Mashka called out, "Все тихо. Тихо. Слушайте. Самолёты летят назад .... Everyone quiet! Quiet! Listen! The planes are coming

back!" For the first time in Sylwester's life he prayed to die. He prayed for a bomb to hit directly on the cellar and kill them instantly. The Russians were atheists and had always teased Sylwester when he said his prayers each morning and night, but now in the face of death, they prayed too. Gripped with terror, they listened to the shrill whistles as the bombs dropped, and begged God to spare them a horrid, slow death.

Bombs were coming down and exploding everywhere. The cellar shook to near collapse. They couldn't see. They were deafened by the noise. A bomb exploded near the door. The force of the blast blew a hole in the doorway, which instantly sucked out the air. Everyone was gasping, gagging, grabbing their throats, trying to breathe something that was not there. The sounds that came from their mouths were the sounds of dying men. The vacuum lasted an eternity of seconds, before the air rushed back in. Everyone started screaming again.

Mashka called out once more, "Все тихо. Я могу увидеть лучь солнца через щель .... Everyone quiet! I can see sunlight coming through the cracks!" The men scrambled, throwing the boulders left and right, not caring about anything except getting out. They madly crawled out through the hole like rats, trampling everything underfoot. Outside they continued running in every direction, trying to get away from the cellar. Herr Schlick shouted for them to come back. He yelled in German, "Halt! Halt! Wir müssen jeden zählen. Vielleicht sind noch welche begraben oder tod .... Stop! Stop! We must count everyone. Maybe someone is trapped or killed." They kept running.

Slowly sanity returned. "Илья. Где Илья? .... Ilya. Where is Ilya?" No one remembered seeing him come out. Two men bravely crawled back into the black cellar. They carefully made their way down the debris calling, "Ilya! Ilya!"

They found his slumped body at the base of the rubble leading to the doorway. A huge piece of metal was protruding from his gut. He had been standing by the doorway when the bomb exploded. No one knew he had been killed. No one noticed his body as they desperately scrambled to get out of their grave. Ilya had been killed by the bomb that had saved their lives.

Four Days Later
The American Fighter Plane

Sylwester awoke to the first day of 1945. A light snow had fallen during the night, and had powdered the ground and the young evergreen forest nearby. Herr Schlick had given everyone the day off. Sylwester quietly jumped from the boxcar, leaving his sleeping comrades, and joined those who were already up. A game of cards was in progress. Sylwester stood behind the men seated on tree stumps, and watched.

As it neared noon, one of the players asked,"Славко, ты можеш идти и достать карточки на пищу? .... Slavka, would you go and get the tickets for the meal?" One meal ticket was issued per man per meal. Without a ticket no bowl of soup was given.

"Да, конечно ... Sure, yes." Sylwester got the tickets from the soup kitchen. The game broke up for lunch. They were in the boxcar getting their soup containers, when American fighter planes swooped down like a swarm of bees. Herr Schlick shouted, "Nicht aus dem Wagon steigen sonnst werdet Ihr erschossen! Bleibt versteckt! .... Don't step out of the boxcar or you will be shot! Stay hidden inside!" There was no way they were going to stay inside with bombs aimed directly at the train. They had been trapped in the cellar only four days before. They rousted the men who were still asleep, and ran. The bombs whistled through the air. Sylwester dove under the trees and covered his head with his hands. The bombs exploded around him. The ground shook beneath his belly and the noise was deafening. Metal, wood and rock shot through the air in every direction. The planes opened fire with their machine guns. The bullets ripped the ground and chewed the branches that hid him.

Sylwester sprinted to a big tree with roots protruding above the ground. He crawled under its gnarled roots. He squeezed his way through the sharp talons anchoring the giant tree and found Mashka covering his head as the bombs exploded. The ground shook. The tree swayed.

Sylwester ran, and an American fighter plane spotted him and opened fire. Bullets spewed out of its machine guns. Sylwester ran for his life, but he couldn't outrun a plane and its bullets. The light snow on the

ground provided no camouflage. He ran into the evergreens again. He had been taught how to play dead. He slid under a pile of stacked boughs, and laid beneath them motionless. He was breathing hard, his mind was racing, his heart was pounding, and he dared not move.

The pilot was not convinced that his target was dead. He made a pass, circled around, and flew low to the ground. The pilot opened fire into the boughs. Sylwester said countless prayers as the bullets sprayed. "Prosię Pana Boga żeby kule mnie nie trafiły .... Please God let the bullets miss me." He wanted to run. Round after round of machine gun fire spewed from the plane, shaking the ground beneath him. The bullets chopped through the branches. The boughs violently shook and hit him as he laid still. The pilot was satisfied and left.

Sylwester stayed under the branches. He did not know if he'd been hit or not. He had been told if a bullet hit him he would feel no pain. He had to know if he was wounded, and ran his hand all over his body. There was no blood. The pilot had missed him.

The men were terrorized by a second bombing in four days. Some remained hidden the rest of the day, too terrified to come out even for food. Sylwester's hunger took over his fear. With so many men not eating, he saw an opportunity to get extra helpings. Thankfully the kitchen of the train had been spared. Sylwester gathered as many containers as he could find, went to the kitchen and explained that he was getting soup for some of the others, and then ate them himself.

Seven men had been killed. Their bodies were carried to the side of the train and laid side-by-side. Sylwester looked at the hollow faces and bony bodies covered in blood. Just a short time before, they had been running and hiding, stricken with panic and fear, just as Sylwester had been. He cried. Not far from the train, a German army transport was moving soldiers, trucks, artillery, and tanks. They had been bombed by the same planes. Many German soldiers were killed.

After the bombing, local farmers arrived with their horse-drawn wagons to help in whatever way they could. Hay would be needed to line the mass grave. Grave diggers were needed to dig the huge pit. Sylwester remembered the advice his father gave when he was taken from his home

in 1942, "Jak potrzebują ochotnika to ić i bendzie Ci za to wynagrodzone .... If they need a volunteer, go and you will be rewarded." The Germans asked for five volunteers and Sylwester heeded his father's advice. It took hours to dig a pit large enough to bury so many men.

January 3, 1945
The Mass Burial

Wagon loads of straw were delivered to the grave site by the farmers. The hay was thrown into the grave. Sylwester set to work making a bed of straw for the dead. The bodies were not wrapped; there was nothing to wrap them in. The corpses were covered in blood, and some were horribly mutilated. Sylwester and the four other gravediggers covered the bodies with a final layer of straw. As he climbed out, he realized how easily it could have been him laying there with these men. A few inches closer and the bullets would have ripped him to shreds.

A group of German soldiers dressed in full uniform approached the burial pit. They wore short military jackets. The soldiers stood at the edge of the grave and sang, "Unsere lieben Freunde, Auf Wiedersehn .... Our dear friends, goodbye." They raised their rifles in a farewell salute, fired three rounds and stepped aside.

Sylwester made the sign of the cross, and shoveled dirt over the bodies with the other gravediggers. German soldiers and Russian prisoners were equal, and at peace, as they lay side by side in death. Why could it not be so in life? Young Sylwester was at a loss to find any logic to war. There was no reward for digging the grave, except a feeling of peace for having lain his comrades to rest.

Before leaving Mainz, camouflaging for rockets that were hidden near the city had to be replaced. Huge branches were cut and bundled, dragged to the road, and loaded onto trucks. The Germans transported the

branches to the secret rocket site and assembled the camouflage without the workers.

Part 2 - Chapter 5

Düsseldorf, Germany
January 1945

Forced Labour
Outside the German Work Camps

Work Assignment: Building a Floating Barge
Sylwester Drzewiecki - 19 years old

They were moved by train from Mainz to Düsseldorf, in January 1945, and were stationed on the West side of the Rhine River. They no longer slept on the train, but stayed in an old school house. They were to build a floating barge to avoid disruption of German transport, should the bridge crossing the river be bombed.

As they worked on the barge, the Americans were advancing on the German army. The Germans were retreating, and the battle front was getting closer and closer to the Rhine. Sylwester could hear the explosions of the artillery fire. The sound was enormous. If the Americans continued their forceful stance, the front would soon be on them.

The workers had to be moved to the east side, where they slept in a small wooden shack. There was nothing to the structure. The walls were paper thin. They built bunk beds for themselves to make a little more comfort and room. Each day they travelled by tram to and from the bridge, where they continued their work on the barge, and listened to the shelling.

A few weeks later
Sylwester Tries to Escape

While the men rested in their flimsy sleeping quarters, they could clearly hear the shelling. It was incredibly loud. Sylwester not only could hear artillery, he could hear gun fire as well. The Americans were advancing and would be at the bridge any day.

Sylwester decided to escape. He wanted to get across the bridge to the Americans. He had been a slave for three long and horrible years. Liberty was on the other side. He told no one his plan. He knew exactly where he would hide when he reached the west side. He had seen a small building near the bridge, while he had been working on the barge.

He took the tram over the city to the bridge, and showed his workpass. The guard let him through, and Sylwester wasted no time getting across the bridge. The river was wide, and the bridge very long. As he neared the middle, he could not believe his eyes. The Germans were retreating. Men and machinery were funneling onto the bridge from every direction. Thousands of German soldiers were running towards him. The bridge was tightly packed. Sylwester pushed and shoved his way through the sea of men. They were running for their lives and paid no attention to him, as he kept pushing West.

Energized by the revelation of liberty, he ran to his pre-planned hide-out. He didn't care how long he would have to wait, and how hungry he became. He was a free man as soon as the Americans made it to the Rhine. He opened the door of the shack and stopped short. A German foreman was hiding inside the shack; he was a Volksdeutsche - a Pole of German parentage. He too, was trying to escape and join the Americans. The two men stared at each other. The foreman was embarrassed to have been discovered, and instead of admitting his intentions, told Sylwester he should not be there, and took him back. Sadly, the foreman's decision to return would prove tragic.

The Following Day
At the Front Line

The next morning, the workers and Herr Schlick climbed into the tram that took them to the bridge, but they could not go all the way. The tram had been damaged by artillery. They disembarked and walked. About 400 yards from the bridge Sylwester saw a German soldier laying down in the back of a truck. He had an explosive device that looked like a small tank. It was about 2 feet high, by three feet long, by two feet wide, and was full of dynamite. His job was to set the device under an American tank, and blow it up. The soldier ignored the workers as they passed by.

The workers went a little further and were instantly surrounded. German soldiers jutted their bayonets in their faces, shouting, "Halt! Wo gehst Du hin? .... Halt! Where are you going?" Herr Schlick had lead the workers right to the front line of the battle field. He explained that they were to work on the barge. "Zeige Deinen Pass! .... Show us your pass!", demanded the soldier. He showed the pass and several of the soldiers lead the workers to the bridge. It had been completely destroyed during the night. Huge timbers lay heaped and broken in the water. Sylwester looked at the ruins. He would have been on the west side with the Americans right now, instead he was trapped on the east side.

They could not reach the barge on the other side without the bridge. They took their tools and were told to set to work taking apart empty barracks. The bunk houses would be shipped and used elsewhere. As they disassembled the buildings they could see American planes rise up in the distance, assess the situation, and descend again. Sometimes the Germans would fire artillery towards the planes but there was no retaliation. The Americans were waiting.

At quitting time, Sylwester and the workers headed back towards their sleeping quarters. They had walked about a kilometer when the artillery started to fly. The Americans opened fire on the German army right where the men had been working all day. Thousands of shells exploded. The noise was incredible. They scrambled for cover but their flimsy hiding places provided no protection.

One week later
The Artillery Attack

The Americans were gaining ground, pushing the Germans even further back. The workers were ordered to gather their belongings and ready themselves to leave. They were to be transported by tractor-trailer to Bielefeld that night.

Packed and ready, they waited inside their sleeping quarters for their transport. The Volksdeutsche foreman, Józef Dubitski, and a few others, sat around the table in the middle of the room playing cards. Others were on their bunks.

Sylwester shared a top double bunk with Balabon, the young fellow who had crawled into the storage compartment with him in Mainz to steal the military jackets. The two were on their bunk. Balabon was next to the wall, laying on his back, with his feet flat and his knees bent. Sylwester was on the outside of the bunk, fully stretched out with his hands under his head. All was quiet as they waited.

The quiet instantly turned to bedlam. An artillery shell exploded in the centre of the room, smashing the table, and critically wounding every man who had been playing cards. Some were killed. The men cried in agony. Their bodies were ripped and mutilated. The foreman who had ordered Sylwester back after trying to escape, lost his leg. Blood gushed from the stump. Józef Dubitski was down. He had one side of his buttocks blown off. Sylwester and Balabon sprang from their bunk. Blood was everywhere. They madly tied tourniquets around the wounds as fast as they could. Only a handful of the men were spared. The wounded had to be moved to the concrete bunker outside. More artillery fire was sure to fly at any moment.

Sylwester and Balabon lifted one of the worst of the casualties. With his arms around their necks, they dragged him between them. They made a run for the bunker. They were almost there when Balabon collapsed. Shrapnel had ripped through his knee when he was lying on the bunk. In his state of shock, he hadn't realized that he had been hit. Sylwester supported one man on each side and got them both to the bunker. The artillery let fly! Shells were exploding with such magnitude, the blasts lit up the night. It was as though night had turned into day. The

manic scene was inconceivable to Sylwester. They were in the direct line of fire at the front.

They had to save the wounded and themselves. Their only hope was the concrete bunker. The noise drowned out their yelling. Blasts exploded, sending shrapnel and debris in every direction, as Sylwester and the few others carried the wounded to safety.

The bunker was filled with agonizing groans. They tended the wounded with rags. The shelling continued outside, but the bunker held tight. Sylwester went to his faithful friend Józef Dubitski, who had protected Sylwester many times from his first days at Küstrin Neue Stadt. It hurt to see his guardian in excruciating pain. Dubitski spoke. "Panie Drzewiecki, zostawiłm Moje rzeczy w pokoju. Prosie Cię przinieś .... Mr. Drzewiecki, I left my things in our room. Would you please get them for me?" Their few meager possessions were all they had. Sylwester told his old friend he would go.

He had barely stepped out when he flew back in, slamming the door shut. The artillery was even more intense than before. Search lights now scanned the ground. To venture out would be suicide. There was absolutely no chance of making it back to their room. If the artillery didn't kill him, bullets certainly would. He could not help his dear friend. He went to Balabon. His bandage was bloody. The boy was in terrible pain and Sylwester felt helpless.

The night was long with suffering. German soldiers found their way to the bunker as well. A German First Aid attendant arrived. He went from one man to the next throughout the ugly night, but there was little he could do to help.

The following day the tractor-trailer arrived and took only the able-bodied men. The wounded stayed behind in the bunker with the First Aid attendant. Their sleeping quarters had been reduced to a pile of splinters. It was sorrowful saying goodbye to Józef Dubitski. He truly was a good man.

The tractor-trailer pulled away. The Americans would be there any day. Sylwester had some peace knowing that Józef Dubitski and Balabon would soon be liberated. He was on his way to Bad Oeynhausen.

Dubitski was older than Sylwester yet he never called Sylwester by his first name. He only addressed Sylwester formally as Pan, or Panie Drzewiecki. Sylwester forever remembered Pan Dubitski's kindness and protection. He never saw Józef Dubitski or Balabon again. Their fate is unknown.

Part 2 - Chapter 6

Bad Oeynhausen, Germany
April 1945

Forced Labour
Outside the German Work Camps

Work Assignment: Repairing the Railroad Station and Track in Lohne.
Sylwester Drzewiecki - 19 years old

From Düsseldorf, they were sent by train to Bad Oeynhausen. During the entire journey, they were immersed in war. Air raid sirens and bombing raids abounded.

The workers bunked in an empty health spa in Bad Oeynhausen. The once popular mineral baths were now empty and abandoned. The men placed boards across the tubs which served as their beds. They walked three kilometers each day to the nearby town of Lohne where they were to repair the main railroad station.

En Route to Bad Oeynhausen
Locked out of the Bunker

The train stopped en route, in the town of Bielefeld. The men were not to disembark. As they sat waiting inside the boxcars, the air raid sirens blared again. There was a bunker near the train station, and everyone sprinted for the bomb shelter, German soldiers and workers alike. The soldiers were safely inside, while the workers were still running. They could hear the planes.

They hurriedly opened the door and stopped short. The Germans aimed their machine guns at the desperate Poles and Russians.

They would not let them in. Their choices were suicidal; either stay outside and get bombed or push their way in and get shot. There was no time to waste. The workers desperately fled for any cover they could find.

The bombs whistled through the air as Sylwester cowered against a wall, covering his head with his hands; he had no cover. The bombs exploded one after another. The ground shook. The explosions were deafening. He wanted to be inside the bunker, but his life meant nothing to the Germans sitting safely inside. A dog would have had better treatment. Sylwester remained huddled against the wall with his hands covering his head as the bombing continued. He was completely exposed to whatever flew at him. He felt hopeless and doomed, and did not stop praying for a moment.

When the bombing stopped, Sylwester could not hear for his ears were ringing from the explosions. Slowly the terrorized workers gathered. Luckily, the bombs had exploded far enough away that they had been spared.

The prisoners were ordered back into the boxcars. They never came face to face with the German soldiers who had denied them refuge in the bunker. It would have given Sylwester some satisfaction to show them that they had survived.

The train moved forward, and Sylwester continued on his way to Bad Oeynhausen.

In Lohne
The Pedestrian Bridge

As the men repaired the main railroad line in Lohne, the air raid sirens screamed again. There was no concrete bunker in sight. The men were out in the open with nowhere to hide. There was a pedestrian's bridge, about 200 yards long, near the train station. It lead to a field which lead to a forest. The foreman ordered the men to run for the cover of the trees. They wasted no time. They could hear the drone of the bombers overhead. They ran across the bridge, through the field, and into the woods. Nothing happened.

A cannon was fired, signaling that the bombers had left and the men were to return to work. However, the fighter planes remained in the air. The men could hear them. Sylwester stayed put. He had come too close to the spray of bullets from the same kind of plane in Mainz. He would rather take his chances in the forest than venture out into the open. Not one of the men returned. They were too afraid.

Slowly the men started to feel a little more at ease. Feeling protected by the trees, they started a game of cards. As the game progressed, a man dressed in rags appeared out of nowhere. He was filthy and looked tired and gaunt, older than his years. His face was unshaven and black with dirt. His hair was a mass of grubby tangles. The men stopped and stared as the vagrant approached.

The man spoke perfect Polish and Russian, and told them that he worked with the underground of the British Intelligence. He pulled out a map, and spreading it before them, showed the men where the American, Russian and British armies were positioned. He said that the allied forces would arrive in two days, no longer. He carefully folded the map, and was gone. It was as though he had vanished.

The workers looked at each other. They would soon be free; liberated from slavery. They would not return to work. They would wait in the forest until the allied forces reached them.

Within a few minutes of resuming their game of cards, armed German soldiers materialized from every direction of the forest. Their

bayoneted rifles pointed directly at Sylwester and the others. In seconds they were surrounded, and their short-lived dream of freedom was gone. With rifles and bayonets pointing at the workers, they ordered, "Zurück zur Arbeit .... Back to work!" The men had no choice, and obeyed.

They walked out of the forest and back across the field towards the pedestrian bridge. As they neared it, they could see two rows of uniformed men, standing on either side of the bridge. They had no idea who the men wearing the dark uniforms were. Were they railroad workers?...Firemen? The uniformed men watched the unsuspecting workers approach. The German soldiers continued to move the workers forward with bayonets pointed at their backs. As they drew nearer, they recognized the dark uniforms of the German Secret Service. The SS men were spaced apart every few feet over the entire span of the bridge, each was armed with a club, and each had a menacing look.

Sylwester realized what was about to happen. Their only chance was to run as fast as possible to the other side. Bayonets were behind them, and clubs were ahead of them. The workers started to run. The SS chased them and beat them with their clubs. The first man onto the bridge was the luckiest. He received his share of flogs but didn't get held down. He ran across quickly. The rest were not so lucky. Sylwester was near the middle of the pack. Everyone was getting clubbed over their heads, their backs, their shoulders, wherever. The SS men did not care where the blows fell, as long as they fell hard. Those who were grabbed and held were given no mercy.

Sylwester ran with his arms crossed over his head. A hard whack on his skull would kill him. The SS were swinging their clubs with all their might. He was hit on all sides. His tormentors were ruthless. He couldn't get across quickly enough. There was no way to avoid the battering. He had to endure the painful blows until he reached the other side. As long as he avoided a direct hit to the head, and was not grabbed, he could make it.

The workers ran back to their work site at the railroad station, afraid that the SS would chase them, but thankfully they did not. When Sylwester reached the railroad station he knelt down on the railroad ties

and wept. Three years of pent up anger raged within him. He had reached his breaking point. He was no longer a naive sixteen-year-old farm boy. He was a cruelly educated, nineteen year old man. He wanted to kill the SS who had mercilessly clubbed him. Kneeling on the railroad ties, he swore before God that he would murder a German before the war ended. He had never made a death wish before.

Three days later, bruised and aching, Sylwester was liberated. The Americans had arrived in Bad Oeynhausen. He was not only liberated from slavery, but liberated from doing something he would have regretted the rest of his life.

In Bad Oeynhausen
Liberation

The day after the clubbing, the Americans were very near Lohne and Bad Oeynhausen, just as the ragged man in the forest had said. German army trucks arrived to move out the many slave labourers. The workers were ordered to climb into the back of the trucks.

Sylwester did not want to go, with the Americans so close. He wanted to be free and this was his chance. He knew well how to sneak around and hide. He watched and made his move. Sylwester, and a few others, ran and hid in a small basement. Some workers from other work groups, Russian women as well as men, found their way into the basement as well. They had no food, but they had become accustomed to the constant state of hunger. They waited and tasted freedom.

They stayed hidden for one day and two nights. The morning following the second night, they heard a plane flying low overhead. In every language it announced, "Don't walk on the streets. The American forces are entering the city." When Sylwester and the workers heard this, they were ecstatic. Freedom was on its way. An hour later the American tanks rolled into Bad Oeynhausen. The rumble of the approaching army was music to their ears. The Germans put up no resistance. Bad Oeynhausen surrendered.

The Russian women went out to meet the Americans first; they had a better chance of receiving a friendly welcome. They quickly returned and eagerly called into the basement, "Товарищи выходите. Американцы здесь. Вы можете идти в магазин и взять что вам нада .... Fellows come out. The Americans are here. You are allowed to go into the stores and get yourselves whatever you need."

Everyone in the city was hungry and a grabbing frenzy ensued. It was chaos in the stores. People madly took whatever food they could. Sylwester anxiously ran to the grocery stores, but by the time he arrived the shelves were bare. The Russian women had grabbed shirts for the men. They could see there would be nothing left if they did not seize things instantly.

They converged back in the basement. Food was shared and devoured. One Russian girl gave Sylwester a shirt. He thanked her and hurriedly put it on. He marveled at its cleanliness and newness. His tattered, filthy rag lay heaped on the floor. The girl's kindness, and his newly found freedom, overwhelmed him with such emotion that he wept uncontrollably.

The Americans would begin organizing the displaced people into nations of origin in a few days. The refugees had to fend for themselves during this time. They slept and ate in the basement. They shared their food and rationed what they had collected to last three days. On the third day the Americans called the refugees and the German civilians to assemble. The Americans ordered the German people to feed the homeless until the time came when they could be transported out.

Lice infested all of them, and they had to be doused with the powder disinfectant. They had become accustomed to lice, just as they had become accustomed to hunger, hard work, and cold.

People were organized by their country of birth. The Poles were grouped with the Russians as there was no Polish group in Bad Oeynhausen. Sylwester was thinking of Poland and home, but was classified as Russian.

Sylwester sat down near a ditch, and took out his official identification work book, which he had carried with him every day for the past three years. It was thin, like a passport, and had the Nazi insignia on the cover. He had been issued it when he was taken from Rudnia in 1942. He looked at the book thoughtfully, turning it over and over, flipping through the pages. He read his name, Sylwester Drzewiecki, his birth place Rudnia, his town Kołki, his province Wołyn. Each German city where he had lived and worked was entered. Each camp and work assignment was listed.

Sylwester wanted to rid himself of his Russian classification and his record of slavery; he was Polish and he was free. Three years of hell were in those pages. He angrily ripped them up and threw them into the ditch. It felt good to tear the book to shreds. He buried them and walked away a free man....with no proof of who he was, where he was from, what he had done, or where he had been.

Germany 1945
Fallingbostel
Berlin
Poland 1945
Minden
Werl
Paderborn
Frankfurt
Mannheim
Note: This map is not to scale

Part 3

Chaos After The War

Sylwester Drzewiecki
Mój Ojciec - My Father

Determination and Perseverance,
Give us wings to fly.

-Mary Drzewiecki, 2000

Part 3 - Chapter 1

The Russian Refugee Camps
Minden and Fallingbostel, Germany 1945 - 1946

Introduction
Sylwester Drzewiecki - 19 years old

The Second World War ended May 8th, 1945. From Bad Oeynhausen, Sylwester and the Russian workers were transported to a refugee camp in Minden, Germany. There he learned of the horrors of the Ukrainian uprising in Eastern Poland; that entire villages had been completely destroyed and the people slaughtered. He wanted to know the fate of his family, but he had no way of finding out if they were alive or dead. He felt compelled to return to his homeland.

In the first weeks after liberation, Sylwester regretted his hasty decision to destroy his Russian identification papers in Bad Oeynhausen. Without official papers it was mayhem. His freedom was neither immediate nor easy, and returning to Poland was not guaranteed. His work papers, issued by the Germans in 1942, had stated that he was from Rudnia near the town of Kołki. Now he had no way of proving he was a Pole, let alone proving his name.

There were thousands upon thousands of refugees from all over Europe in Minden. Each nation had its own camp. Organizing the massive numbers of displaced people was an immense undertaking for the Allied Forces. In the midst of the chaos, Sylwester's identity was not believed. He spoke perfect Russian and was classified as such. He was placed in a Russian refugee camp, and slept under a massive, big-top tent with the other workers. The Russian army organized its citizens for deportation. Sylwester was slated to be deported to Russia on the next train. He did not want to go to Russia. He wanted to go home. He felt trapped, like a prisoner once again, and was miserable. He waited in the camp in Minden for three weeks.

Russia had been ravaged by war. Skilled workers and manual laborers were needed to rebuild the country. The Russian authorities asked their citizens their occupations. They would be placed in positions where they were most needed upon their return. Sylwester was not going to say he was a farmer as he had done in 1942, and end up with a pick and shovel. If he was going to Russia, he was going to learn a trade. He had always been intrigued by machinery, and had been fascinated by the machinists working the lathes in the pulp mill in Küstrin Neue Stadt. He had wished he could have run the machines that built the mechanical parts. The job engrossed him. The Russian official asked Sylwester, "Какая ваша робота?..... What is your occupation?"

"Я машинист ..... I am a machinist." The man wrote it down and went on to the next.

Army trucks arrived to transport the Russians from Minden to Fallingbostel, where a train to Russia was leaving in three days. The train would travel across Poland, and then disappear inside Russia, with Sylwester.

Three Weeks After Liberation
The Polish Flag

In Fallingbostel, each man was issued a seven day ration of food. Sylwester looked inside his bag and was overwhelmed. After living on next to nothing for three years, there was enough food to last him a month. He knew hunger too well and would ration carefully. Once he was on the train to Russia, he did not know when his next meal would be.

The evening before departure, Sylwester was so unhappy thinking that he would be living in Russia for the rest of his life. He forlornly walked the compound which was fenced, and had a guard at the gate. This was not the freedom he had dreamed of. The Russian flag flew overhead. He looked out and saw the flags of other countries flying over their camps. He was thinking of his fate when, in the distance, he saw a Polish flag. He stared in disbelief. It was definitely a Polish flag, with a white

strip across the top and a red strip across the bottom. His heart soared. It had to be flying over a Polish compound, and Sylwester was determined to get into it. He walked towards the gate. The Russian guard ignored him, because he wasn't carrying anything that needed to be checked.

Sylwester felt liberated all over again when he entered the Polish Army camp. Everyone around him was speaking Polish. He was at home. He spoke to a Polish guard, and was elated to hear that Polish civilian refugees were entering the camp and being accepted each day. He had to return to the Russian camp for his meager belongings and his bag of food, but would immediately return. He was free. The train would leave for Russia in the morning without him. Sylwester was going home to Rudnia.

1945
Stopped at the Gate

Sylwester re-entered the Russian compound as effortlessly as he had left. He entered the big tent and went straight towards his comrades and his belongings. The morning train would take the men that he had lived and worked with, to their Russian homeland. They would never see each other again. The Russians tried to convince Slavka to go with them to Russia. They told him he was foolish and making a big mistake. Sylwester replied, "Я жил с вами ребята и вы мои товарищи, но я другой. Я поляк. Я принадлежу Польше ..... I have lived with you boys, and you are my friends, but I am not one of you. I am Polish. I belong in Poland." They embraced and said their goodbyes.

The Polish flag waved in the distance. Sylwester strode towards the gate, with his bag in full view. The Russian guard stopped him. "Стой! ..... Halt!" No one had permission to take things out of the compound. The guard questioned what he was carrying, and where he was going. No Russian was permitted to join a Polish camp. He could not tell the truth, or he would be on the next train to Russia. "Видеш я уезджаю в Россию утром. У меня есть одежда которая мне не нужна.

Там много одежды в России. Я думал что я пойду в польский лагерь, продам одежду и куплю водку от поляков .... Well, you see, I'm leaving for Russia in the morning. I have some clothes in here that I don't need. There are lots of clothes in Russia. I thought I'd go over to the Polish camp, sell the clothes and buy some whiskey from the Poles."

The guard's eyes lit up at the mention of whiskey. He told Sylwester that he too was leaving on the train in the morning, and he would like a drink. Sylwester could see the guard had taken the bait, so he continued, "Хорошо. Как долго ты будешь на посту? .... That's good. How long will you be on duty?"

"Полтора часа .... Another hour and a half."

"Я вернусь назад через пол часа и мы выпьем за наш отьезд .... Well, I'll be back within half an hour, and we'll have a drink to our departure." Sylwester said cheerfully. The Russian guard was pleased with the idea and let Sylwester out of the gate, thinking of the whiskey only thirty minutes away. Sylwester immediately put the guard out of his mind, and headed straight for the Polish Army camp, and home.

The Polish Camp

Sylwester had to register. He spoke Polish, explaining his history and his situation to the Polish officials. Three years had passed since he left Poland and he rarely had the opportunity to converse in Polish. Without even realizing, he was mixing Russian words and phrases in with his Polish.

The Polish officials were not convinced. He had no papers with which to prove his identity, and they rejected him. He was not Polish. They would not allow a Russian to infiltrate the Polish Army camp.

The Poles did not want him, and he did not want to return to the Russian camp. The train was leaving in the morning. He was desperate.

The same young Polish guard, whom he had spoken to earlier in the Polish camp, saw Sylwester's gloom. "Oni mnie nie przyjęli .... They did not accept me," Sylwester sadly said.

The guard believed Sylwester was telling the truth, and wanted to help him. He leaned close to him and whispered that Polish civilians from the German farms were brought in almost every day. He told Sylwester to stay in that particular area of the camp, and when a new group of workers was brought in, to mix with them. No one would know he did not belong and he would be accepted.

Sylwester liked the plan. He did as the young man advised. He stayed hidden in an empty barrack, and waited. He looked out the narrow window for the expected arrivals, but no one arrived. He opened his food bag and ate sparingly. He was prepared to wait a month if needed. He knew he could make his seven day ration of food last that long.

Day after day Sylwester stayed in the barrack waiting. Finally on the morning of the seventh day, he awoke to sunshine and the sound of trucks coming into the camp. He hurriedly rolled off the wooden bunk and over to the window. How he prayed this would be the day. He watched the trucks drive by, and stop. He would not make his move until he knew the time was right. Many people disembarked. There were men and women of all ages, and children. There was a large group of men from a concentration camp. They were emaciated and their heads were shaven completely bald. Sylwester carefully listened. They were all speaking Polish. He grabbed his bag, went outside, and mingled with the Poles.

He made his way towards the group of men from the concentration camp. Sylwester had a full head of dark hair and was rather conspicuous beside them. "Dlaczego Ty masz włosy .... Why do you have hair?" they asked. "Pracowałeś na gospodarstwie? .... You worked on a farm?"

"Nie, ja pracowałem jako cywilny robotnik .... No, I was slave labour."

The Polish officials began organizing the civilians; women and children in one area, men in another. Sylwester went with his group to their assigned barrack and stood in front of it, waiting for the Polish offi-

cial to come. Sylwester was nervous but kept telling himself to stay calm and to remember to speak only Polish. What if the Polish official today was the same man who rejected him seven days before? What if he was recognized? What if, what if...?? Polish. Polish. He must remember to speak Polish. He became more and more nervous.

Sylwester breathed a sigh of relief. He had never seen this official before. The men lined up and he asked each man in turn his name and birthdate. Birthdays were not celebrated by Sylwester's family in Rudnia. Sylwester knew the year he was born and the season but no specific date. When it was Sylwester's turn to answer he said, "Urodziłem się w roku 1925. Może w lipcu .... I was born in 1925. Maybe in July."

The Polish official looked at Sylwester quizzically. "Chłopcze zapomniałeś przez wojnę kiedy żeś się urodził. Ty się urodziłeś trzydzi-estego pierwszego grudnia, dwudziestego piątego roku! .... Young man, through the war you have forgotten when you were born. You were born the 31st of December, 1925!" He wrote it down and moved on. Whether it was true or not, Sylwester's birth date remained December 31st, 1925, for the rest of his life. It was stamped on every official paper from that day forward. *Perhaps the Polish official chose that date because New Year's Eve is known as Sylwestra in Poland.*

Sylwester had cleverly infiltrated the Polish Army camp. He was Polish once again, and had papers to prove it.

Part 3 - Chapter 2

The Polish Refugee Camp
Fallingbostel, Germany
1946 to 1947

Introduction
Sylwester Drzewiecki - 20 years old

Maintaining law and order in a time of food, housing, and clothing shortages, with thousands of displaced people to relocate, was chaos. Thefts were rampant. There were shortages of every kind. Looters broke into German homes and stores and helped themselves, feeling justified in their revenge. People worked the illegal black market selling stolen contraband; food especially, was at a premium.

Many British people worked in Fallingbostel. The peacekeeping forces tried to enforce law and order by instilling stiff sentences on thieves. Sentences of ten and twelve years were common for minor crimes. There were hundreds of civilians who were imprisioned immediately following the war.

Help was needed everywhere. Sylwester worked as a camp policeman in Fallingbostel for one month, until he learned that a British woman who ran a soup kitchen for orphans, needed help. Sylwester jumped at the opportunity to work where there was plenty to eat. He and a friend, Józef Antczak, worked in the kitchen spooning food to the orphans. It was heart breaking seeing so many children with no parents. Sylwester believed the children were the worst victims of the war, for they were totally helpless. The two young men fed the hungry children, and fed themselves as well. Sylwester could not get enough; he savored the feeling of a full stomach, but always wondered if he would eat again the next day. He worked in the kitchen for six months, and for the first time in his life, started to gain weight.

There were dances in Fallingbostel for the refugees. Sylwester taught himself to dance in his room, using a broom for a partner. He sang and whistled as he spun the broom around. He learned the Slow Waltz, Viennese Waltz, and Polka in this way, and was popular on the dance floor.

Relief organizations distributed Red Cross food parcels to the refugees. Sylwester and Józef each received one. They decided to save their packages, for they had enough to eat while working in the kitchen. They carefully hid their food parcels, because Red Cross packages were greatly sought on the black market. Unfortunately, Sylwester and Józef would pay dearly for theirs.

March 1946
The First Janka

Sylwester had seen few girls during the war and here they were, at every glance. He liked what he saw and began his romantic pursuits. His first girlfriend was Janka, not Janka Horoszkiewicz whom he married, but another girl with the same first name. To avoid confusion I will use Sylwester's nickname for her, Pyra. She was from the region of Poznan. When Sylwester learned from Pyra, that the people of Poznan called potatoes pyra, rather than kartofla, like they did in Rudnia, he lovingly named her Pyra - Potato.

Sylwester liked Pyra's company. They walked and talked together. It was wonderful to be treated kindly and to be loved. Sylwester had been abused his entire life, and delighted in her display of love and affection. In his heavenly state, Sylwester wondered if he and Pyra would marry.

Shortly After
The Bottle of Whiskey

Sylwester was moved from the Polish Army camp to a Polish civilian camp in Fallingbostel. There he met Piotr - Peter Konopatcki, who was about the same age as Sylwester. The entire Konopatcki family was together in the camp: The mother, father, and four children. Pani Konopatcki made whiskey from beets, and used it as currency to trade for bread, meat, or anything else the family needed. She needed bread for her daughter's wedding. There was a good bakery in a village nearby, where Sylwester and Peter had twice previously traded whiskey for bread. Off the two friends went with another bottle for the baker.

Unknown to the boys, during the night the small village had been looted. The British military police were everywhere. As the boys were walking into the village, they were stopped by two British MPs in an army jeep. The MPs grabbed the two boys without questioning them, and laid them on their backs in the jeep. They didn't have a clue what was going on.

Sylwester and Peter lay scrunched in the back. The boys didn't question authority; besides, the British only spoke English and they would not be able to understand them. They were certain when they arrived wherever they were being taken, that the bottle of whiskey would be taken from them. Better the boys to have it than the British. Peter marked the bottled half way down with his thumb; half for Peter and half for Sylwester. Peter glugged away, checked how far he had gone, and glugged some more. Sylwester polished off the remaining half. The jeep stopped at the station in Walsrode with two drunkards who could barely stand and who needed to vomit. They threw up all over the place. The British had quite a time managing the inebriates inside. The fire was going in the stove, and it was very hot inside the station. The boys' drunken stupor made it feel even hotter. The two boys collapsed on bunks and slept until 4 p.m.

An interpreter was brought in and the boys explained about the wedding, the whiskey, and the bread. Obviously these were not the robbers that had plundered the village during the night. Sylwester and Peter

were released. The MP's gave the two boys tickets for the train back to Fallingbostel. With their heads pounding, and feeling quite ill, they climbed on board. It was a long time before they had a drink of whiskey again.

Peter and his entire family immigrated to Australia, and contact was lost with them.

May 1946
Guilty Until Proven Innocent

The refugees in Fallingbostel were to be sent elsewhere. Pyra and her family were being sent to Peine, near Hannover. Sylwester and Józef decided to go to Mannheim, to the American zone, to check if they would be accepted to work in the peacekeeping forces. There they would have clothes, food, and a bed. It was worth a try.

The British woman who ran the kitchen, gave them some bread and butter for their journey, and a pass to prove the food was theirs; without a pass, the food would be assumed stolen and confiscated by the military police. Their Red Cross packages, that they had saved, would be ideal for the trip. They rooted them out of their hiding place and were off on their adventure to Mannheim. They securely clutched their parcels and their kitchen lunch, for there were many thieves.

Sylwester and Józef luckily caught a ride in a British ambulance to the train station in Minden. The railroad station was swarming with people and the two watched their bags like hawks. British military police were everywhere, searching for stolen packages. Sylwester and Józef were unaware that they should have asked for a pass for their Red Cross packages before they left the camp. Nor did they take the name of the British woman or the telephone number of the soup kitchen where they had worked.

A British MP searched their belongings, asking to see their passes. They showed the officer everything, but he had dealt with innocent look-

ing thieves before. Their day of fun and adventure instantly turned into a nightmare.

They tried to explain, but their pleas fell on deaf ears. They were arrested, and accused of stealing the parcels to sell on the black market. The British woman could verify their innocence but no one cared enough about them to pursue the truth. It was quicker and easier to lock them up and forget about them.

They were charged as thieves and thrown into a tiny cell in the Minden jail to await trial. After three horrible and hungry days, Sylwester and Józef were taken to an English court. They did not have a lawyer to represent them. Sylwester did not even know what a lawyer was. How could he? He had only experienced Rudnia poverty, German slavery, and post war chaos in his short twenty years of life. Sylwester and Józef stood before the British judge, with a Polish interpreter beside them. They wanted to plead their innocence but the interpreter told them to plead guilty. He assured them they would be put in prison for years if they pleaded not guilty. He had seen it before.

Sylwester was crying. He pleaded, "Panie, dostaliśmy to w obozie Fallingbostel .... Sir, it was given to us in the Fallingbostel camp." The British woman could instantly clear them if someone would only look her up, but nobody did. The judge was in a hurry. He had no time for discussions before the bench. It was a complete sham. The interpreter approached the bench and told the judge the two boys pleaded guilty. Down the gavel came. "Six months." They were treated like criminals. They were handcuffed and escorted from the courtroom to an awaiting vehicle that took them to the prison in Werl. It was a four hour drive away.

The prison was called Zucht Haus and suitably nicknamed 'The Beehive'. Sylwester and Józef were thrown into separate cells which were already occupied by long term inmates. Sylwester was miserable. It was May 7th, 1946, and he was a prisoner once again. He sat down in his cell and wept. He hated every moment of his unjust sentence.

The time dragged as he sat cooped up in his cage, waiting for six months to go by. Pyra sent him letters. He consumed every word, and read the letters over and over again. The intolerable boredom made the

weeks and months drag. There were some Polish books, but reading could not fill the hours in his day. He sat and waited. A priest came to the chapel of the prison each Sunday, and Sylwester faithfully attended mass and sang in the choir.

The guards took the prisoners out for a walk around the compound only three times a week. On one of his walks, Sylwester met two young Polish brothers who were serving twenty-five years for break and entry. They had worked as a team; one brother stood watch outside a house, while the other looted. The sentences were harsh for everyone, but even more so for Sylwester and Józef because they were innocent.

The boredom was intolerable, but the starvation was worse. The British officials weighed the prisoners once a week, on shower day. If a prisoner lost too much weight, his food ration was slightly increased. Ironically, Sylwester was more hungry in the British jail during peace time, than he was during the Second World War in the German forced labor camps. At least in Germany he could steal potatoes.

Living waiting, is wasting living.
- Mary Drzewiecki, 1994

October 6, 1946
Released from Prison

On October 6th, 1946, Sylwester was released from the Werl Zucht Haus. He was a skeleton after six months of starvation spent cooped up in a tiny cell. From Werl, he and Józef were given train tickets to Paderborn, where there was a Polish camp. Sylwester devoured the food given to him in the Paderborn camp. Thankfully there was enough to eat, and he gradually gained weight over the three months he was there, but he was still dreadfully thin. He continued to correspond with Pyra but could not visit her from Paderborn. He hadn't seen her for a long time.

In late December, 1946, Sylwester and Józef had to report to the headquarters in Lahde. They were assigned a room in the Polish camp in Raderhorst, just north of Lahde. While in Lahde, they chanced to meet two Raderhorst camp policemen wearing MP arm bands.

The two MPs had been sent to Lahde to get produce for the Raderhorst camp. Their wagon, pulled by a tractor, was piled high with potatoes, turnips, and beets. They were friendly and offered the boys a ride. They sat with the produce. Sylwester glanced at the MPs to make sure they weren't looking, and quickly stuffed potatoes down his shirt. He knew starvation all too well and was not going to pass an opportunity to collect food. One of the MPs, named Zygmunt, saw him but looked the other way. Sylwester was unaware that he had just met his future brother-in-law, Zygmunt Regulant.

Germany 1947
The Brother-In-Laws
Zygmunt Regulant and Sylwester Drzewiecki

Late December 1946
Sylwester 21 years old
Raderhorst Camp

In the Raderhorst camp, Sylwester met a Polish family from Omelanka, which was 40 kilometers from Rudnia. The family had fled their village in July, 1943, during the Ukrainian uprising, and after hiding in the forest for one week, had found their way into Germany. The father, Adam Horoszkiewicz, knew Sylwester's father Jan Drzewiecki. This made the two men feel connected. In fact, Adam Horoszkiewicz and Jan Drzewiecki had tried to pursue the same girl when they were young. Sylwester was welcomed by Adam into his home. Adam introduced Sylwester to his youngest daughter Janina, and his bachelor days ended.

Part Four

Born and Raised
Under a Straw Roof
A True Legacy of the Human Spirit
WOLYN
Krakow
POLAND ~ 1939
Mary A. Drzewiecki

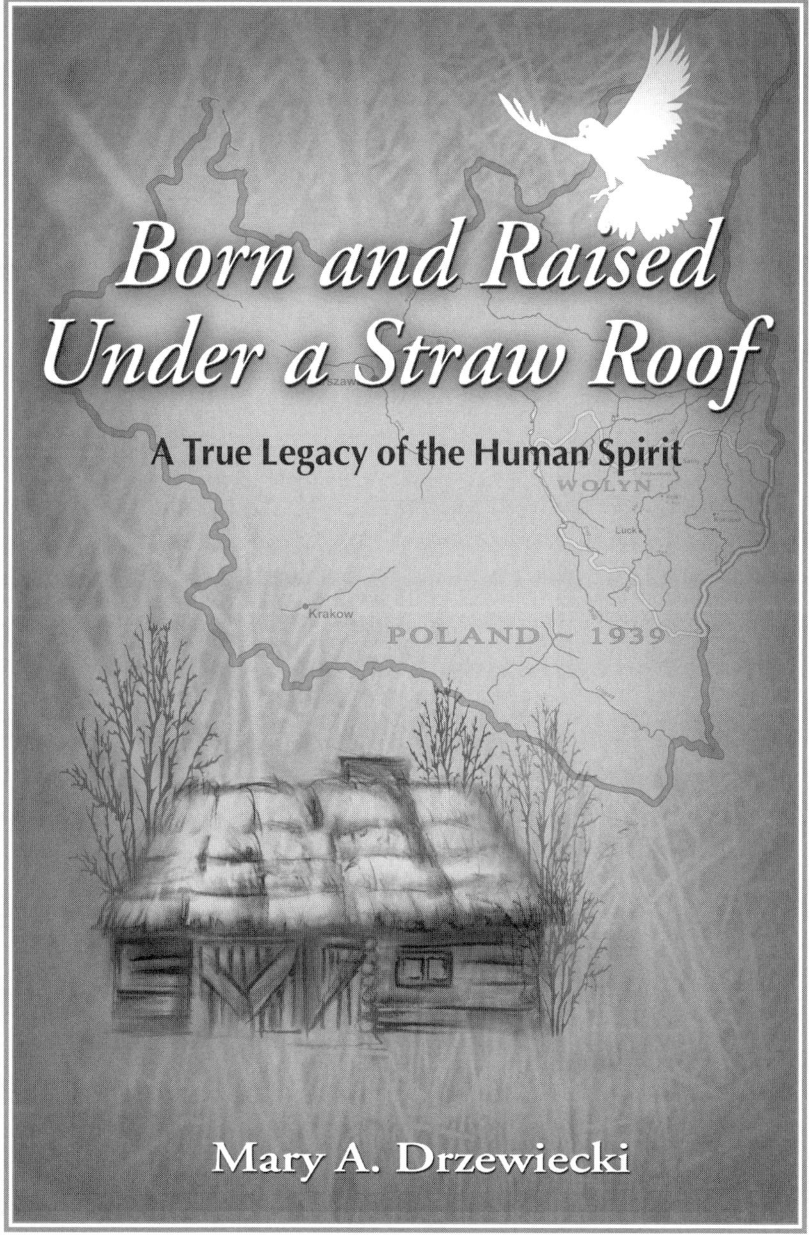

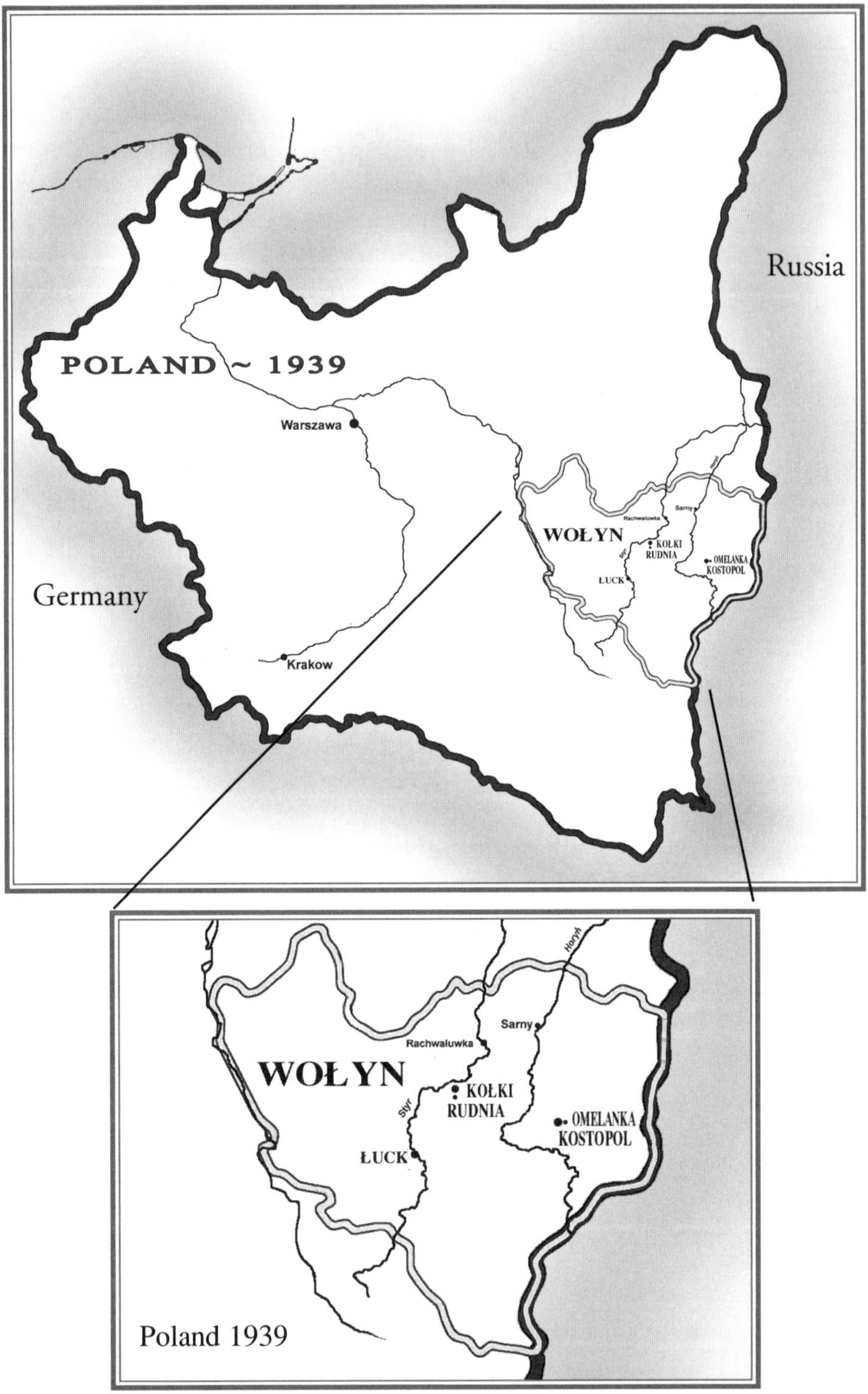

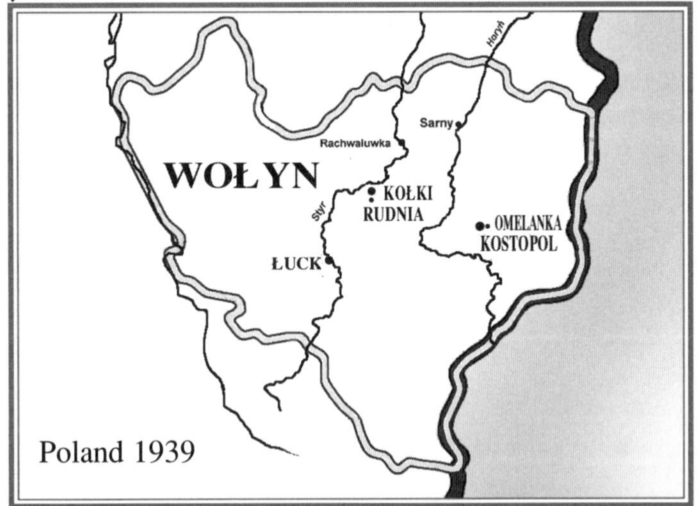

POLAND ~ 1939
Russia
Germany
Warszawa
Krakow
WOŁYN
Rachwaluwka
Sarny
KOŁKI
RUDNIA
ŁUCK
OMELANKA
KOSTOPOL
Styr
Horyń
WOŁYN
Rachwaluwka
Sarny
KOŁKI
RUDNIA
ŁUCK
OMELANKA
KOSTOPOL
Styr
Horyń
Poland 1939

Part 4

Omelanka, Eastern Poland to Germany
1943-1945

Janina Horoszkiewicz
Moja Mama....My Mother

Look through the windows of the past,
But leave there not your heart,
For moments vanish into many tomorrows,
And we can only grow moving with them.

- Mary Drzewiecki, 1994

Part 4 Introduction

Growing Up In Omelanka

Part IV takes place in my mother's home village of Omelanka in Eastern Poland, during the Ukrainian uprising in the Second World War. It tells of her home life, how she and her family fled their home and hid in the forest to escape the Ukrainian insurgents, and how they were taken to Germany to work on farms as forced labourers.

Again my parents and I wish to emphasize that the intent of this book is NOT to condemn the nations as a whole under whom they suffered. We again emphasize the importance of forgiving the perpetrators of their crimes. Peace can only come through forgiveness.

The Introduction tells of my mother's home life, some of her childhood experiences, and introduces family members, before moving on to Chapter 1 when Omelanka burns, and my mother flees her home where she was *Born and Raised Under a Straw Roof.*

The village of Omelanka was in:

Gmina Stydyn - Municipality of Stydyn
Powiat Kostopol - Region of Kostopol
Województwo Wołyńskie - Province of Wołyn
Wschodnia Polska - Eastern Poland

It is helpful to know the following events as they directly affected Janina and her family:

July 1943   The village of Omelanka is attacked by Ukrainian insurgents. The Horoszkiewicz family flee and hide in the forest for one week.

July 1943   Janina's father, Adam Horoszkiewicz, leads the family through the forest at night to the town of Rachwaluwka. They are transported by train to Nienburg - Weser,

Germany, then by horse-drawn wagon to Steinbrink, where they work as forced labourers on German farms.

1945   The Second World War ends. The Horoszkiewicz family is placed in a refugee camp in the village of Lahde, near Minden, Germany. There are refugee camps in Raderhorst, Frille, and Ilzehade.

1947   Janina meets Sylwester Drzewiecki. They marry on Easter Sunday, April 7, 1947.

Note: Janina preferred to be called Janka in this book.

Janina Horoszkiewicz:

Birth date: August 1, 1926
Birthplace: Wioska Omelanka - Village of Omelanka
                            Wschodnia Polska - Eastern Poland
Nicknames: Her family called her Janka or Jasia.
                            In Germany she was called Johanna.
                            In Canada she was called Janina or Jenny.
Pronunciations: Janina - Yu-nee-na
                            Janka - Yun-ka....short vowel sounds
                            Jasia - Yu-sha
                            Johanna - Yo-han-a
                            Horoszkiewicz - Ho-ro-shke-veech
Immigrated to Canada: July 25, 1949

Janka had a loving family and did not live in dire poverty as did the Drzewieckis forty kilometers away. As much as Sylwester's father was abusive, Janka's father was gentle and kind. She had one sister, Stasia. Her home had a thatched roof and a clay floor, and was partitioned like a duplex. Janka's side of the house had one big room, and two small sleeping rooms. Stryjek - Uncle Kajetan's family, and her Babcia - Grandmother Horoszkiewicz, lived on the other side. The farm provided well with the two families working together. The work was constant, but food was plentiful. The home had simple furnishings made by hand: a large closet, two beds, a table, chest, and a couch.

Janka was compliant, and content with her simple life. The Horoszkiewicz family went to market, and attended the Roman Catholic church in the nearby village of Huta Stepanska. Janka was taught to serve and to please others, which she did her entire life. School and endless chores left little time for play. The clay floor was polished smooth. She chopped and stacked kindling, milked and fed the cows, and helped in the fields and in the house. There were also chickens, swans, pigs, and one horse to feed. Her pet was a grey milking cow, with gorgeous brown eyes. Stryjek Stanisław had given it to her as a gift. Janka had hand fed her and cared for her since she was a tiny calf.

Spring was Janka's favorite season, when everything came alive after the long winter. She loved the blossoms on the trees and the wild flowers in the fields. She sat on the grass and made chains of daisies for her hair, or picked flowers for her mother. She loved watching her mother combing her dark, waist-length hair, and putting it up in a bun on the crown of her head.

At sixteen, when Omelanka was attacked by Ukrainian rebels, Janka was blossoming into a very attractive young woman. She was five feet four inches tall, with a shapely figure, and long, dark hair. Her gentle, quiet nature made her even more attractive. The young men's heads turned, but Janka didn't notice.

Janka did not travel beyond Huta Stepanska before fleeing Omelanka in 1943. She grew up sheltered and protected, and was very naive about life and the world. That would all change.

Adam Horoszkiewicz:
Janka's Father

Birth date: December 17, 1898
Birthplace: Wioska Omelanka - Village of Omelanka
                     Wschodnia Polska - Eastern Poland
Pronunciations: Horoszkiewicz - Ho-ro-shke-veech
Height: Five feet, eight inches
Immigrated to Canada: October 31, 1956
Died: May 13, 1987 in Ladysmith, BC, Canada
                     89 years old
                     Buried in Cedar Valley Memorial Gardens,
                     Cedar BC, Canada

Adam Horoszkiewicz was a quiet, peaceful man. He was a skilled woodsman and knew every turn in the forest near Omelanka. His detailed knowledge of the woods, and his bravery, saved his family during the Ukrainian uprising in Eastern Poland in 1943.

Adam was born when Poland did not exist as a country. He lived under the rule of Czar - Tsar Nicholas II, Emperor of All Russia, until he was twenty years old. Schooling in the Polish language was forbidden. He learned to read and write in Russian at school, and in Polish secretly at home.

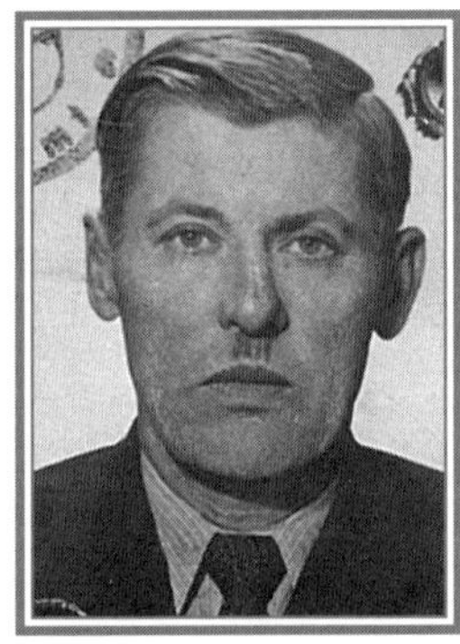

Adam Horoszkiewicz

First World War 1914 - 1918

In March, 1917, when Adam was eighteen years old, he was conscripted into the Russian army. The new recruits had to be trained to be disciplined Russian soldiers and to fight with sabers in hand-to-hand combat. Adam travelled nineteen days by train deep into Russia, to the military school in Krasnojarod. He was to be in the infantry. His training lasted eight long months. He was a gentle man, and the thought of killing another with a sword was repulsive.

During Adam's training, the Czar and his two eldest daughters honored the military academy with an imperial visit. The formal inspection took place near the train station in Krasnojarod. Every cavalryman and every mount was detailed to perfection. Every infantryman was flawlessly polished. The Czar, in full dress uniform, sat regally upon his steed inspecting his cavalry. His two daughters rode in a carriage behind. The infantry stood at attention in reverence of the Emperor of All Russia. Adam was curious to see the princesses and was disappointed to find that, in his eyes, they were not pretty. There were much prettier Polish farm girls at home.

Adam's military training finished during the First World War, in October, 1917. Wearing his Russian uniform, he was transported by train to battle at the Austrian front. His training had not prepared him for the gore he was about to witness. He did not want to be killed, but he did not want to kill anyone either. Praying kept his sanity. His division was not ordered into the slaughter and the mutilation on the battle field. They were to stay in the trenches and wait for the command to attack. Hundreds upon hundreds of young men were cut down with bullets and shredded with swords before him. Hearing and seeing death was morbid. The fortunate died instantly. The wounded lay helpless, suffering torturous mutilations. Gangrene was rampant. Death from infection was ugly and mean. There was little morphine. Medical teams often had to amputate without anesthetic. Bodies of comrade and foe lay side-by-side. Blood of friend and enemy flowed together. Horse carcasses were strewn over the field. The entire horror was barbaric.

While Adam was at the Austrian front, the Bolshevik revolution of 1917, was in full thrust. Lenin was the founder and leader of the Russian

Communist Party known as the Bolsheviks. The Bolshevik Revolution started in March, 1917, and collapsed the Romanov dynasty of Czars in Russia. Czar Nicholas II was forced to abdicate. Military units joined the rebels, and the revolution continued. The Imperial Family was transported to Siberia, and later to Ekaterinburg in the Ural Mountains, where they were executed.

The soldiers battling at the Austrian front knew nothing of the Bolshevik revolution and the fall of the Czar until November, 1917, when word reached the trenches. Adam wanted to escape the Russian army and return to Poland. Other Poles at the front wanted the same. In the confusion, Adam and many other Poles in Russian uniform, returned by train to their homeland. Adam was home in Omelanka one week before Christmas, 1917.

The First World War ended on the 11th hour, of the 11th day of the 11th month, 1918. It was said to be the war to end all wars. After 123 years of foreign rule, Poland was once again recognized by the world as a country.

The Battle of Warsaw 1920

In 1919, Adam was enticed to join the Polish army with a promise of free land to those who gave one year of military service. He enlisted in the cavalry for he loved horses and was an able horseman. The First World War had just ended, and he thought he would serve his time without event, and have a plot of land when he finished. It was not so. In the summer of 1920, Russia invaded Poland and advanced to the gates of Warsaw. The famous Battle of Warsaw, known in Poland as Cud nad Wisłą, had begun.

The Russian army, of infantry and cavalry, was massive. It was divided into four armies, and each was heavily armed in artillery, machine guns, and swords. The Russians outnumbered the Poles in a four to one advantage. They marched towards the capital. The Poles were dispersed in thin lines along the 200 mile front and were no match for the

Red Army. The Poles suffered high casualties and were pushed back. The Red Army continued its onslaught and advanced within a few miles of Warsaw, at which point the war reversed itself.

Adam's cavalry of 300 men was ordered to stay hidden at the perimeter of a forest adjacent to an open field. They were to ambush on command. The Poles had transported seven machine guns across the field by horse-drawn cart, and were ready at the edge of the woods. The machine guns aimed across the open field. A massive Russian regiment was on the other side.

Adam was on his horse, with his saber ready. The Russians were given the order to attack. Hundreds upon hundreds of swords raised into the air at the same time. The blades glistened in the sun. The light was blinding. As the Red Army advanced, they cheered themselves on, "Hurrah! Hurrah! Hurrah! " The chant was continuous as they moved forward onto the open field. They marched one line behind the other shouting, "Hurrah! Hurrah! Hurrah! " The machine guns waited for the command to fire. The Polish cavalry stood silent. The Russians kept moving forward.

The Poles manning the machine guns were ordered to aim for the horses' chests; when the horses fell, the men would come down with them. They fired. The seven machine guns cut down row after row of the approaching Russian Army. The Russians continued their chant, "Hurrah! Hurrah! Hurrah! " as the machine guns fired non-stop. The Polish cavalry stayed put in the trees watching the massacre. They were ready to ambush on command, but no command was given. The Russian leader, Budenny, continued to order his men forward. The Polish commander, Halerczyk, could not believe the insanity of his command. He was sentencing his men to death. No one could escape the barrage of bullets flying across the open field. The field was heaped with bodies and horse carcasses, and flowing with blood. When one regiment fell, another one was ordered forward. The new divisions crawled over their dead comrades trying to get across, using their dead comrades' bodies as shields. Their chant went quieter and quieter: Hurrah.... Hurrah.... Hurrah...... until it was silent. Every Russian in that regiment was killed. Thousands died. No one even got close to the Poles.

Adam remembered his Polish commander telling his men, "Jak ktoś ma mocny żołądek, to tam niech idzie i popatrzy co myśmy dokonali .... If anyone has a strong stomach, go and see what we have accomplished." They could see enough from the forest and were sickened by the sight.

The Battle of Warsaw was powerful. It continued as the Poles relentlessly pushed the other Russian armies back. Adam's division remained hidden. His Polish commander would give the order to ambush when the retreating armies were positioned just where he wanted them. When the signal came, Adam's cavalry brigade of 300 strong men, came out of the forest with their sabers in the air. They ambushed the unsuspecting Russians and fiercely fought with steel against flesh. Cavalry, seated high on their mounts, had the advantage over infantry. Adam was in the midst of battle, when he and a few others were targeted by a large group of Russian cavalrymen. The Russians came after them at full speed. Adam's group was outnumbered. If the Russians encircled them, they would be cut to pieces. They spurred their mounts to a full run. The Russians were excellent horsemen and were close on their heels. The chase was fierce. The Poles could not shake them. Their only hope was the forest; their knowledge of the woods would give them the advantage.

They maneuvered through the trees at break neck speed, and dodged their pursuers. They took one road and the Russians another. The Poles made it safely back to camp, but the Russians had taken a road that lead directly to a Polish village about two miles away. They feared for the villagers, so Adam and four other cavalrymen were sent to scout and to report back.

They quickly made their way along the road towards the village. They lost the cover of the forest, and were again out in the open. They continued to ride forward. All was quiet in the village below, but it was surrounded by forest. The Russians could be anywhere. Adam spotted thirty Russian cavalrymen mounted on their steeds. They were on a road, on the other side of the village, with the forest at their backs. The Poles had to report back to camp.

They turned their horses and spurred them to a full run, but the horses were tired from the intense chase just moments before. Adam's

horse was especially tired and lagged behind. Two Russians detected him and took up the chase. Adam was an easy target.

He glanced back. The Russians' horses were strong and gaining. His four comrades were a good distance ahead. He would be cut to pieces if they reached him. His only chance was the forest. He abruptly turned his horse to cut across a field into the woods, but as he turned, his horse caught its leg in a ditch and violently went down, taking Adam with him. Adam's leg was trapped beneath his horse. The Russians were galloping towards him with their swords high. The ground thundered. He was helplessly pinned to the ground.

His Polish comrades sharply veered their horses and turned back towards the two Russians. They fiercely approached, but before they reached him, one of the Russians brought his sword down on Adam's back, and the two Russians got away.

The Poles rapidly dismounted their horses. Adam was faint. They feared a mortal wound, but found no blood. The Russian's sword had ripped Adam's shirt but did not cut him. Adam was so weak from fright, that he could not ride back unassisted. He rode back to camp with one comrade on each side, holding him up under his arms. He did not realize until he returned to camp, that he had soiled his pants.

The spot where the Russian's sword had struck, developed into a small black blister and left a permanent scar on Adam's back; a reminder of the day he was nearly killed. His comrades teased him, saying he was lucky that the Russian's sword was dull.

That was the last day Adam saw the Russians. The Red Army retreated from the capital. Many dropped their weapons as they fled, and the Poles used the Russian guns against the Russians. After the Battle of Warsaw, hundreds of Polish villagers came from the surrounding areas to assist the Polish army in hauling the dead bodies away. The horse carcasses were cut into pieces and thrown onto carts. It was a gruesome and sickening task. Massive pits were dug. Soldiers and horses were buried together in the mass graves. In the two months of battle, in July and August of 1919, the small Polish army, poorly equipped and outnum-

bered, had stopped the Red Army and the advance of communism across Europe. Unfortunately, Europe neglected to fully acknowledge or appreciate the significance of this political and military victory.

Adam was in the Polish army from July 1919 to September 1921. He served double the time required to receive the parcel of land for his service. He applied for his due reward but was told he was too young to claim it. He had to be twenty-three years old, and he was twenty-two years and nine months. He was shy by three months, and was given nothing.

———

Filipina Myszakowski-Horoszkiewicz:
Janka's Mother

Birth date:	May 15, 1904
Birthplace:	Wioska Omelanka - Village of Omelanka
	Wschodnia Polska - Eastern Poland
Pronunciations:	Filipina - Fi-li-pee-na
	Myszakowski - Mee-shu-kov-ski
	Horoszkiewicz - Ho-ro-shke-veech
Height:	Five feet, four inches
Immigrated to Canada:	October 31, 1956
Died:	November 27, 1998 - Nanaimo, BC, Canada
	94 years old
	Buried in Cedar Valley Memorial Gardens,
	Cedar, B.C., Canada

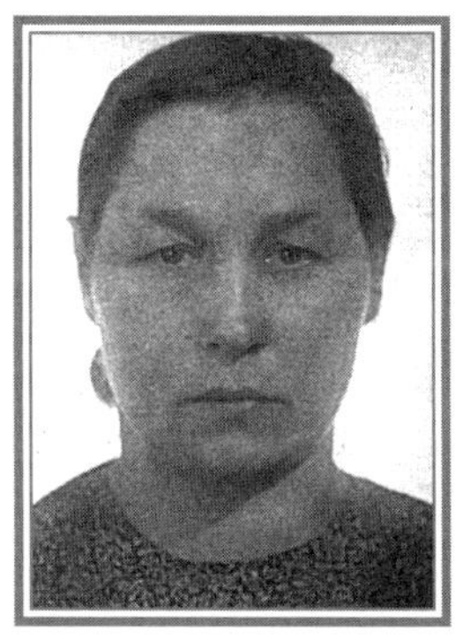

Filipina Horoszkiewicz

Filipina Myszakowski-Horoszkiewicz had a tragic childhood. Her mother died in childbirth when Filipina was only four years old; the baby died two weeks later. There were six children at home, aged one to ten years. Her father, Gracian, was a peasant farmer and could not care for his children and work the farm that provided for them. Sadly, the children had to be dispersed amongst family who lived in and around Omelanka. Gracian's sister cared for Filipina. Filipina was so happy whenever her father came to visit.

Born in 1904, Filipina lived the first fourteen years of her life under Russian rule. She had no formal schooling, but her aunt secretly taught her to read and write in Polish using the bible. In 1914, her father remarried, and the children returned to live with him.

Filipina was eighteen when she married Adam Horoszkiewicz, on November 27th, 1922. They had five children, all born at home with the help of a midwife, but only two survived to adulthood: Stanisława - Stasia and Janina - Janka. She took her infants into the fields when she worked, stopping to nurse them when they were hungry.

Filipina lived in a time when five percent of pregnant women died during childbirth, and twenty percent of children died in infancy or child-hood. Their five children were:

Stanisław - male	1923	Stanisław died when he was 11 days old.
Stanisława - female	1924	married name - Regulant
Janina - female	1926	married name - Drzewiecki
Micia - female	1928	Micia died when she was 8 months old.
Micia - female	1930 - 1935	

Stanisław, was born two months premature. Filipina kept him warm by leaving the oven door open and keeping his crib near by. He was nursing well and growing nicely. He seemed to be thriving, but sadly, he died when he was eleven days old.

The first Micia was a plump and healthy eight-month-old, who became critically ill with pneumonia. Without doctors or medicine, the baby tragically died.

Everyone loved the second Micia. She was a beautiful child with a happy disposition and platinum blonde hair that flowed in natural curls down to her waist. At the age of five, she became mortally ill with Scarlet Fever. She laid across her bed, thrashing violently and pulling her hair. After she died, clumps of hair were found behind the bed.

In the fall of 1939, Filipina was at her father's bedside when he died. Tears filled his eyes as he spoke his final words to her, "Ja dzisiaj mam 75 lat, i ja myślę że ja już będę umierał. Jak szybko czas zleciał. Mnie się wydaje że ja byłem tylko jedną noc z końmi na noclegu .... I am 75 years old, and as I look at myself, I think I am going to die. How fast the time went. It seems to me as though I was only in the fields with the horses for one night." Gracian died in his home the following morning at 10 a.m. Filipina held her father's hand until his last breath.

Filipina's Father
Gracian Myszakowski - Poland
1864-1939

Stanisława Horoszkiewicz:
Janka's Older Sister

Birth date: December 1, 1924
Birthplace: Wioska Omelanka - Village of Omelanka
                       Wschodnia Polska - Eastern Poland
Nicknames: Her family called her Stasia.
                       In Canada she was called Stella.
Pronunciations: Stasia - Sta-sha
                       Horoszkiewicz - Ho-ro-shke-veech
Height: Five feet, two inches
Immigrated to Canada: April 20, 1950

Stasia Horoszkiewicz

Stasia was very capable and independent. When she was an adolescent, she took tailoring classes in the village of Thory, fifteen kilometers away, and became a very skilled seamstress. She lived with her Stryjek - Uncle Mieczysław Horoszkiewicz and his family. Stasia learned everything about sewing, from drafting a pattern, to tailoring a suit. Janka was too young to be sent to the classes, and at the time the family only had enough money to send one daughter.

Stasia and Janka were playmates while growing up. When all the housework and farm chores were done, there was very little time to social-

ize with others. The double bed that they shared had a firm straw mattress. One night when they were in their early teens, they were especially playful. They were crawling over and under each other, switching sides of the bed and giggling non-stop. Adam told them several times to be quiet. The girls would quiet down for a few seconds, burst out in giggles, and start the game again. Adam had had enough. When Janka and Stasia heard their father walk across the floor they pretended to be asleep. They knew they had pushed him too far. Janka was on Stasia's side of the bed. They closed their eyes and softly snored.

Adam rarely spanked his girls but he had had enough of their ruckus. He came down with the strap over the down quilt, on Stasia's side of the bed. It didn't hurt a bit; the padding was too thick. Janka cried, "Tato to ja, to nie Stasia! Tato, to ja! .... Daddy it's me, not Stasia! Daddy, it's me!" Stasia laid stiff as a board on Janka's side. Adam went back to bed, and the two sisters pretended they were crying. They pulled the quilt over their heads to muffle their giggling as they started once more. Adam called out, "Bądźcie cicho bo dostaniecie znowu pasem .... Be quiet or you'll get the the strap again." They finally settled down and let their parents sleep.

The Gołubica River was near their home, and one hot summer's day in 1937, Janka, Stasia and two other sisters went for a swim. The girls didn't own bathing suits and dared each other to go skinny dipping. Janka protested but was outnumbered, and followed the others. They stripped behind a bush and hid their clothes. Making sure the coast was clear, they ran stark naked into the water, laughing and giggling all the way. They stayed submerged. They didn't want to risk anyone seeing them. Stasia mastered dog paddling, while Janka mastered sinking; she never did learn to swim. They were having so much fun playing and splashing that they didn't notice the boys coming.

Janka was horrified when she saw her cousins, Janek and Mirek Myszakowski, and her teacher's son, Zbigniew, sitting on their horses under the bridge nearby. There was no time to run and get dressed. They stayed in the water and told the boys to go away, but the boys were having too much fun tormenting the girls. They rode up closer, laughing and teasing. Spotting the clothes behind the bush, they playfully nabbed them, turned their mounts, and left. The girls desperately pleaded and eventually the pranksters put the clothes back, and rode away laughing.

The four girls waited a long time before they went ashore and grabbed their clothes. "Na drugi raz mamy być ciszej .... Next time we have to be more quiet," they whispered as they hurriedly dressed, and burst out laughing.

After the war, Mirek and Janek Myszakowski, immigrated to Toronto, Canada, with their parents and younger brother. Janka visited them in 1975, and stories of their youth evoked many memories and much laughter.

Janek 1949

Mirek 1948

Zygmunt Regulant:
Stasia's Husband

Birth date: March 28, 1915
Birthplace: Wioska Dombrowa - Village of Dombrowa
                         Wschodnia Polska - Eastern Poland
Immigrated to Canada: August 20, 1949
Died: November 5, 1978 in Ladysmith BC, Canada
                         64 years old
                         Buried in Ladysmith Cemetery
                         Ladysmith, BC, Canada

Zygmunt Regulant - Polish Army 1939

Zygmunt fought in the Polish army in the Second World War. In September 1939, at its onset, he was captured by the Russians and was being transported by train to Russia when the train stopped. The tracks had been destroyed. The Russians ordered the prisoners off the train to fix the rails. It took a few days and there was no food. The Russians ordered the Poles to collect firewood from the forest and to dig potatoes from the farmers' fields. Zygmunt and six other Poles from his region of Dombrowa, volunteered to collect wood. Once they were in the forest, they fled.

They knew their way home but it was a great distance. They travelled at night for safety. On their way, they were stopped by a band of Ukrainian rebels. The Ukrainians demanded their clothing and shoes.

Zygmunt spoke fluent Ukrainian but it did nothing to help them. They were stripped naked, taken into a barn, and locked inside. The Ukrainians left.

One of the Polish soldiers escaped through the roof and ran down the road naked, straight towards a Russian army vehicle. The Russians had no doubt that a mass murder was about to take place. They rescued the Poles and captured the Ukrainian rebels. Their clothes and shoes were returned. The Ukrainians were lined up by the head Russian; he was judge and jury. He read their charge, found them guilty, and opened fire.

Zygmunt and the others continued towards Dombrowa with visions of the war and execution haunting them. It took them three weeks to reach home. They were lucky to be alive.

The Ukrainians attacked Zygmunt's village and the villages in his surrounding area during the night in June, 1942. The slaughter was immense. Those who were fortunate to have escaped, fled. Zygmunt made his way to Omelanka twenty-five kilometers away, and lived with one of Adam's cousins. By the winter of 1942, everyone in Omelanka and all the villages in the district of Huta Stepanska were on alert. People were afraid day and night.

In spite of all the horrors in Eastern Poland in 1942, Stasia and Zygmunt fell in love. Zygmunt was a kind man and was liked by everyone. The young ladies of Omelanka tried to get the attention of the new and handsome young man, but Zygmunt only had eyes for Stasia. They were married on June 20th, 1943, in the parish of Huta Stepanska. Stasia was eighteen, and Zygmunt was twenty-eight. The family and guests returned to the Horoszkiewicz farm for an outdoor celebration. It was a beautiful, sunny day. The presence of the war and the fear of the Ukrainian uprising did not curb their wedding day. The newlyweds resided with Stasia's family. Adam loved Zygmunt like a son.

Early in 1943, before the wedding, a terrified villager ran through Omelanka warning that the Ukrainians were attacking. Panic and terror were instantaneous. The Horoszkiewicz family fled across their field to the forest beyond, and hid. Their relief was indescribable when they learned it was a false alarm. However, in July, 1943, one month after the wedding, it

became a reality. Omelanka and every village in the district of Huta Stepanska were set ablaze.

Part 4 - Chapter 1

Omelanka Burns
July 1943

Introduction:

In 1943, the full force of the Ukrainian uprising was felt in Eastern Poland. Entire villages were set ablaze. Men, women and children were mercilessly killed. There were no warnings of the attacks. The rebels came during the day or night. It was a killing and burning rampage.

There were no radios, but news of the massacres had travelled to Omelanka. Poles who had fled other villages told of the horrors. Janka was terrified. She was afraid to go to sleep. Every night she knelt beside her bed and prayed for God to protect her family. When morning came she thanked Him for their lives.

When Zygmunt's home village of Dombrowa was attacked in 1942, many of the villagers fled to Omelanka for safety. People took in as many refugees as they could. The Horoszkiewicz farm was refuge to many. People slept in their wagons, in the granary, the barn, wherever they could.

An inhumane nightmare was unfolding. It was mayhem beyond imagination. The entire Powiat - Region of Kostopol was set ablaze, and thousands of villagers were murdered.

The following villages in the region of Kostopol were completely destroyed:

Omelanka	Tresten	Siedlisko
Huta Stepanska	Zakuscie	Usowicze
Lade	Hrada	Olosik
Słone Błoto	Styrtka	Borek
Temne		

Only one month after Stasia and Zygmunt's wedding, Omelanka was brutally attacked by Ukrainian insurgents. Janka and Stasia were in the kitchen making bread with their mother. They had just finished putting the loaves into the clay oven with a long wooden paddle, when their father ran into the house and told everyone to run into the forest. Janka was only sixteen years old.

Note: My parent's home villages of Omelanka and Rudnia were both in the province of Wołyn. The province of Wołyn burned during the Ukrainian uprising.

<u>*Sylwester Drzewiecki:*</u>　　　　<u>*Janina Horoszkiewicz:*</u>

Wioska - Village of Rudnia　　　*Wioska - Village of Omelanka*
Gmina - Municipality of Kołki　*Gmina - Municipalityof Stydyn*
Powiat - Region of Łuck　　　　*Powiat - Region of Kostopol*

Województwo Wołyńskie - Province of Wołyn
Wschodnia Polska - Eastern Poland

July 1943
Hiding In The Forest

Adam Horoszkiewicz	44 years old
Filipina Myszakowska-Horoszkiewicz	39 years old
Janka Horoszkiewicz	16 years old
Stasia Horoszkiewicz-Regulant	18 years old
Zygmunt Regulant	28 years old

Adam was working in the fields when he heard gun shots, and saw smoke in the distance. He raced towards the house to warn his family. He flung the door open and frantically yelled, "Ukraińcy atakują! Podpalili domy. Uciekajcie! Idźcie i zchowajcie się w lesie .... The Ukrainians are attacking! They have set fire to the houses. Leave now! Run and hide in the forest!" Petrified, the women grabbed blankets and fled. They ran past the cows and the chickens, the barn and the pond, and into the field

that led to the woods. The forest was one mile away. Adam yelled to Zygmunt to quickly help him get the cows. They could not be left. The cows would destroy the garden, which the family depended on for food. The two men, madly drove the cows with sticks. The grey one was pregnant with her first calf and due any day. The animals were wild with fright. The women were running ahead in their long skirts and bare feet, with blankets in their arms. The gunshots were getting closer. The killers would soon reach their farm. The forest was their only hope.

Janka glanced back. Omelanka was ablaze. Huge billows of smoke curled into the air. Round after round of gunshots were fired. She was terrified. Into the forest the family fled, farther and farther into the trees. They were exhausted when they finally stopped. They held each other, trying to catch their breath. They were scared beyond comprehension.

The villagers who were lucky enough to flee, either hid in the forest or ran to the town of Huta Stepanska. The majority fled to Huta Stepanska, but several families converged in the forest. Adam's brother, Mieczysław, was visiting Omelanka that day. Mieczysław, his wife, and their three small children, reached the forest safely. A villager named Kazik, met up with Janka's family on horseback; he was born with a deformity and was unable to walk. A young couple, with the woman advanced in pregnancy, arrived. Another family with small children came. The refugees huddled together in their moment of safety.

Ted (pseudonym), a newcomer to Omelanka, also converged. He was sick with worry about his pregnant wife, because she was not with him at the time of the attack. She had fled to Huta Stepanska with her family. Early in the war, Ted had been studying in Warsaw to become a priest, but fled to escape the German forced labour camps. He found shelter with a family in Omelanka, fell in love with their daughter and married. He prayed for their safety, as he had never prayed before.

They could not leave the forest until they were sure the danger had passed. Everyone spoke in whispers. Adam believed the crisis would pass in a couple of days, but they needed food. The sack of dried bread they had saved for an emergency evacuation was left behind. The cows could forage for themselves, but Janka's family had no provisions, only

blankets. Janka was surprised to discover that she had somehow grabbed her birth certificate when she fled. Adam and Zygmunt had to venture back to the farm for supplies, but had to wait until dark.

The Ukrainians could be hiding anywhere waiting for the Poles to return. The two men moved out of the safety of the forest, and cautiously made their way towards their home. It had been spared in the first attack. They crept around, gathering supplies.

Janka was so afraid while her father was gone. She listened to every sound in the forest, and huddled close to her mother and her sister. Her imagination ran wild. Adam and Zygmunt finally returned with the supplies and the bad news. Adam said, "Nie możemy wracać za dwa dni. Jest niebezpiecznie. Musimy być tutaj dłużej .... We cannot go back in two days. It is too dangerous. We must stay here longer." They did not know how long they would have to stay hidden. They rationed the food.

They needed to find out what was happening outside, and the fate of other villagers. Two men left the forest to learn what they could. After many hours, the scouts returned with horrible news. Everyone listened in morbid fear. Most of the Poles who had fled to Huta Stepanska were massacred, including Ted's wife; his grief was uncontrollable. Two families hiding in the woods near Huta Stepanska were fooled by Ukrainians calling in Polish. The unsuspecting families answered and were slaughtered. A newlywed couple from Huta Stepanska, whom Janka knew from church, were shot while fleeing into the woods. The woman's body was left dangling over the fence, her husband's body lay on the ground beside her. Everyone wept. Hundreds and hundreds of villagers had been murdered.

They had been in the forest for several days when it started to rain. It poured all day and all night. They were drenched. There seemed to be no end to the downpour. They sat on the wet ground, under the trees, with blankets over their heads as the rain fell. Their hair, clothes and blankets were soaked, and they were chilled to the bone. Janka thought of her warm bed and down quilt. She thought of her house with the thatched roof that kept them dry, and the wood stove that kept them warm. She imagined the wonderful smell of the bread they had left in the oven, and

butter melting into a big piece of it. How she missed her home. The rain continued.

Finally it stopped. Even though it was July, it was cool in the forest. One of the men built a fire to keep everyone warm. They needed more provisions, and they needed an update of the news. That night, Adam and Zygmunt crept back to the farm for food, while the scouts ventured out for information. The rest waited in the forest and prayed.

The woman who was advanced in her pregnancy, went into labour at this dismal time. She lay on the ground, bearing her pain in absolute silence. Giving birth at home, with the assistance of a midwife was dangerous enough, but giving birth in the forest, with no trained assistant and no proper place to give birth, was life threatening to the mother and the infant. Her labour continued, with her husband trying to comfort her.

Adam and Zygmunt found their farm a smoldering ruin. The house and all the farm buildings were burnt to the ground. In the perilous week that they had been hiding in the forest, the entire village of Omelanka had been destroyed. There was nothing left.

The scouts had learned that the Ukrainians were combing the forest on horseback calling out in Polish, as they had done in Huta Stepanska. The Ukrainians were schooled in Polish and spoke the language perfectly. Everyone was afraid. Their situation was desperate. They had to leave immediately in the cover of night. They had to walk through the forest to the town of Rachwaluwka, many miles and many hours away.

They had learned weeks before that the Germans had taken Rachwaluwka, and the train station there. They would give themselves up to the Germans. They gathered their sparse belongings. The family groups had to travel separately as small children were a danger; they might cry out and alert the Ukrainians. The poor woman in labour could not be moved. Her husband stayed at her side. He alone would assist in the delivery of their first child. The families were torn to leave the desperate couple, but the couple bravely urged everyone to quickly go. It was their only chance. It would take them all night to reach

Rachwaluwka. Only God could help them now.

Before leaving, they all knelt in a circle and together made the sign of the cross. "W imię Ojca, i Syna, i Ducha Świętego, Amen .... In the name of the Father, the Son, and the Holy Spirit, Amen." Ted, full of grief over the death of his wife, lead them in prayer like a real priest. He prayed for God's blessing, guidance and protection; he prayed for the safety of the couple delivering their child; and he prayed for peace. They all made the sign of the cross and rose to their feet. Their perilous journey through the forest to Rachwaluwka was about to begin.

The fate of the young couple left birthing in the forest is unknown.

One Week After The Attack
Fleeing Omelanka

Adam lead his family, Mieczysław's family, Ted, and Kazik, away from Omelanka through the pitch black forest. Sorrowfully, the two cows had to be left behind. The pregnant grey one was standing alone as she watched the family walk away. She would have to deliver her calf on her own, which was due any day. Janka looked at her gentle and beautiful pet for one last time. She hugged and kissed her goodbye, and cried. The sad sight of abandoning her pet, and her sorrowful brown eyes, haunted Janka. She vividly remembered the depressing scene for the rest of her life.

Adam knew every turn in the forest and had a mental map that would lead them to Rachwaluwka. They walked in silence, holding hands and carefully listening. They had no footwear. On and on they followed Adam; only he knew the way. The adults took turns carrying Mieczysław's young children. Kazik helped carry the little ones on his horse. The Ukrainians would be hunting the Poles on horseback in the morning. They were tired, but drove themselves forward.

After several hours they rested, but they could not stop for long. They had to reach Rachwaluwka before daylight. Stasia sensed some-

thing was wrong. She peered into the darkness but could see nothing. She became anxious, sure that something was not right. She pressed her father to leave at once. Adam sensed her urgency; perhaps he felt something too. He wasted no time. He immediately motioned everyone to move. They held hands and ran. Moments later they heard screams and gunshots in the distance. The bandits were somewhere in the forest. They did not stop running. Exhaustion was overtaking them.

Where was little Jasia!? Stryjek Mieczysław's two-year-old daughter was missing! The terror at finding the toddler gone was insurmountable. Mieczysław and his wife were in horror. They had to find her, but how? The forest was pitch black and the Ukrainians were somewhere in it. They held hands and made a chain as Adam retraced their steps. They called her name in whispers, looking under bushes, around logs and trees, but there was no sign of Jasia. The frantic search continued. After a frightening hour they found the little girl sitting quietly under a bush, hugging her knees up to her chin, waiting for someone to find her. Mieczysław and his wife cried as they hugged their baby girl. Everyone wept.

They had to move on. The villages of Styrtka and Temne had horridly met with the same fate as Omelanka. The smells of charred ruins and rotting remains reached them. It was ghastly. They walked the forest beyond the ruins of Temne, and heard the sound of the Czapelka River. They were nearing the village of Siedlisko. It was too dangerous to use the bridge; the rebels might be waiting. Adam lead everyone down river. He stopped where the water was calm. A wheat field grew tall near the shore. No one knew how to swim, including Adam, so the water had to be shallow to cross. Adam found a long stick. He told Kazik to cross on his horse; the horse would swim if the water became too deep. Adam would follow Kazik, while testing the depth of the water with the stick. The rest were to stay hidden in the wheat until he returned.

Kazik rode his horse into the river, and Adam waded in, ignoring the cold. Farther and farther they went, while the families hid in the wheat and stared into the darkness where the two had disappeared. Adam carefully moved forward. He plunged his long stick ahead of himself with each step. The river was too deep.

Only Adam returned. Kazik had made it across. "Nie możemy przejść przez rzeczkę bo jest za głęboko. Zostańcie tu i ja pójdę do mostu i zobaczę czy jest bezpiecznie .... We can't cross here. The river is too deep. You stay here and I'll go to the bridge and see if it is safe." He would not risk taking anyone with him. The three men, Zygmunt, Mieczysław, and Ted had to protect the women and children if anything happened. Adam was wet and cold as he crept towards the bridge. The Ukrainians knew the bridge was an exit for many of the villages of Wołyn. They could be hiding and waiting. Adam was afraid.

He hid in the bushes near the bridge and listened. The smell of decay surrounded him. He saw no one, but had to be absolutely sure it was safe. He was incredibly cold, but didn't dare move. Faintly, he heard a woman calling in Polish to her daughter far off in the distance. When Adam heard the woman's voice, he was positive there were no Ukrainians nearby. He hurried back to collect everyone. They had to be fast. The situation on the bridge could change by the time they returned. When they neared the bridge, Adam motioned for everyone to stop. He once again intensely listened. The rotting stench was unbearable as they moved closer. Decomposing bodies lay mangled on the bridge. The dead villagers had been viciously murdered. It was morbidly frightening. Adam waved everyone forward. They hastily ran to the other side. Lying across Janka's path was a rotting corpse. She covered her mouth to muffle her cry, made the sign of the cross, and quickly stepped over him. They had to hurry to the forest on the other side. There was very little night left. The Ukrainians would be hunting at daybreak.

They had walked the entire night. Adam had brought them all safely to Rachwaluwka, just as morning broke.

The Following Day
Rachwaluwka

The German soldiers looked ominous with their rifles and machine guns. Everyone was afraid as they followed Adam and approached the town. There was no guarantee of safety, but they had to turn themselves in. It was their only hope of escaping from the Ukrainians.

The Germans were already aware of the mass slaughter and the burning of the villages in the region of Kostopol. Refugees from Omelanka who had already arrived, had told of the murders and the ruin. Janka spotted her teacher, Pani Bielawska with her son, Zbigniew. The families embraced and tears flowed. They recognized other familiar faces too. They shared their horrific ordeals that brought them to Rachwaluwka. So many had been killed.

The Poles would be transported to Germany by train to work as free labour; it was better to slave than to be killed. The train was due in Rachwaluwka in five days. The refugees were bunked in one room, and slept crammed on the floor. There was very little food, but they were alive and safe from the Ukrainians combing the forest.

There were many people, but there was room to move inside the boxcars. Benches skirted the perimeter and some benches ran down the center. The train stopped for more people in Sarny, in Eastern Poland. Adam's older sister, Bronisława Filinska, lived in Sarny, but it was not possible for Adam and Mieczysław to be reunited with their sister one last time. They had to remain on the train during its two hour lay over. Bronia had no way of knowing that her brothers and their families were sitting in a boxcar at the station. The train left.

They disembarked in Ruwno, Poland, where they remained for one week, waiting for another train to take them to Germany. They had escaped the Ukrainians, but what lay in store for them in Germany they did not know. A passenger train arrived. Adam's family and Mieczysław's family were separated. It was the last time they ever saw each other. Adam, Filipina, Janka, Stasia, and Zygmunt boarded the train. They were going to work as farmhands somewhere in Germany, but they did not know where.

The fates of Kazik and Ted are unknown.

Mieczysław Horoszkiewicz
Poland

Three weeks after Omelanka was attacked
Arriving in Germany

Sixteen-year-old Janka looked out the windows of the train as it took them into Germany. What was going to become of them? They were all strong and capable farmers. Adam was skilled in logging and tool sharpening. The concern was not the hard work, but the thought of separation and the unknown. The chances of one farm needing five hands was slim.

The train stopped in Nienburg, Germany. Men and women were separated for showers and for disinfection. Janka was very modest, and was embarrassed to go into the showers together with the other ladies. They spent that night on the Weser River. In Nienburg, they had their pictures taken for the first time in their lives. The photos were for their German work record and identification books. They stood with their identification number displayed across their chest. Adam's number was 10491. Filipina's was 10492. Name, birth date, and birthplace were recorded in their booklets. They were each given a badge reading OST - East, to identify that they came from the East. They had to visibly display the badge on their chest wherever they went.

Adam and Filipina Horoszkiewicz, 1943
Photos for their German Work Books

The Cover of the German Work Book

Adam's German Work Book page 1

Adam's German Work Book pages 2 and 3

They were being sent to the village of Steinbrink, near Nienburg-Weser, but as they had dreaded, they were separated. Five farms in Steinbrink could use one extra farmhand. They would work and live on different farms.

Several German farmers came by horse-drawn wagon to collect the workers. The Horoszkiewicz family climbed into the back of one wagon. It bumped its way along to Steinbrink and the five farms that awaited them.

Part 4 - Chapter 1 - Epilogue

Omelanka Burns
1943

Of the Horoszkiewicz family who immigrated to Canada between 1949 and 1956, only Stasia returned to Poland. In 1973, she was reunited with family she had not seen since hiding in the forest and fleeing Omelanka, in July 1943. She saw Stryjek Mieczysław's three grown children, Jasia, Mirka, and Czesiek. They were preschoolers when they had all fled through the forest to Rachwaluwka. Jasia had been the lost toddler in the forest.

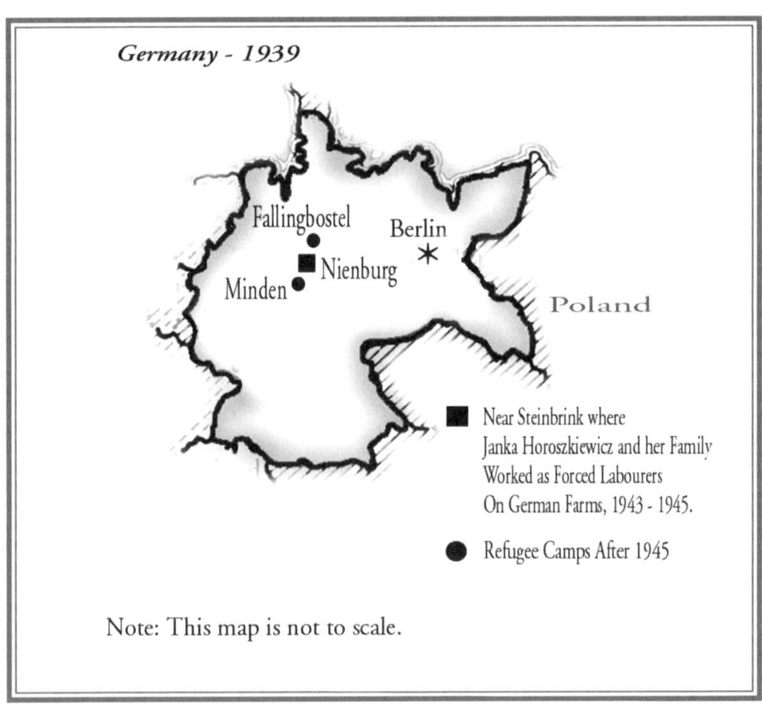

Germany - 1939
Fallingbostel
Berlin
Nienburg
Minden
Poland
Near Steinbrink where
Janka Horoszkiewicz and her Family
Worked as Forced Labourers
On German Farms, 1943 - 1945.
Refugee Camps After 1945
Note: This map is not to scale.

Part 4 - Chapter 2

The German Farms
Steinbrink, Germany
1943 to 1945

Forced Labourers on the German Farms in Steinbrink 1944
Janina is standing in the back row, wearing a dark coat, sixth from the right.

Introduction:
Janka Horoszkiewicz - 17 years old

Janka, Filipina, and Zygmunt worked for kind German families who fed them well. Stasia, unfortunately, was placed on a farm run by a heartless woman, Frau Lieschien. She gave Stasia minimal rations and was very unkind to her. Adam alternated between two different farms. He worked three days on Filipina's farm and three days on another. A Polish woman named Hanka was already working on the small farm where Filipina and Adam were placed. Their German farmer was a widower whose only son was tragically killed on the battlefields. Hanka was his

housekeeper. His farm was too small for Adam to work there full-time. Miserably, the farmers at the other farm where Adam worked, did not feed him well. He was hungry, but he was resourceful, and snuck milk from the milking parlor, eggs from the hen house and potatoes from the garden. He boiled the eggs and the potatoes on the wood heater in his tiny room. The room was barely big enough for his cot.

The five farms bordered each other. During the summer evenings the family members visited. Sunday was their day of rest, but the cows still had to be milked. Janka milked her cows in the morning and then was free to visit until it was time for the evening milking. There were many Poles on different farms in Steinbrink, who visited with the family.

Janka worked on two different farms in Steinbrink. The first farm was owned by the Williams family. It was very big and needed several farmhands. It had a big farm house with many rooms, and accommodated many people. There were two prisoners-of-war working on the farm when she arrived. One was a Frenchman named Jean - John. The other was a Russian named Slavko. Janka worked on the Williams' farm for over a year. The second farm where she worked was much smaller, but near the first farm. The Williams' elderly relatives ran the small farm. Janka worked for the elderly couple until the end of the war.

The Williams worked equally as hard as their farmhands. Oma - grandmother, the 23 year old daughter-in-law, Getra, and Getra's five year old daughter, lived on the farm with Mr. and Mrs. Williams. Their son, Villy, was fighting at war. Janka called the grandmother Oma.

Janka had her own little bedroom, with a feather bed and feather comforter. Each night she said her prayers, crawled into bed, and sunk deep down into the mattress. It was very different from her firm straw mattress in Omelanka.

In the winter the house was not heated, only the kitchen was warm. There was electricity in the big house, but during the long winter evenings they would all sit quietly in the warm kitchen, illuminated by a dull light from a kerosene lantern. They were not allowed to brightly illu-

minate the house with electrical lights for safety reasons. They could not use a radio; Janka wondered if the family even had one, for she never saw one, nor heard one playing. Janka never saw any candles in the house, and found her way to her cold room in the dark, where she would quickly jump into bed.

Oma worked all day in the house doing all of the cooking and baking, while the rest of the family worked on the farm. The family and their farmhands ate five meals a day, at 7 a.m., 10 a.m., noon, 3 p.m., and 6 p.m. At 7 a.m. they had bread and molasses, and sometimes jam. At 10 a.m., Frühstück, Brot und Leberwurst .... breakfast, bread with liver wurst; Janka loved the liver wurst. At noon and 6 p.m., they ate thick soup. Their 3 p.m. meal consisted only of bread. They also ate a lot of preserved fruit.

Oma made a different soup every three days. Most of the soup was made with a pork base. The pork halves were smoked and hung high up in the barn. Even though the meat was cured, maggots infested the meat. Janka shuddered when she first saw them in her soup. She watched the others scoop the maggots out and set them aside. After awhile she too became accustomed to finding the creatures and scooped them out like everyone else.

An extra special meal was served at noon on Sunday: chicken, vegetables, potatoes and gravy. Coffee and a very special cake called Kuchen, was served each Sunday afternoon at 3:00. The Kuchen had a cake base with rows of sliced apple, and lots of sugary crumbs sprinkled on top. It was delicious. She looked forward to her Sunday Kuchen all week. Janka worked unbelievably hard, but ate well and put on weight. She would have liked to learn to cook, but the closest she came to working in the kitchen was splitting the kindling each day for the wood stove.

Janka was happy that her own family lived down the road. It was her first time away from her parents, and although her room was cozy and the German family was kind, it was not her home. She was thankful they were all alive and safe. They were so lucky to have escaped the Ukrainians. Ironically it was the Germans who had saved them.

August 1943
The First Farm
Janka's First Day

Oma knocked on Janka's door at 5 a.m. and said in German, "Johanna wache auf .... Johanna wake up." It was the first time she heard her new name. Johanna went to the kitchen and found Getra up and ready to show her the barn. Getra had been the milkmaid prior to Johanna's arrival. It would now be Johanna's job. The two women went into the barn in their wooden shoes; the shoes would take some getting used to.

The long barn was attached to the house. High in the barn hung the smoked meat. On one side of the barn were the pigs and horses, and on the other side were seven milking cows. Milking was going to be a very big job. Getra showed Janka where everything was kept. She introduced her to the farm dog. He was so friendly, and Janka loved him right away. Janka understood what she was to do, even though there was no common language. She sat down on the milking stool with a metal bucket under the cow and started squirting the milk. Getra was pleased that Janka knew what to do. With wild gestures, Getra pointed to the cow that was nearly impossible to milk. Janka understood the warning, and Getra went back to the farm house to help Oma.

She quietly milked and thought of her two cows, abandoned in the forest. She wondered if her grey one had had its calf. She would never forget her eyes as she walked away from her. She continued to milk, saddened by the memory, and cried. By the time Janka reached cow number seven, her hands hurt. It was painful to finish, and to make matters worse, the cow would not stand still. She kicked defiantly just as Getra had warned. The bucket of milk spilled everywhere, and Janka fell off the stool. The cow kept kicking, forcing Janka to quickly move out of the way.

Janka loaded the three heavy milk cans onto a little cart, harnessed the farm dog to it, and together they walked from the barn to the road; it was quite a distance. The German Shepherd was a beautiful dog, and she loved him. He strained as he pulled, but liked to work. He knew exactly where to go, and where to stop for Janka to unload. She set the cans by the roadside for the pickup at 7 a.m.

Her next job was to chop kindling to restock the woodpile for the kitchen stove. She neatly stacked the wood under a small, protective roof, and then went in for breakfast. Jean and Slavko, who were farmhands also, joined them for the meal; they lived in the prisoner-of-war camps nearby. Jean and Slavko arrived each morning for breakfast, worked all day, and went back to their camps after supper.

After breakfast, Janka, Getra, Jean, and Slavko went to work in the field. Four nationalities with four different languages, Polish, German, French, and Russian, worked side-by-side. Jean and Slavko could speak some German. Janka found the Russian language similar to Polish, and was able to slowly communicate with Slavko, but the French and German languages had her baffled. The four field-hands spent most of the day working in silence. Getra worked equally as hard as the others. Janka liked Getra, for she treated them fairly.

Everyone sat at one table for meals, except Slavko. He was segregated and ate alone at a small table in the kitchen. Janka felt terribly sorry for him. It was horrible seeing such discrimination. Even the German family who set him aside felt awful. It was mandated that the farmers not allow any Russian prisoner-of-war to sit at their table, so they had to abide.

The following morning, Oma knocked on Johanna's door to begin her second day. "Johanna wache auf .... Johanna wake up." Oma woke her every morning that way. Janka's hands hurt from all the milking the day before, but she went out to milk the seven cows. She was afraid of the crazy cow, but she milked them all. She harnessed the dog to the cart, and spoke to him in Polish. He knew what to do, and went ahead. She ran after him, and found him waiting for her at the unloading site by the road, his head turned back to see where she was. She unloaded the big cans, and the two friends headed back to the farmhouse.

Her hands were so badly swollen from the milking, she could not bend her fingers. As she chopped the kindling, she could hardly hold the axe. She stacked the wood for Oma and went into the kitchen for break-fast. When Getra saw her hands, she knew Johanna could not continue milking two times a day. Getra took pity on her and resumed the milking

job for two weeks while Janka's hands healed, after which they shared the job. Janka's hands gradually became accustomed to milking seven cows, and she became the full-time milkmaid on the farm once again.

A few months after arriving on the first farm
The Wooden Shoes

Janka awoke to a freezing cold room. A thick layer of ice frosted her window. She tucked her head under her down quilt for one more minute, and peeked out to find her clothes. She only had one dress that she wore each day. It would not keep her warm today. She jumped out of bed and wasted no time getting dressed. It was so cold she could see her breath. She quickly pulled her dress over her head, smoothed it out, brushed her hair, and headed down the hall to the kitchen in her bare feet. The cows would be fussing soon, and she had to chop more kindling for the big kitchen stove.

Oma was already lighting the fire. She was wearing her black shawl; most of the women in the village wore black during the war as a symbol of mourning. Soon the kitchen would be warm and breakfast started. They greeted each other, "Guten Morgen .... good morning." Janka put on a sweater that was hanging in the porch. A light snow was on the ground. She slipped her bare feet into her wooden shoes which were kept at the back door; she had no stockings. The hard shoes bashed her bare ankles and made them bleed. She finished her milking, and took the big cans out to the road with the faithful dog.

Directly across the road from the farm was the Russian prisoner-of-war camp. The German guard was calling the roll, while the prisoners stood at attention in a straight line. The guard lead them to the gate. Slavko came out of the compound, and Janka and he walked to the farmhouse together. He accompanied Janka like this many times in the year they worked together.

Janka walked to the woodpile, anticipating the next blow against her ankles. She wished for some wool to knit herself stockings, but was too unsure of herself to ask Oma or Mrs. Williams.

As Janka was splitting the wood, Jean arrived. He watched Janka working in her bare feet and saw her bleeding ankles. Without mentioning anything to her, he went into the house and asked Oma for some stockings. Oma dug out a pair of long black woolen socks and Jean took them out to her. She was so happy, and thanked him repeatedly. She cleaned the blood from her ankles and put the stockings on right away. They went past her knees. They were wonderful!

Janka finished splitting the wood, and carried a bundle of kindling into the kitchen. She thanked Oma. "Danke schon, danke schon ....Thank you, thank you." Language was a terrible barrier, but kindness needed no words.

1944
Adam and Filipina

During one of Adam's three-days of work on Filipina's farm, Steinbrink was bombed during the night. There was no air raid siren, just a tremendous explosion. The walls and windows shook. Adam and Filipina jumped out of bed and grabbed their clothes. It was pitch black; all the windows were covered. Filipina grabbed her dress from the chair and Adam grabbed his pants. They hurriedly pulled on their clothes as they ran out of the house. Another bomb blasted. It sounded like it was right on top of them. Filipina ran, putting one arm in one dress sleeve, then the other, but the dress wouldn't go over her head. Adam tried putting on his pants, but couldn't find the leg. Frightened and undressed they kept running.

The bombing stopped after the second blast, and they looked at their clothes. Filipina had her arms stuck in Adam's pant legs, and Adam was holding her dress!

Every household had been awakened by the two explosions. The homes and barns had been spared; no one was hurt. The bombs had landed far out in a farmer's field. The following day everyone gathered at the bombing site. It was frightening to see the size of the craters left by the explosions; a house could fit inside one of the monstrous holes.

Some time later
Villy Comes Home

The Williams' son, Villy, had come home for two days. The family rejoiced in his return. Villy helped on the farm during his stay. Getra told him about the young cow that was surely mad. She explained how neither Johanna nor she could milk the animal, and how they were afraid of her. Being an expert farmer, Villy did not believe that a cow could not be milked. He was going to show Getra and Johanna how it was done.

Villy sat on the stool with the bucket under the teats and started to pull. He was surprised when the cow kicked and bucked and refused to be milked. He settled her down, but not for long. As soon as he started pulling, she began kicking. Villy grabbed a rope and tied her back legs together. He finished milking her, and was about to show off to Getra and Johanna, when the cow, tied legs and all, kicked again. The bucket and milk went flying, soaking Villy and smacking him hard in the knee. Villy relented. Getra was right. He sold the cow, making Johanna incredibly happy.

Villy returned to duty and was sent to the Russian front. His fate is unknown.

Spring 1944
The Lady from Hannover

The city of Hannover had been bombed. The Williams took in a woman with two daughters, eighteen and twelve, who were left homeless. The woman's husband was at war. The mother was refined and educated, and she and her daughters were strikingly beautiful. They had lived their entire lives in the city, and knew nothing about farming, but they learned, and they worked as hard as everyone else. The lady was a lovely person and Janka liked her very much.

When the soup was served at the noon and 6 p.m. meals, the lady cringed when she saw maggots in her soup. She watched the others lift them out and set them aside. She too, got used to them after awhile, and

removed them from her dinner. She gently put one on the side of her plate as she sat beside Janka. She whispered to the maggot, loudly enough for Janka to hear, "So kannst Du weiter leben .... Now you can live on." They both laughed.

In early spring, 1944, Janka and the lady were sorting a big mound of potatoes into seeds and edibles. The large ones were for cooking and the small ones for planting. They were both kneeling on the ground getting their hands dirty. They could partially converse, for Janka was beginning to understand some German. The poor woman was desperately worried about her husband. She loved him dearly and wanted him home. He was somewhere in action in Russia. She said to Janka, "Der Krieg ist bald zu Ende, kaput .... The war will soon be over, kaput." It would be wonderful when it was. The lives of millions of people, regardless of nationality, had been shattered by the war.

They continued sorting and talking. As they worked, a uniformed man walked down the driveway carrying a black envelope in his hand. The women froze as they watched him walk towards the house. A black envelope meant a soldier had been killed. Was it the lady's husband, or Getra's husband?

Without opening the black envelope, the lady from Hannover knew that her husband was dead. She went to her room with the letter. Her daughters joined her. Their grieving was great. Janka felt their pain, and cried too.

The lady and her two daughters worked on the farm with Janka until the end of the war. They parted and never saw each other again, but Janka remembered the beautiful lady and her two daughters from Hannover, forever.

Sometime Later
The Second French Prisoner-of-War

Janka was surprised to find a different Frenchman on the farm one day. His name was also Jean, but I shall call him Johnathan for easier reading. The first Jean had gone to a different farm. Johnathan fell in love with Janka.

Johnathan was 20 years old. He was immediately taken with the pretty Polish girl, and her gentle nature. He gazed at her whenever he could. She was beautiful in every way.

The French prisoners received wonderful parcels from France. Janka thought Johnathan was just being nice when he brought her chocolates. She was unaware that he was trying to court her. He tried to work near her whenever he could, and was happy just to be in her presence. In the weeks that passed, he continued bringing her chocolates and other gifts. One day he brought her the most beautifully colored towels she had ever seen. They were gorgeous. The two talked in broken German. "Das ist fur Dich, Johanna. Bitte nehme sie .... These are for you, Johanna. Please take them." It meant a great deal to Johnathan for Janka to accept his gift. She blushed and thanked him very much.

The weeks passed into months. Johnathan's heart was captured by Janka and he had to express his love. "Nach dem Krieg komme mit mir nach Frankreich, Johanna. Wir werden ein gutes Leben haben .... After the war, come with me to France, Johanna. We'll have a good life together."

Janka was so surprised she blushed a bright crimson. She had no idea Johnathan was in love with her. She was lost for words and stared at him in silence. Janka liked him very much, but she did not think of him as a potential husband. She gently replied, "Oh Jean, nein. Ich kann meine Familie nicht verlassen .... Oh Johnathan, no. I cannot leave my family." Johnathan did not give up. He patiently waited and continued to bring little gifts to his beautiful Johanna, hoping she would change her mind.

Stolcenal Hospital Outside of Steinbrink
Stasia Horoszkiewicz-Regulant - 19 years old

In April 1944, Stasia was advanced in pregnancy. She believed she was due in early June, but a visit to the doctor told her she was due any day. She was huge. Stasia told the woman for whom she worked, Frau Lieschien, that she must go to the prisoner's hospital in Stolcenal, near Steinbrink.

A Ukrainian woman, Józefka - Josephine, who worked on a neighboring farm, told Stasia she would go with her because she was going to have a baby too. Stasia looked at her in surprise. Where was the baby? She didn't look at all pregnant. Her stomach was flat, but her chest and breasts were huge, and her feet and legs swollen.

The prisoner's hospital was an army barrack, with a high barbed-wire fence all around, and minimal medical staff. They were met by a Polish nurse and a Russian doctor. The doctor did not examine the women. He just looked at them and made his diagnosis. He told Stasia she would be delivering twins any day, and he told Josephine she should return to the farm. Josephine argued and cried that she was going to have a baby at any time. The doctor admitted them both. Josephine was placed in the room across from Stasia.

Patients who needed assistance yanked on a cord in the hallway. The cord ran down to the nurse's station and had a bell on the other end. Stasia yanked on the cord and rang for the nurse many times during her six week stay.

April 29, 1944
Stasia Assists in Her First Delivery

Stasia was awakened from a deep nap the following afternoon, by muffled moans. She was in a sleepy stupor and didn't know what the sound was. Through the doorway she could see the foot of Josephine's bed. Josephine was kicking and moving from side to side. Stasia quickly

ran to help her. The baby's head was already beginning to show. She wildly yanked on the cord in the hall to call the nurse, and then ran back to Josephine. No doctor was on call. When she returned, the baby's entire head and one shoulder were exposed, and they were dark blue! The umbilical cord was wrapped around the baby's neck. Stasia was rapidly unwrapping the cord as the nurse walked into the room.

The nurse quickly ordered Stasia to get a basin of cold water. She ran, and was back in time to see the delivery. The nurse immediately dunked the infant into the cold bath several times to start him breathing. Finally he cried, and the three women cried as well. Disregarding her white uniform, the nurse sat down on a chair with the newborn across her lap, blood, cord and all.

Josephine's chest heaved with sobs. She told Stasia and the nurse that she was not married, and had tried during her entire pregnancy to miscarry the baby. She tried to abort it by wearing a tight corset for nine months, and she didn't call anyone when her time came because she wanted the baby to die during child birth. She cried and cried. She was so ashamed and remorseful at what she had tried to do. She had a beautiful baby boy weighing more than nine pounds. He was destined to live, and she loved him as soon as she saw him. She named him Józef after his father.

Josephine returned to the farm with her son, but Stasia waited six weeks before her baby was born. She welcomed the bed rest, but did not like being confined indoors. She was not permitted to go outside for a walk, or to go to church. During her first month in the maternity ward, she assisted in the delivery of three babies.

Stasia remembered the boy's birthday every April 29th, for the rest of her life.

Two Weeks Later
Stasia's Second Delivery

A tall Russian woman, advanced in pregnancy, was admitted to Stasia's room. She did not change into hospital garments nor did she lay down. She paced back and forth for hours at the end of her cot, wearing a long, heavy, dark coat and high, black boots. One arm was across her back and the other across her stomach. Occasionally she moved her index finger up to her lip as though she was deep in thought, but then moved her hand back down to her stomach. Hour after hour she paced without uttering a sound or changing her expression. Her behavior was definitely strange and Stasia felt uncomfortable.

Suddenly the woman broke her pace, left the room, and went into the bathroom. A few minutes later, Stasia heard the woman scream and a baby's cry. Stasia ran to the bathroom. The Russian woman was standing in her long coat and high boots with a crying baby on the floor between her feet. The umbilical cord was still attached to the placenta in her womb! Stasia wildly yanked on the rope in the hall to call the nurse.

The nurse picked up the baby with the cord still attached to the mother. She walked stooped over holding the infant, while Stasia guided the woman to the bed. The woman was in shock and Stasia backed her up to the end of the cot; it was as though she was frozen. The nurse told Stasia to give the woman a hard push on her chest. She fell straight back onto the bed and her big black boots flew straight up in front of Stasia's face. The nurse put the baby on the bed so that she could undress the mother, and remove the placenta. She pushed down in circular motions on her abdomen until it came out.

After a few days, the Russian woman took her baby and left. She never uttered a sound except for that one scream during her entire stay.

Two Weeks Later
Stasia's Third Delivery

A petite young mother, about Stasia's size, arrived. She went into labour, and suffered an entire week without any medical aid. Stasia stayed beside her and nursed her with kind words. She held her hand and wiped her forehead with a cool cloth. The poor girl was in absolute agony. The contractions continued hour after hour, day after day. The baby's head emerged and disappeared several times, and no one was there to help. The girl was exhausted. Both the mother and Stasia wondered if the baby would ever be born. Stasia was worried that the mother and baby might die. After seven horrible days of labour the baby's head started to come out for the last time. Stasia knew what to do. She yanked on the pull cord, got a basin of cold water, and waited for the nurse.

The last delivery frightened Stasia. She was worried that her small frame would complicate her delivery too. She looked down at her rotund belly and knew that her baby was big. She was going to have a difficult time.

May, 1944
Janka's First Bike Ride

Janka wanted to visit her sister, but the hospital was thirty kilometers away. There was an old bicycle on the Williams' farm, and Janka was determined to learn to ride. She climbed on, and immediately crashed. Cycling was not as easy as it looked. She steadied herself on the fence, and then pushed herself off. The handlebars wobbled. She tried to balance herself again, and crashed repeatedly. When she finally managed to stay up, she proudly cycled around the yard.

With permission from their farming families, Zygmunt and Janka cycled to Stolcenal at the end of May. They awoke early Sunday morning, packed a lunch, displayed their OST badges, and climbed onto the farm bikes. Janka was definitely a beginner, and her handle bars still wobbled, but she was sure she could make the sixty kilometre round trip.

The bikes were old with wide seats, fat tires, and heavy frames. The chains needed oil and there were no gears, but the entire route was flat farmland. Janka and Zygmunt were very strong from all of their manual labour, and confident they would reach Stolcenal on the old bicycles. They pedaled past many farms, and a pretty lake on the way. The German countryside was beautiful. After several hours they arrived.

Stolcenal Hospital
The Abortion

Janka gave Stasia and Zygmunt some time to themselves and went down the corridor. In the room next door, all alone, was a beautiful seventeen-year-old Polish girl. She was in her bed crying. Janka went to her and gently asked what was wrong. The girl said, "Oni zabili dzisiaj moje dziecko .... They killed my baby today." Janka was horrified and asked why. The girl said, "Ja nie wiedziałam co oni robili. Ja pracowalam na gospodarce. Właścicieli przywiózł mnie do szpitala. Dostałam zastrzyk, ale nie wiedziałam dlaczego. Ten zastrzyk zabił moje dziecko. Moja mama i moj narzeczony nie wiedzieli o tem .... I didn't know what they were doing. I was working in the fields. The farmer came over and took me to this hospital. I was given an injection, but didn't know why. The injection killed my baby. My mother and fiancée do not know." The poor girl sobbed. She told Janka to see what they had done.

The girl was near the end of her third trimester of pregnancy. She was lying on her back, with her knees bent, and her legs apart. A sheet covered her from her neck to her knees. Janka went around the bed. What she saw, remained etched in her mind the rest of her life. The baby's tiny leg was tied with a string, and coming out of the mother. A heavy weight was tied to the other end of the string and hung over the edge of the bed. Janka did not tell the girl what she saw, nor did she ask any questions. She sat beside her and they wept together. She wiped the girl's forehead with a cool cloth. She was so young and so pretty. Janka felt terribly sorry for her and tried to comfort her, but the girl's grief was inconsolable. While Janka was in the room, the girl's mother and fiancée arrived. How

they cried when they saw the heinous act. They had no human rights. Their baby was dead.

Janka left the grieving family and went back to Stasia's room. She was shaken and walked back in silence. She could not remove the horrifying scene from her mind.

All Janka knows about the abortion is what the girl told her, and what she witnessed. She did not know any more medical details, but she remembered the Polish girl, and the atrocity, for the rest of her life. Both she and the girl had been seventeen years old.

Sunday, June 4, 1944
Stasia Goes into Labour

Stasia was becoming depressed from being confined to the hospital for six weeks. She desperately needed to get out, and was at the point where she didn't care if she was caught leaving the hospital. It was Sunday, and she was going to church.

She was so glad to be out of the hospital, breathing in the morning air. She waddled down the road with her round belly swaying with each step. She was tired by the time she got there. She quietly entered the church, made the sign of the cross, and knelt. It was peaceful there. She no sooner started praying when a jolt of pain seized her belly. She held her stomach as the pain subsided. She continued praying. A few minutes later the pain grabbed her again. Stasia panicked. The baby was coming. She reached the door of the church when the third contraction hit.

Her contractions continued as she walked. She was on the road alone and in labour. She stopped several times, doubled over in pain. Stasia thought she might not make it. The road seemed much longer going back than it did the other way. She slowly took one painful step after another.

She was relieved when she laid down on her bed. She endured her contractions alone hour after hour. Her labour continued into the next

day. The nurse occasionally looked in on her, but assessed it would be a long time before the baby was born.

Wednesday, June 7, 1944
Stasia's Third Day of Labour

On the third day there was still no baby. She was exhausted. As her labour continued, the air raid sirens blared. There was nowhere for her to go, for the bunker was only for the Germans. She was terrified as the American bombs whistled through the air. The walls of the hospital shook and the windows rattled. The noise was deafening. She was helpless and alone. She screamed and cried, and pleaded to God to let her die, before the baby was born. She did not want to leave a helpless infant behind. She repeated her prayer again and again, as the explosions continued.

The hellish nightmare finally ended. When all was quiet, she felt another strong contraction, and her torment continued into the fourth day.

Thursday, June 8, 1944
Stasia Delivers

The nurse helped deliver Krystyna Regulant on June 8th, 1944, at 7:15 a.m., four days after Stasia's labour began. Stasia cried at the sight of her baby. She sent word to her husband and family.

The Russian doctor's initial diagnosis of twins and an early delivery was wrong; his diagnosis was six weeks early and one baby too many.

Sunday June 11, 1944
Janka's Second Bike Ride

Janka and Zygmunt could hardly wait to visit. The following Sunday, they once again packed their lunches, displayed their OST badges, and pedaled to Stolcenal. Zygmunt took the lead and checked on his sister-in-law. Even though Janka had cycled the sixty kilometers two weeks earlier, she was still a novice; her handle bars wobbled before she got going. On they rode through the pretty German farmland. They rounded a bend and passed the little lake. They would soon be in Stolcenal.

Stasia looked exhausted but happy that it was all over. They listened to her relive her ordeals. Zygmunt wished he could have been with her during that time. Stasia and Krysia would be home soon. They took turns holding the newborn.

Zygmunt and Janka climbed back onto their bikes and pushed off. Zygmunt once again took the lead and Janka tried her best to keep up. He glanced back from time to time, but he was thinking of his wife and baby. There were long intervals between his glances and soon Zygmunt was well ahead. He passed some people standing on a curve near the lake. He followed the bend and was out of sight.

Janka was not paying attention to the road up ahead. She had her head down looking at her front tire turn around and around. It was rather hypnotic. When she finally looked up she was heading straight for the pedestrians. The road curved to the left, the people were in the middle, and lake was on the right. Everyone jumped out of Janka's way as she whipped by them completely out of control. Janka, bike and all, did a nose dive into the lake. She stood up, coughing and gasping. Luckily for her the water was shallow, for she never did learn how to swim. Her baggy dress clung to her and her hair was plastered over her face. The onlookers burst out laughing, and Janka did too.

When Zygmunt couldn't see Janka, he turned back. He found her standing in the lake, soaking wet, holding her bicycle. She looked so funny he burst out laughing. "Co ty tu robisz? .... What are you doing here?"

"Dobrze że ja się nie utopiłam .... It's a good thing I didn't drown!'', laughed Janka, as she pushed her bike out of the water.

"Teraz się patrz gdzie ja jadę i gdzie będę skręcać na drugą drogę .... Now you watch where I'm riding, and when I turn on a new road," said Zygmunt.

"Ja będę blizko ciebie. Ja już nigdzie nie będę skręcać żeby znowu nie wjechać do wody .... I'll stay close to you. I won't ride into the water again," Janka assured him. They both laughed and continued on towards the farm. It was a cool ride all the way home.

The humorous episode ended Janka's cycling days. She never rode again.

Shortly After
Stasia Brings Her Baby Home

Zygmunt and Janka travelled by train to Stolcenal to bring Stasia and the baby home. Krysia was baptized in the Catholic Church near the hospital before they left. Janka was the godmother and one of Zygmunt's brothers, was recorded as the godfather.

Frau Lieschien, who ran Stasia's farm, had no children and her husband was away at war. Stasia and three other farmhands worked on Lieschien's farm. Stasia had a very difficult time with Frau Lieschien. She worked incredibly hard and was not given enough food, even when she was pregnant. When she came home from the hospital with the baby, the heartless woman did not like having Krysia in the house. Stasia had to continue to do her regular workload while taking care of her newborn. She rushed her meals so that she could feed Krysia, or rinse out her diapers. A German lady on a nearby farm, gave Stasia a few baby clothes. She was thankful, as there were extreme shortages, and she would have had nothing for the baby.

She tried nursing Krysia for six months, but had to stop. Due to poor nutrition, she did not produce enough milk. The woman allowed only one pint of cow's milk per day for the baby. Stasia supplemented the baby's diet by boiling and mashing carrots. She strained the carrots and

made a formula by mixing the carrot stock with the milk, so that there was enough food for Krysia for the day.

Stasia kept Krysia beside her as she worked, but sometimes Krysia had to be left with the mean woman. One day Stasia had to work far from the house. Frau Lieschien promised that she would feed the baby. Stasia prepared everything. When she returned from the fields at 6 p.m., she found Krysia asleep in her buggy under a tree, with her untouched formula beside her. The woman had left Krystyna outside all day and had neither fed, nor changed her. It was obvious Frau Lieschien did not want Krysia on the farm, and Stasia started to fear for her daughter's safety.

She continued working long after bed hours to prepare Krysia's food. She made carrot juice, mashed potatoes, and mashed soup. She started spoon feeding her when she was still very tiny. Autumn brought cold weather and there was ice on the walls in her room. To keep the baby warm, they slept together. She laid Krysia on top of her stomach and wrapped the blankets around the two of them. She was worried she might roll over onto the baby, so she did not sleep well. Keeping the baby warm while bathing her was also a challenge. To bathe the baby, she laid her on the bed fully dressed. Stasia wore a sweater unbuttoned down the front, leaned over Krysia, and flipped the back of her sweater over her head making a tent over the baby. Breathing on Krysia to keep her warm, she undressed her and quickly gave her a sponge bath.

Stasia had to somehow get away from Frau Lieschien. She was afraid.

July 1, 1944
Janka's Operation

While working in Steinbrink, Janka developed severe abdominal pains. The pains worsened, and Slavko was worried. Sometimes she doubled over in agony. Something was terribly wrong. Slavko spoke to Oma in German and told her that Janka must see a doctor.

Mrs. Williams took Janka to the doctor. The doctor examined her and discussed her condition with Mrs. Williams. Janka could not understand what was being said in German. She was booked for surgery July 1st, 1944, without any explanation as to what was wrong with her, or what they were going to do.

Janka was afraid to have an operation after witnessing the abortion only one month earlier, and cried into her pillow. She never met the surgeon. The entire procedure was absent of any feeling. She felt helpless as she was taken into the operating room.

She awoke with a burning fever, and a huge bandage over her abdomen. A male nurse looked in on her, but did absolutely nothing. She continued to feel helpless and alone. She was in pain, and there was no medication to help. A young Russian girl was in the hospital at the same time, with a broken arm. She nursed Janka and tried to break her fever. She brought two basins of cold water and dipped Janka's wrists into them. She put cold compresses on Janka's forehead. She brought cool water to drink. Slowly Janka's fever passed. The girl watched over her, while the nurses did nothing.

Janka felt horrible, but better. She was able to sit up in bed for short spells. One day while sitting in bed, a French prisoner looked in the window and saw her. (The French prisoners were not as tightly monitored as the Russians.) The Frenchman went back to his barrack, and returned with some chocolates. Janka was deeply touched by his kindness. The candy was delicious and such a rare treat. He visited her each day and always brought her something: chocolates, bread, an orange.

The Frenchman spoke German, but Janka's German was too poor to have a conversation. The Russian girl spoke German better than Janka. Janka could manage a conversation in Russian. Janka wanted to repay the Frenchman's kindness by mending his socks. She passed her message in Russian to the girl. The girl passed Janka's message in German to the Frenchman. The Frenchman replied in German to the Russian who passed it in Russian to the Pole. Somehow it was understood. The Frenchman brought Janka his socks, with a darning needle and yarn. She immediately began darning the holes, which pleased him.

Janka desperately wanted to know what had been done to her during surgery. She slowly climbed out of bed and tried to walk. The incision burned with pain. She stood in the doorway and looked down the hall. It was empty. There was no one in sight. A nurse wearing a white apron, rounded the corner and started coming her way. Janka had never seen her before and asked, "Czy ty byłaś przy mnie jak ja miałam operację? .... Were you beside me during my operation?"

"Tak ...Yes." She was from Warsaw, but a Volksdeutsche - a Pole of German parentage.

"Ciekawa jestem co to była za operacja bo nie widziałam lekarza ani przed ani po operacji .... I want to know what kind of operation I had, because I did not see the doctor before or after the surgery."

The heartless nurse callously remarked, "Ty nie będziesz miała dzieci. Jak będziesz chciała wyjść za mąż to nie mów nic narzeczonemu .... You will never have children. If you want to get married, don't tell your future husband."

She was shocked at what the nurse was saying. She had been sterilized! She did not want to believe what she was hearing. Weakly, she replied, "Ja nie będę kłamać, tylko powiem prawdę jak ze mną jest .... I will not lie. I'll tell the truth of my condition," and went back to her room and sobbed.

The Russian girl came over to her and said in Russian, "Не плачь, не плачь .... Don't cry. Don't cry." Janka told her what the nurse had said. "Ты молода и будешь здорова. Не плачь что ты не будешь иметь детей. Ты будешь .... You are young and will be healthy. Don't cry that you won't have children. You will."

Zygmunt and Filipina came to visit. Janka sadly told them the awful news. Filipina tried to console her daughter by saying that she was thankful she was healthy and alive. But Janka found it difficult to accept that she would never have children.

Mrs. Williams and Slavko came to get her in the horse-drawn wagon. She needed two more weeks at home to recuperate. Oma did not want Janka to sleep alone for the first couple of days. She would share

Getra's big room and big bed. Getra did not mind the company.

Janka was in awe of Getra's big clothes closet. Getra opened it and showed Janka her dresses. She had never seen such a wardrobe; she only had one shabby dress. Janka loved Getra's green dress. It had long sleeves and a raised collar. She could only dream of owning such a dress.

Janka grew brave enough over the next few days to ask Getra about the dress. She offered to buy it for an exchange of work. Getra liked the dress and shrugged in uncertainty, however, the next day, Getra gave Janka the dress as a gift. She hugged Getra and couldn't wait for Sunday when she could put it on.

Stasia was relieved that her younger sister was home. After a few days rest, she brought Krysia to her. Stasia desperately wanted to keep Krysia away from Frau Lieschen. She brought the baby early each morning, and picked her up each evening. Janka loved caring for little Krysia, but was nervous handling such a tiny infant. Janka rested in her bed, or outside on a blanket in the warm sun, with her five-week-old niece beside her. She fed, changed, and lovingly pampered her. Janka was a natural mother.

Janka went back to work after two weeks of rest, but she was not ready for strenuous labour. She felt terrible pain as she milked the cows, and lifted the heavy cans. Her incision was still tender and sore. One month after surgery, Filipina came to visit. It was a beautiful sunny day, yet Janka was depressed. She leaned against the fence and forlornly said to her mother, "Ja nie będę mieć dzieci .... I will not have children."

Filipina understood her daughter's grief, "Bogu podziękuj że jesteś żywa i jesteś młoda, i będziesz zdrowa. Wszystko będzie dobrze .... Thank God that you are alive and young, and that you will be healthy. Everything will be all right."

Janka never did find out what was done to her during her operation in 1944. Her abdominal pain continued throughout her life, right into old age. She had not been sterilized as the cruel nurse had told her, and she had six children to prove it:

		Born in:
Krysia - Krystyna	August 16, 1948	Frille, Germany
Wandzia - Wanda	April 11, 1950	Nanaimo, BC, Canada
Danusia - Daiena	November 2, 1951	Nanaimo, BC, Canada
Marysia - Mary	December 25, 1953	Ladysmith, BC, Canada
Rysiek - Richard	September 28, 1955	Ladysmith, BC, Canada
Roman - Ron	January 13, 1961	Ladysmith, BC, Canada

September, 1944
Slavko, the Russian Prisoner-of-War

Janka and Slavko became friends as they worked together on the farm. He taught her some Russian, as well as the German commands she needed for the farm dog. Janka enjoyed Slavko's company and the language lessons. She learned that he was forty-five years old, and had a wife and two daughters in Russia. He was a gentle man, with a big heart. Slavko desperately wanted to return home to his family. He feared for their safety, for the German army had already advanced into Russia. Slavko wanted to protect his family, but he could do nothing. It was mental torture not knowing their state.

Janka worked with Slavko for over a year, when he started having abdominal pain. Slavko mentioned his pain day after day. It became progressively worse to the point where he was unable to work. Slavko was admitted to the small hospital in Stolcenal for emergency surgery of an acute appendicitis. Janka was so worried about him, and anxiously awaited the results of his operation. Her experiences in the hospital had not been positive, and she feared it would be worse for a Russian military prisoner-of-war.

Slavko died in hospital the day following surgery. No details were given about the operation or his death. Janka deeply mourned her kind

friend. All he had wanted was to return to his wife and children in Russia.

Autumn, 1944
The Sausages

Adam was transferred to a logging camp to sharpen tools, and was given no time to tell his family. He was on a train and gone with no goodbye. The family was upset and very concerned. Would Adam return? Would they ever see him again? They were told nothing. Marian, a Pole who worked on an adjacent farm, was also transported.

A young Pole, Jack (pseudonym), who worked on a farm nearby, told Janka that the men in the camp were poorly fed and almost starving. Janka wanted to help her father, but how? Jack wanted to visit his friend Marian in the logging camp, and asked Janka if she wanted to go with him. He told her it would be safe to take food, and convinced her to steal some sausages from the Williams. No one would miss a few links, and together they would board the train and take them to Adam.

Janka had never stolen anything in her life, but would to feed her father. She trusted Jack. She knew nothing of Nazi concentration camps, or the Gestapo. To steal and deliver stolen food to forced labourers was a serious offense. People were beaten, shot, or hung for lesser crimes. Unknowingly, she was risking her life.

Mr. Williams had slaughtered a huge pig, and many lengths of pork sausage were made. As she worked, she set one length aside. In the evening she returned alone to the barn. She was afraid, and plagued with guilt, as she lifted her baggy dress and wrapped the sausage links around her waist. She had gained weight since coming to the farm, and her waist was thick. The sausages were well hidden.

The workers, with the exception of the prisoners-of-war, could travel on Sundays with permission. Oma gave Janka a little sausage to take to her father, which made her feel even worse for stealing from the family. With the sausages hidden around her waist, and the OST badge on her chest, Janka met Jack early Sunday morning. The two walked to the train station a few miles away.

Janka felt safe with Jack, but when they neared the station, Jack told her they must not walk together any longer. Janka was confused and frightened by this sudden change in plans. "Dlaczego my nie możemy iść razem? .... Why can't we go together?" He explained that if he was searched by the police, they would find nothing on him and they would both be safe. However, if she was searched, then only she would be arrested. He then told her about hangings, concentration camps, and the Gestapo.

Janka was terrified, and kept her eyes glued on the back of Jack's head. He boarded the train, and she followed and sat a few seats behind. She was extremely nervous that there would be a search and her fear showed on her face.

Jack ignored Janka as they disembarked. He continued walking ahead of her. German soldiers and police seemed to be everywhere. The sidewalks were crowded with people. Janka was constantly scanning for trouble.

Janka was so relieved when they finally reached the logging camp. She could hardly wait to see her father, but he was not there. He had been transported to a different camp one week before. Janka wept. She had risked her life for nothing.

She left the sausages with Marian and the other men in the camp. They were all hungry. She wondered if Jack had known all along that her father was not there. She felt used. All the way home, she was wary for police. With or without sausages, she did not feel safe with Jack and never trusted him again.

Adam and Marian worked several weeks in the bush, and then were returned to the farms in Steinbrink.

October 1944
Stasia Visits the Mayor

Nineteen-year-old Stasia bundled Krysia up, and went to see the mayor. He was Getra's father. Stasia explained her desperate situation in broken German; her baby was in danger from Frau Lieschien. The mayor listened but made no reply.

Zygmunt lived and worked with the Kumins, a wonderful German family. Mrs. Kumin knew how wicked Frau Lieschien could be. Two weeks after Stasia met with the mayor, Zygmunt knocked on her farmhouse door. He told his wife that he had just been notified that she and Krysia were to have been at the Kumins a week ago! Her plea to the mayor had worked. Stasia jumped up to go right away, but Frau Lieschien blocked her way. She did not let Stasia go until evening.

With the Kumin family lived the grandparents, daughter-in-law, and grandson. The Kumin's son was at war. Stasia and Zygmunt brought Krystyna to the Kumin's home. They were thrilled to have the four month old baby with them, and she went from one set of arms to the next. They treated her like their own, and grew to love her more and more. Krysia was well fed, bathed, and pampered. Oma Kumin was the main caretaker, but the thirteen-year-old grandson, took the baby for walks in the buggy and played with her, too. As she grew, they built her a little sand box, and protected her play area with a fence. Adam and Filipina's farm was adjacent to the Kumin's. They could see their granddaughter as she played on the other side of the fence. Little Krystyna was safe and surrounded by people who loved her.

Late Fall, 1944
Steinbrink - The Second Farm

Janka had worked on the big farm for over a year, when she was moved to a smaller farm nearby. The elderly couple who operated the second farm were relatives of the Williams. They could no longer manage all of the chores themselves. There were cows to milk, wood to chop,

animals to feed, and fields to tend. The Williams recognized that Janka was a reliable farmhand with a gentle nature, and chose her to help their aging relatives.

Janka left in the fall, and Johnathan, the second French prisoner-of-war who was in love with her, was heartbroken. He would not see his beautiful Johanna each day, but he remained hopeful. The farms were close together and he would still be able to see her and bring her gifts.

The aging relatives, Oma and Opa, welcomed Janka and treated her well. They had no children of their own. Oma and Opa showed her to her room, which had a puffy feather bed and a down quilt, just like her room on the big farm. She felt blessed that she had been placed with two good families since arriving in Germany. The old folks showed her the barn and the two milking cows, which were used as plow animals, and to pull the wagon, just as she had seen in Poland. Opa sat down and began milking. Janka pulled up a stool beside the second cow and milked too. The old man was pleased.

Shortly after her arrival, Oma and Opa went away for the day, and left Janka with the chores. She set to milking the two cows. There was some hay spread in the corner of the barn next to the milking stalls, which completely hid a pit into which the animals' excrements were scraped. It was collected and used to fertilize the fields. Janka finished milking the first cow, and backed around its rump to reach the second cow. She took one step back too many and down she went, into the pool of manure. She was waist high, and her skirt floated all around her. It was absolutely disgusting! She tried to climb out, but couldn't. She needed help, but the old folks were away. Janka grabbed the tail of the cow closest to her and pulled as hard as she could. The frightened cow jerked to the side, and out Janka came.

She was a mess, and smelled twice as bad! She was so glad the elderly people were not home; she would have been embarrassed. She went outside to a big barrel filled with water, quickly pulled off her clothes, and began scraping off the manure, and scrubbing herself. She then heated lots of water on the stove and washed herself again and again.

She was so lucky she hadn't hit her head as she fell in, or that the manure pool wasn't deeper. What a horrible demise that would have been.

Johnathan continued bringing Janka gifts over the months at the smaller farm. When the war ended he went back to France. They never saw each other again.

Part 4 - Epilogue

Omelanka, Eastern Poland to Germany
1943-1945

When the war ended, it was chaos organizing thousands of displaced people into refugee camps by their nation of birth. The Horoszkiewicz family did not immediately leave the farms. They continued working until the fall of 1945, when the situation for refugees in Germany was more organized.

When it was time to leave, the family gathered at the Kumins to be taken to a refugee camp in Raderhorst, near Lahde, Germany. Frania, a Polish girl who sometimes visited from a neighboring farm, came as well. Janka hugged the elderly couple with, "Auf Wiedersehn .... goodbye." She also said Auf Wiedersehn to Mr. and Mrs. Williams, her first Oma, Getra, and her daughter. The lady from Hannover had left long ago. It broke Oma Kumin's heart to say goodbye to Krystyna. She had watched the baby grow into a toddler, and had nurtured her in every way. Oma Kumin cried and hugged them all for one last time. These German families had kept them together and safe from 1943 to 1945.

En route, they met two young Polish men cycling, who had worked on farms in the area and were also on their way to Raderhorst. The boys remained on their bikes, held the side of the wagon, and got a lift. One of the boys, Stefan, was rolling along right beside Frania and was completely taken with her.

From this chance roadside meeting, Stefan Wrzecionek met his wife. They eventually married in Raderhorst.

Three Generations - Germany 1947
Seated: Filipina Horoszkiewicz with her first grandchild, Krystyna
Standing from Left: Stasia and Janka

Late December 1946
Janka 20 years old

In the Raderhorst camp, a young man caught Janka's eye. His name was Sylwester Drzewiecki. Adam introduced his youngest daughter to Sylwester, and he captured her heart.

When battles rage within the mind,
Assailing the heart, making love blind.
Forgiveness releases hurts and wrongs,
And frees the heart of bitter song.

Acceptance and tolerance, nurture peace;
Let hatred and war forever cease.
We share one Earth, as humankind;
Let peace reside in heart and mind.

History has vanished into the past,
Step out of the shadows that it has cast.
With every midnight, dawns morning sun,
And a glorious world, of which we are one.

- Mary Drzewiecki, 2000

Part 5

Germany 1946 - 1949

Sylwester and Janina Drzewiecki
Moi Rodzice .... My Parents

April 7, 1947

The heart was meant to sing in harmony.

-Mary Drzewiecki, 1994

Part 5 - Introduction

Germany
1946 to 1949

Peace was not peaceful in the years immediately following the war. Lahde, Germany, was the headquarters for the refugee camps situated in the surrounding villages of Raderhorst, Frille, and Ilzehade. The British peacekeeping forces organized the displaced citizens into refugee camps by nation of their birth. The Horoszkiewicz family was sent to the Polish camp in Raderhorst. Many German families were evicted from their homes to house the refugees. The Horoszkiewicz family, and five other Polish families were assigned to live in one large house. Each family had one room, but the main areas of the house were shared. Janka and her parents slept in one room; Stasia, Zygmunt, and little Krysia in another.

It was a mammoth task relocating thousands of homeless people. Children were orphaned. Families were separated. Supplying food to the massive numbers of refugees was a colossal problem for the peacekeeping forces. There were severe shortages of every kind, and people traded whatever they had for milk, vegetables, and meat. There was much looting, and illegal buying and selling on the black market. Allied peacekeeping forces stringently enforced law and order to care for the refugees, and to protect the German families. Stiff sentences were given for stealing, and many thieves who had just survived the horrors of war, faced long term imprisonment.

Countries were opening their doors to immigration: Canada, the United States, Australia, New Zealand, Great Britain, France, Brazil, and Argentina. They enticed the displaced Europeans with beautiful pictures and films of industries, farmlands, and sceneries of their countries. Many people began thinking of immigrating, including the Horoszkiewicz family. Adam yearned to farm in Poland again, but even during war time Filipina and the rest of the family recognized that life was better in Germany than it had ever been in Eastern Poland. They did not share

Adam's longing to return. Adam applied twice to return to Poland but both times he was vetoed by the family. With Omelanka destroyed, and Eastern Poland now within the Russian border, immigration represented opportunity and freedom. If they could not immigrate to a new country, they wanted to stay in Germany.

Russian citizens were not given the option to stay or to immigrate elsewhere. They were quickly deported to Russia. The family witnessed hasty marriages take place between Russian women and men from other countries, just so that they did not have to return to Russia; they too recognized that life was better in the West. Many Russian girls went to France with their new French husbands. Some did not care whether the man was young or old, healthy or sick. In many cases the men were sincere, but some of the women were not. Many of the brides left their husbands once they had their official documents.

In 1946, the administration office in Lahde posted that seamstresses and tailors were needed. There was a house in Raderhorst fitted with two treadle sewing machines. Used clothing needed to be repaired. Stasia, Janka and a few other girls signed up. Three young men also applied. The women used one machine, the men the other. Stasia taught Janka and the others how to sew. Janka did not have the same passion for stitching and designing as did her sister, but she enjoyed learning with the rest. The old treadle machines whirred.

Before Sylwester Drzewiecki arrived in Raderhorst in late December, 1946, Janka had several suitors. She had blossomed into a beautiful twenty-year-old woman, and her quiet and gentle demeanor made her even more attractive; Janka was nice to everyone. The pounds she had gained on the German farms had melted away, and she caught the eye of many young men in the camp. In 1946, Haszuk, Władek, and Izydor were in love with her, all at the same time.

Haszuk was a gentleman, and was totally enamored when they met in 1946. He hoped they would marry. Except for Johnathan, Janka had no exposure to men, and Johnathan had just been a friend. She had passionate dreams about the kind of man she wanted to marry, and unfortunately for Haszuk, he was not her ideal. He was genuinely nice, but the chemistry wasn't there. Władek was a romantic, but he was not the one either. Izydor was a friend, who was a secret admirer. He spoke fluent German which was helpful when they traveled to Minden. He was in love with her, but Janka had no idea. Unfortunately for Haszuk, Władek, and Izydor, Sylwester arrived in the camp, and took up the chase.

Janina Horoszkiewicz in 1947

Note: This map is not to scale

The Refugee Camps of:
Lahde, Raderhorst and Frille
were near Minden.

Part 5 - Chapter 1

The Refugee Camp
Raderhorst, Germany
1946 to 1947

Late December 1946
Sylwester Drzewiecki - 21 years old
Sylwester Arrives in Raderhorst

Sylwester Drzewiecki and Józef Antczak arrived at the Lahde Headquarters in late December, 1946, and were assigned a room in Raderhorst which, coincidentally, was occupied by Jurek Regulant, Zygmunt's nephew from Dabrowa.

It didn't take Sylwester long to scout out the pretty Polish girls in the camp, nor for the girls to notice him, but he was still thinking about Pyra. He was now twenty-one years old, and having been well fed in Paderborn, was a very handsome young man. Sylwester was friendly, had a good sense of humor, and loved to sing. His dapper looks and his outgoing personality made him stand out in the crowd, and Janka Horoszkiewicz noticed.

Janka didn't tell anyone that the new young man in the camp had caught her eye. Haszuk was still trying to court her, and convince her that he was the one. Władek did not take rejection well, and was still trying for Janka's hand, and Izydor quietly admired her, but Janka had Sylwester on her mind.

When Adam met Sylwester, he was unaware that his daughter liked him. Adam liked Sylwester, and invited him to come to the house. Janka was surprised and blushed when her father walked in with Sylwester. She was nervous and did not know what to say. Sylwester immediatelyliked her, and thought of her all the way home.

Late December 1946
Peine near Hannover, Germany
Sylwester Visits Pyra

Sylwester wrote to Pyra from Raderhorst to tell her that he was coming to visit her in Peine. They hadn't seen each other for months, and he wanted to know if there were still feelings between them. There were two Polish camps in Peine, named Camp Chicago and Camp Buffalo. Pyra was in Camp Buffalo. Sylwester took the train to Hannover and made his way to Pyra's camp, as her parents made room for their guest. As Sylwester spent more time with Pyra, he realized that his feelings had changed. However, Pyra did not feel the same way.

December 31, 1946
Sylwester's New Year's Eve

It was common for people to masquerade on New Year's Eve, so Sylwester donned a mask and went alone from Pyra's camp to Camp Chicago. It was about one and a half miles away. He joined a party that was already in full swing, and although he was a total stranger in the crowd, bets were flying that they knew who he was. One bottle of whiskey was placed on the table, then two. Sylwester enjoyed the charade, removed his mask, and the two bottles were passed around. Sylwester drank beyond his limit, and sang as he staggered out the door. He stopped in at a krawiec - tailor, and had a drink with him, even though he didn't know the man, but it was New Year's Eve. Before Sylwester left, the krawiec wrapped a piece of pork for him to eat on his way back to camp Buffalo. As he walked, he tried to unwrap the pork, but his fingers wouldn't work. He fumbled, and the food fell to the ground. Sylwester bent down to retrieve it, and collapsed in the snow. It felt like a pillow on his face, and he immediately fell into a drunken sleep, in sub-zero temperatures.

Luckily a night guard cycling by spotted him, for Sylwester would surely have frozen to death. The guard hoisted Sylwester up over the bar of the bicycle, and took him to the police station in camp Buffalo where

he spent the night. The following day, with a massive hangover, he was sent back to Pyra's. Her parents were not impressed.

The Following Day
The Clothes Line

Sylwester and Pyra spent the next day together. After an evening with friends, they walked home. It was already dark and he wanted to catch the train back to Lahde that night. As they stood on the back porch, he told Pyra his feelings and broke off their relationship. Pyra wasn't listening. She was playing with his collar and rubbing the back of his neck. She combed her fingers through his hair and was moving in a little closer. Sylwester told her to stop, but she didn't listen. He backed away, but once again she moved in on him, whispering, "Sylwek", and giddily teasing him. He firmly removed her hands, turned around and ran. Pyra called after him, "Sylwek, Sylwek wróć się .... Sylwek, Sylwek come back." Sylwek kept running. The full moon shed enough light that he could see the ground, but not enough to see the wire clothes line ahead. "Sylwek, Sylwek!" Running at full speed the wire line smacked him right across his forehead and knocked him off his feet! He was stunned, but the sound of Pyra yelling, "Sylwek, Sylwek!", jolted him upright. He took off like a bullet.

Sylwester arrived back in Raderhorst with a big red indentation straight across his forehead. "Co się tobie stało? .... What happened to you?", Józef and Jurek asked in surprise. Sylwester looked in the mirror at his bright red dent. Everyone burst out laughing. Sylwester was lucky the wire had not been lower. It could have slit his throat! He wore the mark of Pyra for weeks, almost up to the day he married Janka.

Dec 31, 1946
Janka's New Year's Eve in Raderhorst

While Sylwester was saying goodbye to Pyra in Peine, Władek asked Janka to go to a New Year's Eve party in Raderhorst. The celebration was going to be held in the common area of Janka's house. Tables

were set and everyone brought what they could. There was much laughing and visiting. It was a festive occasion until Janka overheard Władek bragging to his friends that he would sell his last shirt for a bottle of whiskey. Janka was shocked by his addiction, and immediately left the party.

The following day Władek asked her why she had left. With distaste, Janka repeated the words he had spoken, but Władek did not give up. He continued to write beautiful love letters to her with hearts drawn beside his name, but her mind was made up. Władek was not for her.

February 1947 - Raderhorst, Germany
The Theatre Tickets

Sylwester showered Janka with his charm. He really wanted to win her heart and he did. Janka fell in love with Sylwester, which caused poor Haszuk much anguish and despair. He went to Filipina in hopes that she would influence her daughter's choice. The four sat around the table; Sylwester and Janka on one side, Haszuk and Filipina on the other. Haszuk kissed Filipina's hand, as was customary for European men, and pledged he would provide well for her daughter; Haszuk somehow had money. He vowed she would be treated like a queen and would never do dishes or any other house work. He was sincere in his love and his promises, but while he was swooning Filipina, Sylwester and Janka sat holding hands under the table.

Haszuk was not about to give up. He would show Janka who was the better man. He would shower the entire family with his generosity. Amateur theatre played in the camp and Haszuk bought tickets for everyone, including Sylwester. Stasia, Zygmunt, Jurek, Sylwester, Janka, and Haszuk walked to the playhouse. Naturally Haszuk planned to sit beside Janka, but that was also Sylwester's plan. Sylwester was quick. He grabbed the seat next to Janka, leaving no room for poor Haszuk. Haszuk was a gentleman and gracefully accepted defeat. He left the theatre with a broken heart and gave up his pursuit.

April 7, 1947
Sylwester and Janka Wed

After a three month courtship, Sylwester and Janka decided to marry. They required birth certificates for proof of identity and citizenship. Janka had hers from Omelanka, but Sylwester had nothing. A visit to the camp priest, with fifty marks and two witnesses, would produce the necessary document, and pay for the wedding ceremony as well. Adam and Zygmunt signed before Father Michałowski, that Sylwester was the son of Jan and Michalina Drzewiecki, and was born in Rudnia on the 31st of December, 1925. Sylwester paid the 50 marks and was given his birth certificate, which he kept for the rest of his life. (The priest was not from the Michałowski family in Rudnia.)

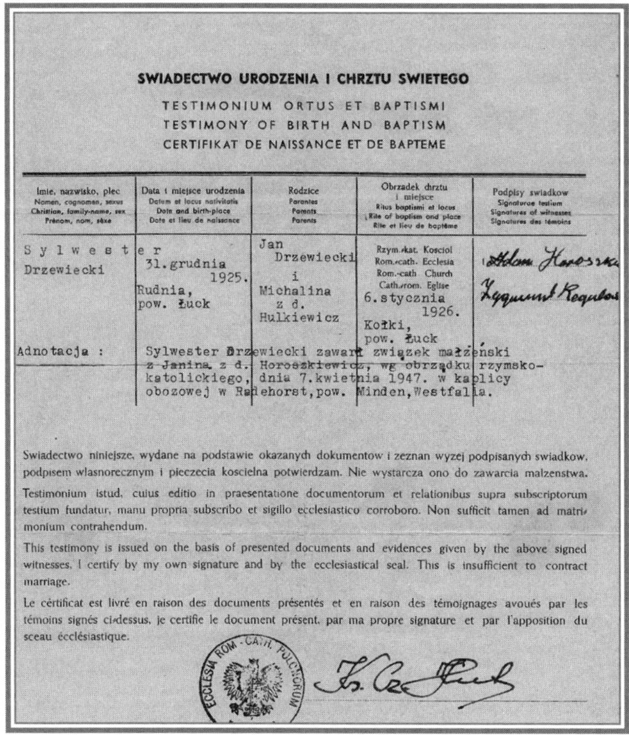

Sylwester's Birth Certificate Signed by
Adam and Zygmunt

*Janina's Birth Certificate with which she fled
from her home in Omelanka in 1943.*

Władek became insanely jealous when he heard of Janka and Sylwester's engagement. He threatened Janka that before she set foot at the alter, she would be dead. She was terrified. He might be crazy enough to kill her, and himself. The threat churned in her mind and she could not sleep, but the wedding plans went ahead.

Stasia and Janka prepared the food, and the main room in the house for the reception. Three long tables were set up around the perimeter for the guests. Filipina, Janka's mother, was in hospital undergoing surgery for a hysterectomy, when the wedding preparations were taking place. She was very ill, but was determined to attend the wedding.

Sylwester borrowed a smart two piece suit. Janka borrowed a wedding gown. She purchased a beautiful pair of hand crocheted gloves to wear on her wedding day. *(She kept the gloves for the rest of her life, and let each of her daughters wear them on their wedding day.)* Sylwester had no money for gold wedding bands, so Zygmunt made rings by filing a pair of two złoty, Polish coins. He worked the soft silver metal into two smooth bands.

On Easter Sunday, April 7th, 1947, the wedding procession lead by the bride and groom, made its way to the church in Raderhorst. The parents, family, and guests walked behind the handsome couple.

It was a double-wedding ceremony. Sylwester and Janka were on the left and another couple, whom they did not know, were on the right. Father Michałowski performed the marriage ceremony as family and guests witnessed the exchanging of vows. Sylwester slipped the silver band on Janka's right hand, as was customary in Poland, and Janka did the same. During the ceremony the candles on their side of the alter went out. Superstitious fears had been part of Janka's life, and she believed it was a bad omen. She immediately feared Władek's threat, but all was forgotten when the priest blessed them as husband and wife. Janka wore her silver wedding band on her right hand for the rest of her life. She never replaced it. It was worth more than gold.

An accordion played, and photographs were taken outside the church. They were given a decorative plate as a wedding gift, which Janka cherished. Everyone returned to Adam and Filipina's home to celebrate the happy occasion. There was much singing, eating, and drinking. Everyone raised their glasses to the newlyweds, Pan and Pani Drzewiecki.

Poor Izydor had painfully watched the woman he loved marry another man. His heart was not into the festivities, but no one knew his secret. Sometime after the wedding, Izydor told Janka he loved her, and how he thought he would die when he saw her marry Sylwester. Janka did not know what to say.

Sylwester and Janina Drzewiecki

Sylwester and Janina's Marriage Certificate
April 7, 1947

From Raderhorst, the entire Horoszkiewicz family was moved to a huge house in Frille, near Minden, Germany. They were given three separate rooms. Six families lived in the big house, and shared the common areas.

Part 5 - Chapter 2

Frille, Germany
1947 - 1949

Sylwester and Janina, 1948

Introduction:

Many changes were taking place in the refugee camps after Sylwester and Janina's wedding in 1947. The British were sending people back to their countries of origin if they did not plan to immigrate to another country. The Horoszkiewicz family had already decided to apply for immigration to Canada and to work in Germany while they waited. Realizing there was nothing left of Rudnia, Sylwester pursued his life-long dream of moving West.

During this time, the British Peacekeeping Forces were organizing guarding forces and transport groups. Many Polish men from the Lahde camps joined the British Civilian Mixed Labor Organization, CMLO. The members of the British CMLO wore dark navy uniforms, while the army wore green. Sylwester had a keen interest in mechanics and naturally signed up for the transport group.

Sylwester loved driving the big trucks. He already had taken some driving lessons from the British, but his opportunities to drive were few and far between. However, in the transport group, he drove every day. A driver's license was not issued until the driver knew the mechanics of the vehicle and how to repair it. His knowledge of auto mechanics was a skill he used the rest of his life, for he not only fulfilled his dream of owning a car, he owned a variety of trucks and cars, as well as outboard motors and all-terrain vehicles. He knew how to fix them all.

Working in the transport group meant that Sylwester had to work away from home, from a few days to a few weeks. Janka lived with her parents so she was not alone. Sylwester brought whatever food he could when he came home, for food shortages continued. Chocolates, apples and vegetables were rare treats.

Sylwester was fed, had a warm bed with clean linen, and was given clean clothing in the British forces. It was the first time in his life that he lived so well. He felt confident and proud of what he was doing. His wages were paid in British pounds, but there was virtually nothing to buy so Janka put most of the money away. There would be many administration costs before they could immigrate to Canada. During 1947, the food supply was so low that Janka could only buy oats. They ate porridge morning, noon and night, day after day. Janka tried to prepare the oats in different ways. She even made porridge soup by adding a little onion and potato that she bought from a farmer, although it tasted terrible.

Sylwester signed with the British forces for two years, until 1949, and worked in the following German cities:

Cuxhaven	Bremerhaven	Wilhelms Haven
Flensburg	Oldenburg	Bremen

Hamburg	Rheine	Walsrode
Fallingbostel	Bergen Belzen	Schleswig
Celle	Hannover	Braunshweig
Kiel	Nienburg	Lahde
Minden	Hamm	Osnarbruck
Gutersloh	Rheda	Werl
Bad Salzuflen	Paderborn	

*Sylwester In the British Peacekeeping Forces
Transport Group, Germany 1947*

December 1947
Sylwester Learns the Fate of His Family

Janka received a letter from a cousin in Poland, explaining the fate of Sylwester's family. Now knowing their whereabouts, Sylwester immediately wrote his brothers and sisters. Roman and Kostka replied and told him the horrible tragedies of Rudnia and Przebraże, and how his brother and his father had died. Jan and Marian had already been dead four and a half years. Sylwester wept.

July 1948
The Four Bombers

Janka and Sylwester were expecting their first baby in mid-August, 1948, and were absolutely thrilled. Janka had lived with the anguish of being told she was sterilized during her operation, and was overjoyed. Sylwester hoped for a son, but Janka just wanted a healthy baby.

Four friends were pregnant at the same time in Frille and were all due within weeks of each other: Janka Drzewiecki, her sister Stasia Regulant, Frania Wrzecionek, and Aniela Kolek. The four pregnant women were quite a spectacle when they went for walks. Heads turned as the 'four barrels waddled down the road'.

One day, the four mothers took a foot path through a farmer's field on their way to buy bread. They were in their last months of their pregnancies, and were huge. A Polish policeman saw the four women and stared. "Wyglądacie jak bombowcy .... You look like four bombers." They all laughed at the comparison for it was quite true. Every few weeks, one of the four mothers was in the hospital in Frille, near Minden, delivering:

Mother:	Delivered:	Named:
Aniela Kolek	End of June, 1948 a boy	Joseph (pseudonym)
Frania Wrzecionek	July 8th, 1948 a boy	*Zbigniew* - Bill
Stasia Regulant	July 29th, 1948 a boy	*Zbigniew* - Bill

Only one bomber was left to drop, and that was Janka.

Monday, August 16, 1948
Janka 22 years old
Krystyna Michalina Drzewiecki is Born

Krystyna - *Krysia* ... Kree-sha

Sylwester was home for the weekend when Janka went into labor but she wanted to be alone. Her contractions continued throughout Saturday and Sunday. When Janka awoke Monday morning, she was relieved to find that her husband had left for work; she did not want him to see her in this state. As she slowly sat up in bed, she felt her water break.

Janka walked alone to the hospital in Frille, as the contractions grabbed her along the way. The hospital was a large, converted house not far from where she lived. Hour after hour went by, as Janka endured the pain alone and in silence all day Monday.

Krystyna Michalina Drzewiecki was born a very healthy ten pounds, ten ounces. Janka was so happy and proud of their baby, who she named after her niece and Sylwester's mother. Babcia - Grandmother Michalina would have been proud of her healthy granddaughter.

Janka wanted to tell Sylwester he had a daughter but there was no way of letting him know. He was working out of town and would not be back until the weekend. Janka recuperated in the hospital and became stronger every day, but postpartum blues set in. She was lonely and wanted to return home. Looking out her hospital window, she watched the Kolek's son being baptized; Zygmunt was the godfather. She sat alone in her room, and cried.

Even though Sylwester wanted a son, he was ecstatic at the news of his daughter. Krystyna Michalina was beautiful, from her head to her toes. He was so proud and celebrated by raising his glass in a toast to his daughter, again and again.

As cute as Krystyna Michalina was, she was a screamer and kept the whole house up. Poor Janka did not know what to do as the baby wailed on and on. Sylwester welcomed the quiet and the uninterrupted sleeps when he went to work, but Janka had no rest, even though her mother was there to help.

Janka was given used clothing by the Red Cross which she used to sew diapers, for there were none to buy. Sylwester found and purchased a used baby buggy, which they needed. Aniela, Frania, sister Stasia, and Janka now went for walks together, each pushing a buggy. It was still quite a sight, but not near the spectacle when they were the four bombers.

Stefan and Frania Wrzecionek immigrated to Canada and settled in Thunder Bay, Ontario, with their son Bill; Frania was one of the four pregnant bombers. In 1975, Sylwester, Janka, and their youngest son, Roman, travelled across Canada in their truck and camper, and visited the Wrzecioneks. Twenty-six years had passed since they had last seen each other in Germany, in July 1949.

There have been subsequent visits between the families. Sylwester flew to Thunder Bay in 1998. The lifelong friends embraced and said it would probably be the last time they would see each other. Frania died the following year. Bill and his family continue to keep in touch.

Frania, Zbigniew...Bill, and Stefan Wrzecionek - 1950

Aniela and Józef Kolek immigrated to Australia, with their young son; Aniela was another of the four bombers. All contact with the Koleks was lost over the years.

1949

The Bread Basket of Canada

Immigrants were essential for the future growth and prosperity of many countries around the world. Countries with government-sponsored immigration programs sent representatives to the refugee camps. They showed posters and films of what their countries had to offer. It helped people make a more informed decision about which country they preferred. Before applying for immigration, applicants had to know where they wanted to go and what type of work they wanted to do.

Each country was beautiful and impressive on film, but when Sylwester saw the film on Canada entitled "The Bread Basket", he was astounded. He watched in awe as mile after mile of prairie wheat fields moved across the screen. Wave after wave of golden stalks rolled like an ocean in the wind. Sylwester saw bread...limitless bread. He loved fishing and the outdoors from his earliest days in Rudnia, and was taken with the sportsfishing and the untouched wilderness of the mountains. Maybe he would be a wheat farmer, or maybe he would settle somewhere near the ocean so that he could go fishing. Canada had a wealth of food and resources. Work in resource based industries such as mining, logging, and pulp and paper, abounded. There would be neither poverty nor starvation ever again in his life. He would provide well for his family. He decided that Canada, whether on the prairies, in the mountains, or by the ocean, was where he wanted to be.

Part 5 - Chapter 3

Applying for Immigration to Canada

1949

Sylwester, Krystyna, and Janka Drzewiecki - Germany, 1949

Introduction:
Sylwester   23 years old
Janka   22 years old

There was rigorous screening before anyone was approved for government-sponsored immigration. Once selected, the government took care of the families until they arrived at their work destination in their new country. Canada treated its immigrants well. They took care of the successful applicants every step of the way. Applicants were given room and board, and transportation to Canada in exchange for twelve months of labour.

The government-sponsored immigration was thick with bureaucratic red tape, and shamefully, money talked. Only young, healthy individuals were approved after thorough medical examinations. The com-

petition to immigrate was fierce. Thousands of young and able-bodied men and women opted for immigration. Disgracefully, hasty approvals of sick and elderly individuals who had bribed the officials, occurred.

Sylwester served his two years in the CMLO of the British Forces and was discharged from Osnabruck, Germany, in June, 1949. He handed in his British uniform and closed the door on a very positive time in his life. His days in the British Forces were memorable ones. He and Janka were now free to go before the Canadian Consul in Augustdorf and apply to immigrate to Canada. However, from Osnabruck, the British sent Sylwester and his papers to the wrong camp. He ended up in Rheine, while his family was in Frille. The British officials bought him a train ticket home, and although Sylwester returned, his official papers did not. His documents were lost.

A bulletin was posted at the administration office in the Frille camp, that dairy farmers were needed in Canada. Married couples with only one child would be considered. Successful applicants had to be young and strong. The men were to help with the milking and farm chores, while the women were to assist with the cooking, cleaning, and homemaking. Sylwester and Janka applied.

Ever since Sylwester's imprisonment in Werl, in 1946, he feared his chances to immigrate were lost, but he would not give up. He had a criminal record that he didn't deserve, but it was real and it was recorded on his misplaced papers that were now somewhere in Rheine. He realized the missing documents would create havoc at the immigration office when the time came, however, without them he believed he had a better chance of being accepted. He had talked himself out of many dilemmas before. Surely his good record in the British Peacekeeping Forces would stand him in good stead to be granted approval for immigration. Maybe, just maybe, he'd be accepted before the documents were found and his criminal record was revealed. Sylwester was determined to follow his dream to live in Canada.

Augustdorf, Germany, 1949
The Canadian Consulate

Sylwester and Janka had been accepted as possible candidates for the dairy farm operation in Canada. They were extremely happy, but there were many more loopholes through which they had to pass. Next they had to travel by train to Augustdorf and present themselves before the Canadian Consul. They bundled up Krystyna Michalina and left. The Drzewiecki family stood before the Canadian representative. They were questioned and physically inspected. Sylwester explained that his discharge papers from the British Forces were being forwarded from Rheine. The missing papers would be demanded when the time came. Right now the Consul was looking for able-bodied couples with a healthy child, and the officials checked for scars, missing fingers, disabilities of any kind.

The Canadian official sat behind his desk and told Sylwester to walk down the hall and back. Sylwester walked down the hallway in his baggy pants as the official watched. The official wanted to make sure his baggy pants weren't hiding any deformities, and he told Sylwester to lift his pant legs above the knees. Sylwester complied and walked, showing two strong legs. The Canadian official asked, "Gdzie się nauczyłeś się doić krowy? .... Where did you learn to milk cows?"

"Moi rodzice mieli krowy i jak poszli do sklepu, zostawili mnie doić krowy i wyprowadzić je na pastwisko .... My parents had cows, and when they went to market, I was left to milk them before letting them out to pasture." Sylwester told the truth, but his perception of a dairy farm, and that which the official had in mind, were at opposite ends of the spectrum. Sylwester knew how to milk one or two cows, but knew nothing about running a fifty or sixty cow operation. The official didn't elaborate on the size of the farm. Sylwester had no idea what he was signing up to do. However he believed whatever he and Janka did not know, they would learn.

They returned to Frille, not knowing if they were accepted until all the applicants had been screened. Ninety families from Frille applied to immigrate to Canada for positions in farming, mining, and logging, and only twenty-eight would be accepted. Zygmunt applied for mining; Adam for farming.

The Drzewiecki family and the Regulant family were notified that they were two of the twenty-eight selected to immigrate to Canada! How they cheered. Sylwester was realizing his childhood dream of moving West; life was better in the West. His children wouldn't live in dire poverty as he had. They would have food and a warm house, clean beds and clothes, shoes on their feet and books to read, school each day, and a doctor when they were sick. What a great country Canada was, and he, Janka, and their children would be part of it. The picture of the golden waves of wheat played over and over in his head.

Sylwester, Janka, and Krystyna Michalina were approved to immigrate together. Even though Krystyna was only a few months old when they heard the good news, Janka patiently started toilet training her. They were very limited in what they were permitted to take, and diapers were bulky. Diapers also posed a tremendous problem in washing and drying. Krystyna was 11 months old and almost completely toilet trained when they departed from Cuxhaven, Germany, in July, 1949.

Pictures were taken for their passage. Krystyna Michalina's picture was taken with her seated upon the blanket Janka had taken from her home in Omelanka when she fled with her family into the forest.

Krystyna Michalina Drzewiecki, 11 Months Old - 1948
Blanket from Omelanka

They carefully planned the essentials they would need to start their new lives in Canada. A tub for bathing and washing clothes was an obvious necessity, as was Krystyna's baby buggy. The small oval wash tub had carrying handles on either end and would act as a packing trunk for their few possessions: a pair of scissors, a tin bowl, the plate given to them on their wedding day, one pot, one frying pan, a meat grinder, a blanket, a change of clothes, and diapers. Each item was difficult to acquire, and precious.

Unfortunately, the members of the Horoszkiewicz family had three different last names; Horoszkiewicz, Regulant, and Drzewiecki. This created confusion in selecting the Horoszkiewicz family as one unit. Sadly, Adam and Filipina were rejected in this wave of immigrants. The twenty and thirty year olds had priority in the selection process. Adam and Filipina were strong and able-bodied but they were fifty and forty-four years old. They remained hopeful that they would be accepted for government sponsored immigration at a later date.

Stasia was pregnant with baby number three, and would not be permitted to immigrate at the same time as Zygmunt. She had to wait until the baby was several months old to ensure that the child was healthy. Stasia remained in Germany with her parents, four year old Krystyna, and toddler Zbigniew - Bill.

Janka's anguish at leaving her parents and her sister was great. They had lived through so much together, and now it felt as though she was abandoning them. Sylwester had had no choice but to sever from his family during the war, but Janka was deeply bonded to her family. Her loving upbringing was foreign to Sylwester's abusive childhood. She was overcome with a great feeling of emptiness which Sylwester could not fully comprehend.

Janina and her Mother Filipina, Germany, 1947

Bad Salzuflen, Germany, 1949
The Polish Consulate and the 100 Marks

The Polish Consulate had to stamp their documents proving that they were married. Without the official stamp, they would be rejected for immigration. There was a hefty fee of 100 marks that went along with the stamp. Sylwester and Janka only had eighty.

The Polish Consulate was forty kilometers away from Frille in Bad Salzuflen. If Sylwester and Janka both traveled there by train, it would cost an additional twelve marks. Janka stayed behind with Krystyna Michalina, while Sylwester traveled alone.

He arrived at the Polish Consulate office at 2 p.m. with seventy-four marks in his pocket. There was a long queue of Poles waiting for their documents to be stamped. Sylwester went to the end of the line. He was anxious. What if the Polish Consul refused to stamp his marriage certificate for lack of money? His family's future was at stake. He was desperate and was prepared to kneel down and beg if necessary. Slowly the line inched forward. The woman just ahead of Sylwester was next. She stepped up to the desk and put her 100 marks on the table. The female official and the woman rattled on in Polish. Sylwester didn't listen, his mind was on his dilemma. Would his seventy-four marks be accepted when there were so many people waiting with one hundred? He prayed for a miracle.

The woman being served was actually German, but she spoke impeccable Polish. The Polish official was so taken with the woman's gifted speech that the questions soon turned to friendly conversation. The woman's Polish husband had taught her the language. Sylwester waited as they talked on and on. Her papers were stamped and the two women continued talking as they walked to the left side of the room, far from the desk. The official had completely forgotten to collect the 100 marks from the table.

The 100 marks stared up at Sylwester and his heart raced. Was this an answer to his prayers, or a temptation from the devil? What should he do? He slowly covered the 100 marks with his right hand, hoping no one saw him. The consequence if caught, would be irreversible; he would never be permitted to enter Canada. He kept his right hand perfectly still on the table, with the 100 marks hidden beneath it.

The official returned, and Sylwester tried to be calm as he handed over his papers with his left hand. He was nervous and answered her questions simply. The woman checked over his documents. "Ja. Acha. Acha. Dobrze .... Yes. Ahha. Ahha. Good," she muttered in Polish. She looked up at Sylwester. "Sto marek .... One hundred marks."

Without saying a word, Sylwester slid his right hand, and the 100 marks, over to the woman. The official took the money and quickly stamped his papers. Kachung. Kachung. Kachung. It was music to his ears. "Dziękuję .... Thank you." He quickly left with his papers and seventy-four marks still in his pocket.

Sylwester thanked God, and the German lady for the miracle. He asked God to bless the beautiful woman for the rest of her life. He and his family were going to Canada!

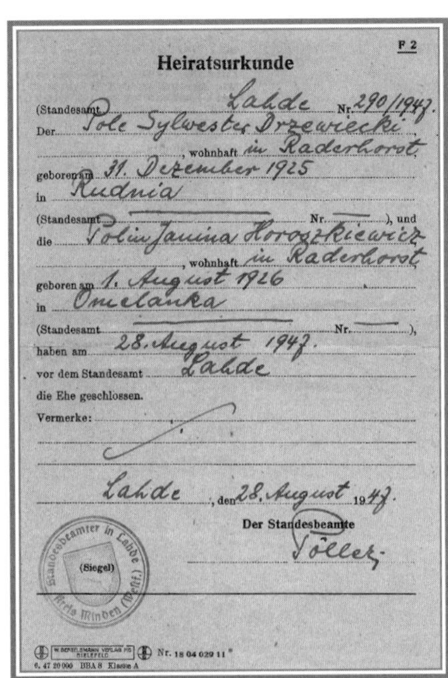

Sylwester and Janina's Marriage Registration, Dated August 28, 1947

International Refugee Organisation British Zone of Germany

Sylwester's Certificate of Identity for the Purpose of Immigration to Canada

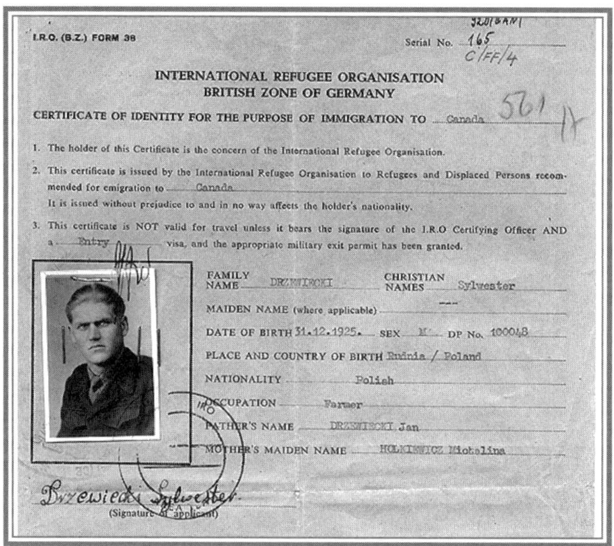

Front - Sylwester Drzewiecki's Displaced Person's Number: 100048

Back - Stamped , Authorized and Recommended for Canada International Refugee Organisation

Janina's Certificate of Identity for the Purpose of Immigration to Canada

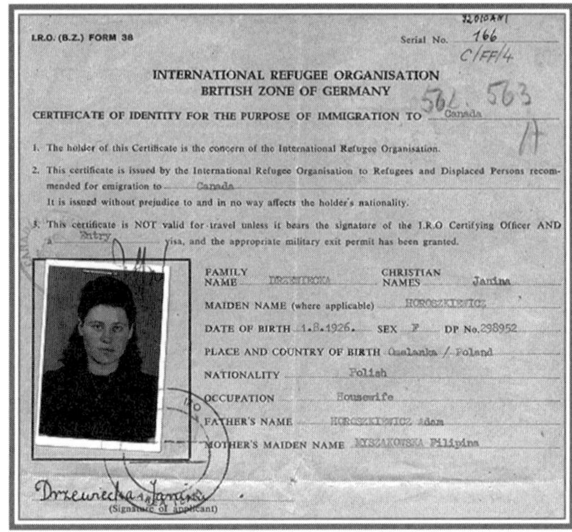

Front - Janina Horoszkiewicz-Drzewiecki's Displaced Person's Number: 298952

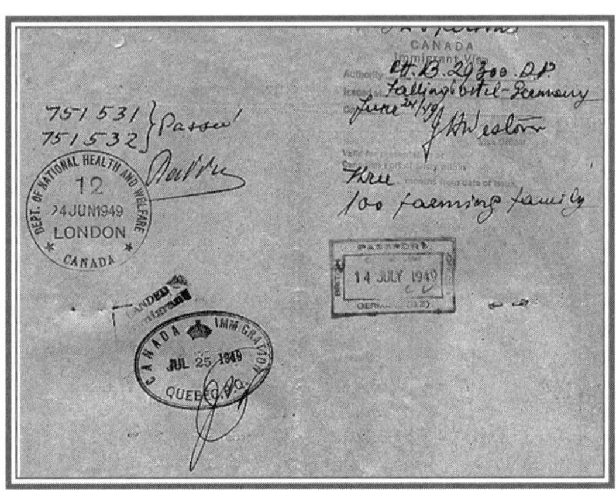

Back

Number 2 Front Reads: "This certificate is issued by the International Refugee Organisation to Refugees and Displaced Persons recommended for emigration to Canada."

Fallingbostel, Germany - The Transit Camp
No Papers...No Medical Exam...No Immigration

The families who were accepted for immigration gathered their belongings, and the British transport took them to a transit camp in Fallingbostel. Sylwester and Janka loaded their wash tub and baby buggy with their few possessions that would start them in the New World. Krystyna Michalina was active and a handful to watch.

In Fallingbostel, Sylwester and Janka had to undergo a rigorous medical examination, and have every official paper scrutinized and stamped. Only when all was approved would they be permitted to board a ship to Canada. They were so close, but Sylwester's missing record that was somewhere in Rheine, brought them to a complete halt. No medical exam would be given until his papers were recovered.

Their ship left. Sylwester repeatedly had to go to the screening room, and was interrogated over and over again. Where had he been? What had he been doing during the war? Why did he have no papers? A second ship left! His story did not change; he omitted his unfair criminal charge and record. A month passed and they were still in Fallingbostel. Sylwester held onto his dream. Finally, the interrogations were complete. Finally, the Canadian officials believed him and issued him new papers.

Sylwester's Medical Examination

Sylwester and Janka were examined by specialists in different medical fields. They had chest X-rays, eye, ear, dental, and heart examinations. Each doctor had to stamp their papers. Sylwester went into the examining room for his complete physical exam and was shocked to find two very young female doctors waiting for him. They were not much older than himself. Female doctors were rare in the 1940's, and Sylwester immediately blushed. They were Latvian and told Sylwester in Russian to take off his clothes. They left the examining room expecting him to be completely naked when they returned. Sylwester was embarrassed. The thought of him standing naked in front of two young women as they prodded and poked

was horrible. Why could he not have been given a male doctor? He hesitantly took off his clothes, but wouldn't part with his shorts. He sat on the table in his underwear and dreaded their return.

The two women walked in. The doctor who had told Sylwester to disrobe was livid when she saw him wearing his underwear. The medical examinations were run like assembly lines and there was no time for such foolishness. Sylwester quickly jumped off the table, pulled off his shorts, and stood stark naked in front of the two doctors. He was so embarrassed. Gentle mannerisms were dismissed as the women examined him left and right, up and down. They had to be thorough, and fast.

One of the doctors lifted his left testicle. She ignored his discomfort. Her commands in Russian were abrupt. "Поверни голову на лево. Покашляй ..... Turn your head left. Cough." Then the right testicle. "Поверни голову на право. Покашляй .... Turn your head right. Cough." Sylwester was at their mercy. If he did not pass the medical examination, he would be denied immigration. "Наклонись .... Bend over." Sylwester was humiliated. It was bad enough having a male doctor, don a rubber glove and do a digital rectal exam, but a woman! He couldn't wait to get out of there. The two doctor's found Sylwester's modesty amusing. Sylwester's embarrassment was multiplied by their snickering.

He retreated as quickly as possible after the examination. He hated ridicule, and the two doctors were masters of it. He was glad he would never have to see them again. He hastily went back to camp, unaware that the two doctors had forgotten to stamp his papers.

Back to the Doctors

Sylwester and Janka were notified that they would be moved from Fallingbostel to Camp Turpits in Bremerhaven, where they would await departure to Canada. Before being transferred to Bremerhaven, their papers were checked again. The official quickly scanned their documents and abruptly stopped. There was no doctor's stamp on Sylwester's medical examination. Sylwester explained that he had had his exam and did not know why his paper was not stamped, but they would not let him pass through.

Sylwester had to hurry. The bus to Bremerhaven was leaving the next morning. He left Janka and Krystyna Michalina waiting in the office, as he raced back to the doctor's office. He cringed at the thought of facing the two women again. The doctors examined streams of people day after day and he feared they might not remember him. The thought of possibly having another physical examination made him wince. Sylwester quickly explained to the doctors in Russian that they had examined him the other day but had neglected to stamp his paper. The physicians looked at each other and laughed. Yes, they remembered him. They quickly stamped and signed his form, and had another good laugh as Sylwester went out the door. He hated them.

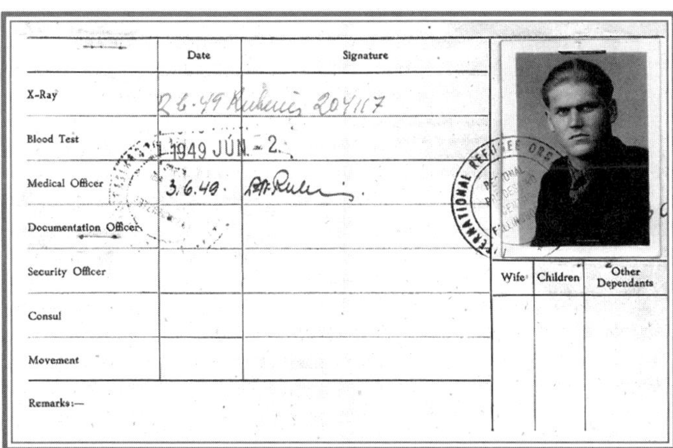

Sylwester's Stamped Medical Card

Separated

At 8 a.m. the following morning, Sylwester, Janka, and Krystyna Michalina boarded the train for Bremerhaven. Buses awaited the passengers at the other end to take them to camp Turpits. "Najpierw matki z dziećmi. Najpierw matki z dziećmi .... Mothers and children first. Mothers and children first." Janka and Krystyna Michalina were quickly shuffled

onto a bus and Sylwester was left behind.

There were only a few buses and many people. Sylwester had to wait his turn as several buses left and returned. All he could think about was finding Janka. He knew she would be worried, plus she had Krystyna to watch. Janka's anxiety at being separated from Sylwester was multiplied when the officials would not permit her into the camp without her husband. They were immigrating as a married couple, and had to present themselves together. Janka looked for Sylwester as each bus arrived. Krystyna was active and hungry. Thankfully she was nursing. Janka was tired and wanted to go to their assigned room, but she had to wait. Hours passed with no sign of Sylwester.

Sylwester immediately began searching for his family when he disembarked from the bus. There were people everywhere. He headed straight toward the immigration office and found a very weary Janka. As soon as she saw Sylwester, she cried. The authorities apologized for their terrible error in separating them, inspected their papers, and let them through.

They were treated well in Camp Turpits with beautiful meals, and movies to watch, as they waited for their ship, the SS Scythia, to dock in Cuxhaven. They had made it, and would soon be on their way to Canada.

Part 5 - Chapter 4

The Voyage to Canada

July, 1949

The SS Scythia 1949
The Ship on which Sylwester, Janina and Little Krystyna Travelled

Sylwester   23 years old
Janina   22 years old
Krystyna   11 months old

When they arrived in Cuxhaven, the ship that would take them across the Atlantic was in port. They felt a mixture of emotions as they boarded the SS Scythia: excitement, fear, happiness, and sadness. Having lived inland their entire lives, the ocean was beyond their imaginations in its enormity.

The ship made a six hour stop in Le Haver, France, to pick up more immigrants before heading out to sea. The excitement and apprehension of the passengers adventuring to a new world was overwhelming. As the ship coursed west, Europe and their old life slowly disappeared over the horizon. In eleven days they would be in Canada.

Sylwester and Janka spoke neither English nor French, and were penniless. They only had each other, and Janka already missed her family. On board the ship, men were in separate sleeping quarters from the women and children. Janka and Krystyna Michalina were given a little room of their own for the voyage. Men had to bunk together, and Sylwester swung his way across the Atlantic in a hammock.

The families visited and dined together during the day. With so many people to feed on the government-sponsored transit, the portions had to be rationed. Sylwester was overwhelmed with the new taste experiences he had on board. He had never eaten oranges in his life and looked forward to the juicy fruit each morning. Unfortunately, he could only have one per day, for he could have eaten a dozen. At every meal music played, including a very beautiful Latin song called La Gondarina. *(Sylwester and Janka remembered that melody for the rest of their lives. It was their song, and it forever reminded them of their voyage to Canada).*

The July weather was fabulously warm, and the ocean was a calm blue as far as the eye could see, but Janka was seasick. She suspected she might be pregnant before she left Germany, and she was. Janka was horribly nauseated. She took Krystyna on deck for some fresh air and sunshine as her stomach churned. Other first-time sea passengers were also sick. Janka laid on the benches with the other green travelers, while Sylwester watched Krystyna.

The hot summer weather continued into the next day, but on the third day it abruptly changed. Black clouds rolled across the sky, and gale force winds whipped the water to a frenzy. The ship's sirens blared. Passengers scrambled to lock themselves in their rooms. The crew frantically worked to secure every porthole and door. The fury of the storm pounded the ship. Petrified, Janka held on to Krystyna and her bed as the old vessel tossed about like a toothpick; she had never been so ill in her life. It felt as though the ship would break in two. The bow slowly rose up, then plunged down. The experience was a terrifying nightmare that lasted two entire days and nights.

Sylwester clung to whatever he could in his room, wishing he could help Janka. He thought the ship was going to hit the bottom of the ocean each time it dove. It was the eeriest feeling.

In spite of all the retching and vomiting going on around him, Sylwester didn't feel ill; in fact, he was hungry! He made his way to the galley as the ship rocked back and forth. Although few passengers made their way to the dining hall, the crew continued preparing meals. At breakfast, Sylwester loaded his pockets with oranges. As much as Janka hated the storm, Sylwester loved it. He got extra helpings of food, and as many oranges as he wanted.

July 25, 1949
Quebec City, Canada
The Ship Docks

On the tenth evening of sail, the SS Scythia entered the St. Lawrence Seaway, and Sylwester and Janka saw their chosen country for the first time. They watched the night lights twinkle on Canada's shore. The ship continued its long journey down the St. Lawrence through the night.

When Sylwester and Janka awoke on July 25th, 1949, the SS Scythia was docked at pier twenty-one in Quebec City. The ship was sitting high on the St. Lawrence River and the view was spectacular. Processing the hundreds of people who arrived all at once was overwhelming. People who had been pre-placed to work in mines, railroads, and factories were off the ship first thing in the morning. After going through Canadian customs and immigration they were immediately transported to their destinations on buses that were standing by. Those who awaited work placements, like Sylwester and Janka, were the last to disembark.

Masses of new immigrants left the ship and queued for document inspection. As the passengers slowly unloaded, so too the crew unloaded the mounds of baggage from the hold. There were hundreds of boxes, bags, and paraphernalia of all kinds to carry into the port warehouse, and the crew were rather reckless. To speed things up, anything with wheels was pushed down the loading ramp and allowed to roll to a stop.

Krystyna's baby buggy was brought out of the hold early that morning. Sylwester and Janka watched in dismay from above, as the buggy was given a hard shove. It jostled down the ramp, rolled across the tarmack, and crashed into the wall of the warehouse. Luckily, it survived the crash.

Hour after hour went by as they waited on board. They went to their rooms to rest. Janka couldn't wait to disembark. She had never been so miserably nauseated in her life, and never wanted to travel across another ocean again...ever. Finally at 3 p.m. they were called.

The ship sat high in the water that morning, but now it was well below the dock. Their first thought was that the ship was sinking but there was no panic. The crew casually directed the passengers off the ship. Sylwester, Janka, and Krystyna hurried for shore. They were baffled as they looked at the water level of the St. Lawrence. How could so much water have disappeared so quickly and where did it go? The concept of tides, shifting entire oceans of water around the world with the gravitational pull of the moon, was mind boggling. They had much to learn.

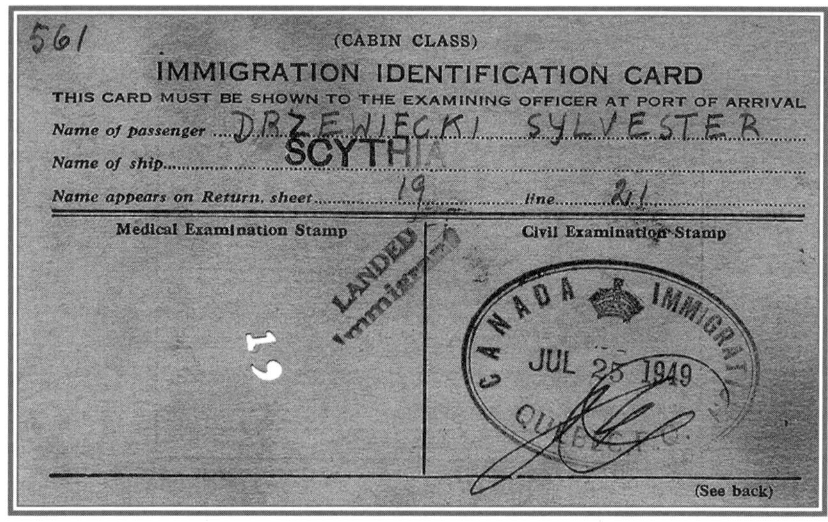

Sylwester's Landed Immigrant Card
July 25, 1949

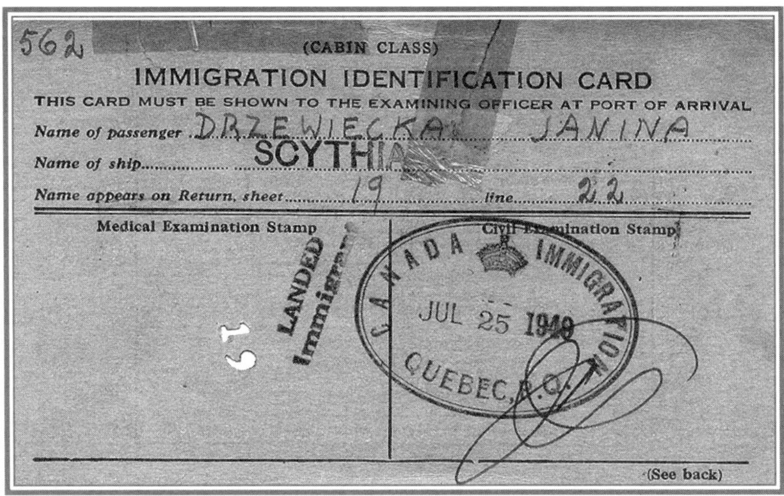

Janina's Landed Immigrant Card
July 25, 1949

They set foot in Canada with a dream of a better life. They had no money, no official language, a baby, and another baby on the way. Their life in Canada was about to begin.

Part 6

Canada

Place your dreams above the crowds,
And live up to the expectations of yourself,
For dreams become reality.....
By choice.

- Mary Drzewiecki, 2000

Part 6 - Introduction

Canada 1949

Sylwester 23 years old
Janka 23 years old
Krystyna 11 months old

The last immigrants to disembark the ship, travelled by train to St. Paul, near Montreal, Quebec, to a camp for new immigrants. Each family was given one loaf of bread and one litre of milk for the long journey. They arrived at 10 p.m., tired and hungry. It was a short walk from the train station to the motel, but automobiles were waiting for families with small children. Sylwester, Janka and Krystyna were driven to the camp. Their names were called and a room was assigned. When they were settled, dinner was served.

The camp was a motel, and home to hundreds of immigrants who awaited work placements. Sylwester and Janka had applied to work on a dairy farm, and were waiting for a farmer to take them. They did not know in which Canadian province nor in which city they would live. Canada spanned thousands of miles from coast to coast. They could end up anywhere.

One week rolled into the next and they were still waiting to be placed. They were anxious to work and start establishing themselves as independent Canadians. The government-sponsored immigration program was massive, and extremely well orchestrated. The future Canadians were carefully guided and cared for every step of the way from Germany to their designated Canadian work sites. In the St. Paul camp, there was an abundance of food: meat, vegetables, fruit, milk, cheese, bread, and desserts. It was not rationed as it had been on the ship. Sylwester enjoyed every bite.

It was a luxury having a private bath in their motel room. Janka washed the family's clothes in the bathtub. There was no clothes line so she draped the laundry on chairs, or laid them on the grass to dry. One hot day in August, Janka carefully laid out a blouse, some diapers, and a pair

of Krystyna's socks on the lawn; she had knitted the socks in Germany. Everything would dry quickly in the summer sun. Janka returned and found the diapers and her blouse full of holes, and all that remained of Krystyna's socks were tiny strands of wool. Grasshoppers had completely devoured Krystyna's socks and chewed through the diapers and blouse. She didn't lay any more laundry out on the lawn.

The director of the St. Paul camp spoke fluent Russian, and he and Sylwester became friends over the next two months. It was wonderful being able to converse with the person in charge. Language was a terrible barrier during the war, and now again in Canada. The English and French languages were very different from the Slavic tongues. Sylwester and Janka slowly learned a few words, but miscommunications were plentiful, and sometimes they were both embarrassing and amusing.

Part 6 - Chapter 1

St. Paul, Quebec, Canada
July to September 1949

August 1949
The Postage Stamp

Janka was thousands of miles away from her parents and missed them dearly. Out of concern, she wrote to tell them that they had arrived safely. However, she couldn't mail the letter because she didn't have four cents for postage. Hopelessly pointing to the envelope, she showed the camp watchman what she needed. He shook his head, indicating no. Dejected, she walked away.

A Polish woman saw Janka's despair and asked, "Czy mogę w czymś pomóc? .... May I help you?"

"Napisałam do rodziców list do Niemiec, a nie mam znaczka .... I wrote a letter to my parents in Germany, but I don't have a stamp," she sadly replied.

"Zaraz dam pani znaczek .... I'll give one to you."

Janka was relieved, but did not mail the letter immediately. She was concerned over her penniless situation, and had an idea. She would write her father's sister in New York, and ask if she would please send her one dollar for stamps for the future. She had never met her Ciocia - Aunt Anastazia Gutkowska for she had immigrated to the United States long before the Second World War.

When Janka opened Ciocia's reply, she found a cheque made out to her for ten dollars! Ten dollars was more than a day's wage for most working people in 1949. Immediately, Janka wrote and thanked Ciocia for her generosity.

Janka was plagued with morning sickness and was too nauseated to go to the bank to cash the cheque. Sylwester took the cheque, signed it at

the bank window, and handed it to the teller. The cheque was made out to Janina Drzewiecki. In his limited English he tried to explain that his wife was ill, but he was sent away. With identification papers, marriage certificate, and his very ill wife in hand, Sylwester returned.

Their first priority was to buy Krystyna a pair of baby boots and wool, and to send the letters to her parents and to her aunt. She remembered her Ciocia's generosity for the rest of her life, but sadly contact was lost over the years.

Early September 1949
The French-Canadian Dairy Farmer

Many immigrants with whom they had arrived, received work placements, and new immigrants arrived. Finally after several weeks, a dairy farmer from the Montreal area came to the camp looking for an experienced hand. The officials checked their files and called the Drzewieckis.

The farmer could see they were strong and capable of the hard work that lay ahead. He nodded and spoke his approval in French. They left the camp with the farmer and headed to their new home near Montreal, a two hour drive away. The farm was lush and meticulously kept; like a calendar picture. The farmer ran a huge milking operation. Anxiety set in when Sylwester learned what was expected of him. The wife's brother had passed away and an experienced dairy farmer was urgently needed to run his farm. The brother's farm was nearby and on a similar scale. Sylwester had only milked their cow in Rudnia, and couldn't even pretend to know where to start.

They went into the kitchen with baby Krystyna toddling beside them. The farmer's wife looked disapprovingly at the child. She did not want hired hands with children. Krystyna innocently looked around and, much to the disgust of the woman, peed in the middle of the kitchen floor. At the same time, Janina was overcome with nausea after the long drive, and was vomiting in the bathroom. Their first impression was not good. The wife turned on her husband. She angrily scolded him with sharp words

and hand gestures. Sylwester and Janka did not have to understand French to know they were not welcome. They felt terrible.

They were given supper that night and went to bed, but Sylwester and Janka felt extremely uncomfortable in their home. The next morning, no one woke Sylwester to go to work, but he heard the farmer get up and go outside. Sylwester told Janka, "Ja wstaję i pomogę doić krowy .... I'm getting up to help milk the cows." He approached the barn and heard the farmer and his wife yelling at each other. It was obvious that the woman was not happy with her husband's choice of workers. Walking into the barn interrupted the fight. All the cows were milked by hand, and the farmer was sitting on a stool milking into a bucket. He stood up and motioned to Sylwester to sit down.

Anyone watching Sylwester as he worked, made him extremely nervous. The couple stared at him as he fiddled with the milking equipment. He sat on the stool, positioned the bucket, and grabbed the cow's teets. Sylwester was so fidgety he couldn't do anything right. He yanked and fumbled with the teets unsuccessfully. When the milk finally did squirt, it missed the bucket completely. So much for convincing anyone he was a dairy farmer. The woman furiously turned on her husband, and stormed into the house.

The farmer was bilingual, and Sylwester laboriously tried to communicate with him in broken English. He suggested that the farmer return his family to the camp, and choose a childless couple. The farmer, wife, and daughter, took the Drzewieckis back to the camp in St. Paul. This time the wife was going to make sure they obtained the right people to work for them. Sylwester and Janka were relieved to be heading back to camp, and Sylwester was adamant that if he was told to return to the dairy farm, he would refuse.

The car was parked in the lot at the back of the motel, and the French-Canadian family walked around to the employment office at the front, but the office was closed on Sunday. Sylwester knew of a backdoor entrance. When he opened the door, he met the Russian director who was surprised to see Sylwester and asked, "Славко, что ты делаешь здесь. Ты ходил на ферму вчера .... Slavka, what are you doing here? You went to a farm yesterday."

"Хозяеба не хотят нас. Жена хочет пару без детей .... The farmer doesn't want us. The wife wants a couple without children," said Sylwester. "Он пошёл искать работу .... He went around the front to the employment office." Without saying another word, the director returned to his office.

The director listened to the farmers and said, "What do you think we are dealing with here? Cattle? Horses? Dogs? These are human beings. You can't choose because of color, nationality, nor because of a child. As long as I am director, you will never get any help from here."

Sylwester and Janka continued to wait in St. Paul.

One Week Later
The Turkey Farm

Sylwester was called again into the office for a job offer. Another Polish immigrant, Antek Pacholczyk, was also present. They were asked through a Polish interpreter, "Czy chciałbyś pojechać do British Columbia? Piękne lato. Tam są owocowe drzewa .... How would you like to go to British Columbia? Beautiful summers. Fruit trees." Sylwester asked, "Jaka praca? .... What kind of job?"

"Karmić indyki .... Feeding turkeys." Sylwester didn't care what the job was as long as it wasn't milking cows or working on a railroad. He swore he would never do either one of those jobs ever again as long as he lived. "To lepiej jak doić krowy. Tak, my pojedziemy .... That's better than milking cows. Yes, we'll go." The Drzewieckis were going to British Columbia. Sylwester and Janka were destined for Cedar, just South of Nanaimo on Vancouver Island; the Pacholczyks for Vancouver.

DEPARTMENT OF LABOUR
NATIONAL EMPLOYMENT SERVICE

CANADA

PLEASE DIRECT BEARER
WHOSE SIGNATURE APPEARS BELOW

TO

NATIONAL EMPLOYMENT OFFICE

AT __Post Office Bldg.,__

__NANAIMO, B.C.__

OR, IF MORE CONVENIENT
TO NEAREST NATIONAL EMPLOYMENT OFFICE

Brzewiecki Sylwester.

SIGNATURE OF BEARER

__Sylvester& Janina DRZEWIECKI__
NAME IN FULL
& child

INDEX № ON ARRIVAL	DATE OF ARRIVAL
92-561& 562	July 25, 1949

EMPLOYERS	
NAME	ADDRESS
Mr. E.H. Martin,	R.R.#2 Nanaimo, B.C

Sylwester and Janina's
Canada Department of Labour Employment Card

(Employer: Mr. E.H. Martin, RR 2, Nanaimo, BC)

Part 6 - Chapter 1 - Epilogue

St. Paul, Quebec, Canada
July to September, 1949

Zygmunt Regulant arrived in Canada one month later, on August 20th, 1949. Unfortunately, he did not have the opportunity to see Sylwester and Janka, for he was taken directly to work in a gold mine in Val-d'Or, Quebec. It was eight months before Stasia was reunited with Zygmunt. She lived in a barrack in Augustdorf, Germany, with her two children and her parents. The barrack was big with many rooms, and home to many families waiting to immigrate. Aniela and Józef Kolek were there, awaiting immigration to Australia. It was there that the Horoszkiewicz family met their life-long friends, Stanisława and Wawrzyniec Witczak. The Witczaks had also worked as forced laborers on German farms during the war.

Stasia gave birth to Zygmunt Regulant II in Augustdorf, Germany, on January 20th, 1950. The infant became very ill, and in the middle of the night, Stasia, the Witczaks, and the Koleks, trudged through knee-deep snow to get him baptized in the church. Aniela and Wawrzyniec were asked to be his godparents. Thankfully the baby recovered.

Stasia immigrated to Canada with her three young children on April 20, 1950 on the ship the SS Samarian. One can only imagine how difficult it must have been for her to travel alone across the Atlantic Ocean with three small children. The Regulants lived in Val-d'Or, Quebec, for one year before moving to British Columbia.

Names:	City of Birth and Date:	Travel Age:
Krystyna - Christine	Stolcenal, June 8, 1944	6 years old
Zbigniew - Bill	Minden, July 29, 1948	21 months old
Zygmunt - Zyg	Augustdorf, January 20, 1950	3 months old

The Regulant Children Canada, 1950
From Left: Zbyszek, Zygmunt II, Krystyna

Adam and Filipina desperately wanted to be with their children and grandchildren, but were left behind in Germany for an additional five and a half years after Stasia left, before they were authorized to immigrate. It was a very difficult time for them. The Witczaks and the Horoszkiewiczs had bonded like family in Germany. Adam and Filipina cared for the Witczak's four children whenever needed. They supported each other emotionally.

The Witczaks were in Canada by April, 1951. Wawrzyniec Witczak immigrated in October, 1950. His wife, Stanisława Witczak, immigrated with their four children ranging in ages from 19 months to 9 years, in April, 1951. The Witczaks settled in Ladysmith. They were godparents to two of the Drzewiecki children, Mary and Richard, and remained friends for life.

The Witczak Family - Germany 1949
From Left: Mary, Wawrzyniec, Bill, Krys, Stanisława, Jasia
Their fifth child, Ed, was born in Canada in 1957.

Part 6 - Chapter 2

Travelling Across Canada
September 1949

The Drzewieckis and Pacholczyks travelled by train across Canada. Their itinerary was explained in English, without a Polish interpreter. Sylwester's English was better than Janka's, Antek's, or Stella's, but it was still barely enough to get by. The official told them they would disembark and change trains in Winnipeg, before carrying on to Vancouver. Sylwester said he understood everything, when he really understood nothing.

On a gorgeous sunny day in late September, 1949, Sylwester, Janka, Antek, Stella, and thirteen-month-old Krystyna, boarded the Canadian Pacific Rail train in Montreal. They each wore an identification badge, and the railway employees were instructed that anyone wearing the special ID was to be fed and well looked after. They were to be called for meals, and have their transfers announced.

The train made many stops for passengers to get on and off. A group of extremely jovial French-Canadian lumberjacks boarded. They were 'out of the bush and into the sauce'. They whooped and hollered in high spirits. They were wearing red checkered jackets, and Sylwester decided that he would one day have such a beautiful coat, which he did. The lumberjacks were showing off rolled wads of cash. They were definitely happy and having a very good time.

It was getting late, and they settled into their seats for the night. The lumberjacks kindly purchased pillows for them. During the night the joyous loggers began tossing bills into the air. Antek awoke to a ten dollar bill by his feet; the loggers had already disembarked somewhere in Quebec. He pocketed the money as the train rambled on. The Drzewieckis and Pacholczyks slept through Ontario, and awoke to the Manitoban wheat fields. Waves of golden grain touched the horizon and followed the train mile after mile, just as they had seen in the film, "The Bread Basket".

The sun travelled with them all the way across Canada. The train stopped in Winnipeg, where they were to disembark and board another train, but Sylwester completely misunderstood this instruction. Instead, they went sightseeing, believing they would be called when it was time to leave. While they were looking around Winnipeg, their train and all of their possessions left for Vancouver.

They enjoyed walking through the stores and looking through the windows; there were no shortages here. Anything they could possibly dream of was in Canada. Sylwester and Janka bought a small bottle of milk for Krystyna, which she quickly drank in the store. They wanted to buy her another, but didn't have enough money for the bottle deposit. The shop keeper told them that if they brought back the empty, he would not charge the bottle deposit. They continued strolling by the shops, when they realized something was not right. It was getting cold and dark and no one was coming for them. They hurried back to the station and found the train long gone. The bare tracks travelled straight as an arrow, as far as the eye could see. They were alone and stranded in Winnipeg, Manitoba, and night was falling.

They went inside the station looking for help, regretting that they couldn't return the empty bottle as promised. One English word that Sylwester knew and thought he could read, was unemployment. He had heard the word in St. Paul many times, and had seen the unemployment sign hanging in the camp office. He walked around the train station, trying to recognize any words, but the English signs were complete gibberish until he spotted an unemployment sign. He looked at the letters carefully. Yes, the letters looked right. The people in unemployment would help them.

It was after work hours, so they all sat in front of the door, beneath the unemployment sign, waiting for the office to reopen. Unknown to them, the English sign didn't read 'Unemployment', it read 'Employees Only'. It was close, but not quite right. They patiently waited, thinking they were in the right place.

Once night fell, the men and women were separated on opposite sides of the waiting room. The security guard came up to the five people sitting under the 'Employees Only' sign, and motioned for them to move. Sylvester tried to speak in English, but gave up. It was too difficult. He tried German, then Russian, Polish and Ukrainian. Someone had to understand that they were stranded and had missed their train. They had to get to British Columbia. One man was able to understand a few words in Ukrainian, but his comprehension was minimal. His mother spoke Ukrainian fluently, and he brought her to the station.

When it was finally understood that they had missed their connecting train to Vancouver, there was immediate action. The Canadian National Railway had a train arriving in Winnipeg in twenty minutes that would take them to Edmonton. In Edmonton, they would have to transfer to another train that would take them to Vancouver. The woman explained in Ukrainian, "З Вінніпеґу поїдете в Едмонтон .... From Winnipeg you will go to Edmonton." Sylwester listened and repeated, "Edmond."

"Hi, ні, Ед-мон-тон .... No, no, Ed-mon-ton," she slowly said. It still sounded like she was saying Edmond so he again repeated, "Edmond."

Finally Edmonton was understood. They were to get off the train in Edmonton, and wait two hours for the second train. The station employee pointed to Sylwester's watch to make sure he understood at what time they must catch the train to Vancouver. They weren't going to take any chances that the Drzewieckis and Pacholczyks would get stranded in 'Edmond'.

Edmonton

They arrived in Edmonton in sunshine, and remained there for two hours waiting for the train to Vancouver. They climbed aboard and Sylwester chose a window seat as they travelled west, through the Rocky Mountains. They were surrounded by the grandest mountains and deepest valleys they had ever seen. The train curved around one mountain after the next. Sylwester was gazing out the window when the ground beneath them disappeared! They were in mid-air over a monstrous chasm. He thought

they were going to plunge! Grabbing Janka and Krystyna, he jumped over to the other side of the train, but there was nothing over there either! Other passengers did the same. Then, it was completely dark! Unknown to them, the railroad line was to be riddled with giant wooden trestles and long, dark tunnels. It was an eerie sensation looking out both sides of the train and seeing nothing holding them up.

It was night when the train stopped in Lytton, B.C. Sylwester looked out his window, but only black space stared back at him. He had never seen such darkness. He looked up and saw towering mountain peaks and thousands of beautiful stars. Where on earth were they? They had traveled many hours since leaving Edmonton, and were still in the mountains.

The train departed just as dawn was breaking. The fertile Fraser Valley was the most beautiful place Sylwester had ever seen. Lush, green farmland stretched from foothill to foothill. Cattle grazed. A river flowed. Sylwester stared as the train passed one beautiful farm after another. The farmland was flat like Rudnia. He wanted to jump off into this paradise. He did not want to go on any farther, but he was committed to work elsewhere. Sylwester sadly watched the beautiful Fraser Valley being left far behind.

Vancouver

The sun was still shining when they disembarked at the train station in Vancouver. The long journey had come to an end for Antek and Stella Pacholczyk. Their farmer was at the train station waiting for them. However, the Drzewieckis were to continue traveling to Nanaimo, on Vancouver Island. The Pacholczyks and Drzewieckis said goodbye. Two years passed before they saw each other again.

A man, either from immigration or unemployment, they didn't know which, was waiting for the Drzewieckis in Vancouver. He hired a taxi and they travelled to the Canadian Pacific Railway Ferry terminal. He told them the trip across the Georgia Strait would take two hours and gave them two dollars with which they were to buy themselves lunch on the ship. He said goodbye and wished them well. They were alone.

As the ferry pulled away from the dock, Sylwester turned to Janka and said, "Ile mórz musimy przekroczyć? .... How many oceans do we have to cross?" They had already crossed the Atlantic Ocean, traveled across Canada by rail, and now were faced with another two hour sea voyage. They did not buy lunch, but kept the two dollars with which to start their new life in Nanaimo. It was all the money they had.

They had never heard of Vancouver Island, Nanaimo, or Cedar, yet it would be their home for well over the next fifty years.

From Left: Stella and Antek Pacholczyk,
Janka and Sylwester Drzewiecki - 1960

The Pacholczyks settled in Vancouver and remained friends. They were godparents to two of the Drzewiecki children, Mary and Richard.

Part 6 - Chapter 3

Martin's Turkey Farm, Cedar, B.C.
September 1949 - July 1950

Aerial Photo of Martin's Turkey Farm
The centre back cabin is where Sylwester, Janina, and Krystyna lived.
Note all the turkeys in the foreground.

Introduction:

In late September, 1949, Sylwester and Janina entered the Nanaimo harbor. The first landmark they saw was a church spire, welcoming them to their new home. The CPR Ferry docked, and the new immigrants entered the terminal. They were alone in a foreign country, with a new language, a baby, and two dollars in their pocket. They slowly walked around, hoping someone would be there to greet them. Mr. and Mrs. Martin, the farmers for whom they would be working, had been waiting at the termi-

nal and easily spotted the young Polish family. Mrs. Martin said, "Hi Sylwester. Hi Janina."

To have total strangers speak their names in such a friendly way was a welcomed surprise. It was customary in Poland to address people by their last names until very well acquainted, or to simply call them Pan or Pani. "How do you know our names?" asked Sylwester in surprise, in broken English.

"You will be working for us," said Mr. Martin with a big smile. How happy they were to be met by the farmers themselves, and how surprised they were that the farmers traveled by car. They were expecting to be transported to the farm by horse and wagon!

Edwin and Mary Martin's turkey farm was about seven miles south of Nanaimo, in the small rural community of Cedar. Mr. Martin turned his car off the highway onto Cedar Road. It was a gravel road, with thick, virgin forest on both sides. The damp coastal climate produced extensive evergreen and deciduous growth. The trees towered overhead, and the forest floor was thick with bushes and ferns. Cedar was very unpopulated and neighbors were few and far between. Sylwester and Janka could not believe that out in the middle of nowhere there would be such a fine gravel road, hydro electric power, and telephone service. Sylwester looked at the telephone and hydro poles alongside the road. This was unheard of in Eastern Poland. "Jaki dobry kraj. Wszędzie jest swiatło elektryczne i telefon .... What a good country," he thought to himself, "Everywhere there is electricity and telephones."

They arrived at the Martin's farm on Holden Corso Road and were greeted by the Martin's five children ranging in ages from five to eighteen years. The eldest was Everett, then Albert, Vivian, Twyla and Gilbert. Mrs. Martin was expecting her sixth child at the beginning of April. Charlene was born one week before Easter and Janka was due the following week. The Martin children were excited and curious to see the new family. The children welcomed Sylwester and Janka and immediately began entertaining Krystyna. She loved all the attention. The Martins gave them a tour of the farm. Janka was shown the house where she would help Mrs. Martin with the cooking, cleaning, and laundry. Sylwester was introduced to the

3,000 turkeys he would tend, and immediately discovered that they were horribly ornery birds. They bit him countless times over the months he worked there. He kept his eyes wide open whenever he was in their pen, but they still poked and bit. Tending turkeys was another job he never wanted to do again.

In addition to their transportation to Canada, Sylwester and Janka were given room and board and a combined income of forty-five dollars a month, in exchange for twelve months of work. The Martins provided them with a small three room cabin, that was nicely remodeled and very clean. It had linoleum on the floors, and the walls were painted white. There was a little kitchen with cupboards and a wood stove. The cabin was sparsely furnished, but it was all they needed. They carried in their wash tub and the baby carriage packed with their few possessions. They were home.

Sylwester and Janka were able to save most of their wage because food and shelter were provided. They ate lunch each day in the big house with the Martin family, but had dinner in their own home. Sometimes they had picnics under the big maple tree in the field behind the barn. *(The huge tree still stands today.)* Mr. Martin gave Sylwester permission to hunt the wild rabbits which were prolific on the farm.

Work was plentiful. Sylwester cleared boulders from the field and dumped them near the creek where they would be used for a road. Lifting the heavy rocks for days on end was back breaking work. He helped in the fields and mended the fences. The work days were long and hard, but he was happy to be in Canada. Sometimes Sylwester came home absolutely exhausted, flopped on the bed and fell sound asleep. The next day he'd awaken and start all over again.

Whenever Janka and Sylwester rested, Krystyna would take turns laying with each of them. After a few minutes of laying beside her father, she'd say, "Ku Mama....Koo Mama," then run to her Mother and say, "Ku Tata....Koo Daddy." She'd run back and forth between her parents, saying, "Ku Mama. Ku Tata." Only Krystyna knew what the word "ku" meant.

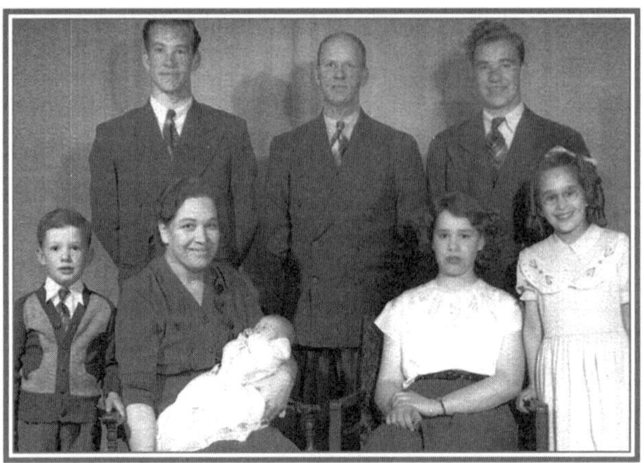

The Martin Family - 1950

Back Row From Left: Everett, Mr. Edwin Martin, Albert
Front Row From Left: Gilbert, Mrs. Mary Martin,
baby Charlene, Vivian, Twyla

Sylwester Drzewiecki working on Martin's turkey farm - 1949

A Few Days After Arrival
Janka's First Apple Pie

Janka and Mrs. Martin were peeling apples to bake several pies for dinner. Hand gestures helped them understand each other. Janka's experience in cooking was minimal, and she did not know what they were making for she had never seen an apple pie. She fondly remembered the German apple Kuchen, that had apple slices placed in rows on top of the cake, but a pie was something new.

Mrs. Martin placed flour, shortening and salt in front of Janka, and demonstrated how she was to mix the dough with her hands. She then walked over to the sink, and motioned, "No water." Janka didn't understand how the dough was going to stick together without any water, but she did as she was told. Mrs. Martin left Janka on her own. She measured and poured everything into a large bowl and started to squeeze the flour, salt and shortening through her fingers. She tried pressing the dough in her hands to make a ball but the crumbs just fell apart. She continued mixing, but it wouldn't stick. Janka called Mrs. Martin. Mrs. Martin added a little water and began rolling the dough out for the first pie.

Janka was anxious to please and to do things right. Remembering the German Kuchen, she assumed she was to neatly arrange the apple slices in rows on the pastry shell. She carefully placed the slices on the bottom and sides of the pie shell, and felt proud when she was done. Mrs. Martin was busy rolling out dough, and fitting the pastry into the other pie plates. She was about to dump apples into the pie shells when she noticed Janka's pie. She smiled at her creation, and let it be. Janka looked at Mrs. Martin's beautiful pies. They did not look anything like hers, nor like a German Kuchen.

After dinner, Mrs. Martin served a thick slice of apple pie to each person, and then brought out Janka's. With a smile she said, "And here's the pie Janina made." Everyone laughed. Janka was embarrassed, but laughed too, for it did look funny.

Her cooking improved. There were eleven people to feed, and she prepared three meals a day with Mrs. Martin and Vivian, the eldest daugh-

ter. Wonderful smells wafted daily from the kitchen. Janka became an expert pie maker and made thousands of deep dish apple pies in her lifetime, and she learned how to make Kuchen too.

Shortly After Arrival
Snakes in the Grass

To Janka's horror, she was to discover that the damp climate and cool forest in Cedar was the perfect breeding ground and habitat for snakes. She had only seen one snake in her entire life before immigrating to Canada, and it was poisonous. She was a young girl in Poland, and had been so frightened by the snake, that her fear developed into a phobia. Janka's first encounters in Canada with harmless, timid garter snakes were terrifying, for she believed they were poisonous.

Janka called Sylwester, who was fixing a fence on the other side of the field, to watch Krystyna while she made lunch. The toddler went off into the tall grass, to meet her father. When lunch was ready, Janka went out to fetch them. When she stepped into the tall grass, a huge black snake slithered across her path, and she leapt out, screaming. She could see Sylwester but Krystyna was hidden in the grass, and so was the snake. Frantically she yelled to Sylwester, but he did not hear.

Eighteen-year-old Everett Martin had been walking towards the field when he saw Janka jump out of the grass. He figured she had been scared by a snake, and laughed. Janka grabbed Everett's arm and pointed across the field crying in Polish, "Krysia, Krysia tam! .... Krystyna, Krystyna is there!" Imitating the movement of a snake, she zig-zagged her finger back and forth screaming, "Węże! Węże! .... Snakes! Snakes!" Everett threw his head back and howled. Janka was horrified. He did not understand. She again desperately pointed and zig-zagged her finger, "Krysia, Krysia, tam! Węże! Węże!" She was almost hysterical.

Nothing prepared Janka for what Everett did. He stuck his right hand into his pant pocket and slowly pulled out a snake! She screamed at the top of her lungs as Everett dangled the writhing creature in front of her

face. Everett threw his head back howling, and kept holding the snake as Janka ran towards her house, screaming. Sylwester picked up Krystyna and came running.

Janka had left her cabin door ajar, and there, stretched across the entire width of her doorway, was another black snake! She shrieked as she jumped over it, and slammed the door. Her heart was pounding. They had immigrated to a snake-infested country! Were there snakes in the house? She ran to the window, glancing behind her, and watched Sylwester carry Krystyna home.

Sylwester tried to reassure her that the snakes were harmless, but she did not feel reassured; not even a little bit. Janka was on the lookout for snakes from that day on, and she found piles of them. Each and every one made her cringe.

A few months later
The Old Well

The well that supplied the farm with water was very deep and very old. Its walls were lined with concrete, and a lip of cement jutted above ground. The gaping hole was loosely covered with rotting, slippery planks that were riddled with moss. There were big gaps between the decaying boards. It was extremely dangerous to leave the well in such disrepair with so many children on the farm.

The well was not far from the house, and in full view of the kitchen window. Janka was washing dishes after lunch, when she saw Krystyna jumping up and down on top of the well. The decaying planks bounced with each jolt. Janka flew outside. Mr. Martin was walking from the barn when he too saw Krystyna, and ran like the wind. One slip, and she would be gone.

Janka knew not to startle Krystyna, for she would surely fall. Talking soothingly, she slowly approached, and then quickly snatched her off the well. She sobbed as she tightly held Krystyna and rocked her back and forth. The baby had no idea what was going on.

Mr. Martin immediately replaced the old wooden lid. He shuddered at the thought of what had almost happened.

New Year's Eve 1949

A Polish man named Tomek - Tommy Radziul lived on Hemer Road in Cedar, not far from the Martins. He visited Sylwester and Janka in their little house, and a close friendship began.

A Polish-Canadian New Year's Eve party was planned in Nanaimo, and Tommy asked Mr. and Mrs. Martin's permission to take Janka, Sylwester and Krysia. He arrived at the farm in a taxi with a Polish man from Victoria, and off the five went. Common language brought all the Polish-Canadians together at Bolek and Władka Jedzieczyk's home. Life-long friendships were established that New Year's Eve. A Polish-Canadian club, and yearly Polish picnics by the Nanaimo River began. Sylwester and Janka met:

Immigrated after the First World War:
> Bolek and Władka Jedzieczyk
> Pan and Pani Miroslaw
> Ludwig and Mary Stefanek
> Andy and Zosia Kapala

Immigrated after the Second World War:
> Tommy Radziul's future wife, Mary
> Michal Zwierok and his future wife, Wanda
> Bazyl and Józefina Tarnawski
> Władek Kazanowski
> Jan and Stefka Graczyk

Radziul, Zwierok, Tarnawski, Kazanowski and Graczyk all served in the Polish Army and fought at the famous Battle of Montecassino in Italy, in the Second World War.

March 1950
The Baby Shower

Mrs. Martin hosted a surprise baby shower for Janka in March, 1950. Such a party was unheard of back home. The guests did not know her, yet they showered her with lovely gifts. The diapers were snowy white and soft, not like the ones she had made from discarded clothes for Krystyna. Janka was happy that the guests understood her thanks, but the English language isolated her from conversation.

April 10, 1950
Easter Sunday

Janka was desperately lonely and homesick. Unfortunately, Sylwester did not understand her feelings. His childhood memories of poverty and abuse were not missed. Canada, his wife, and his children were all that mattered to him. Sylwester embraced his new life wholeheartedly, but it was not so for Janka. Sylwester left no one behind in Germany, while Janka left her family.

She yearned for the closeness of her parents, her sister and brother-in-law, and their children. She longed for conversation. Without English, she was a prisoner inside her mind. She only had Sylwester and Krystyna with whom to talk. Everything in Canada was different: the customs, the language, the towering thick forests, the rainy climate, the snakes. The farm was several miles from town so even going to church was difficult. Janka counted her blessings and she did not take them for granted. Canada offered them peace, freedom and opportunities that only came in dreams. However, she felt trapped and alone, and missed her family so much that more than once she had cried and wished she hadn't come.

On Easter Sunday, Sylwester borrowed Mr. Martin's bicycle and pedaled seven miles to Nanaimo to go to church. Janka missed the comfort of Sunday worship, where everything was familiar and language barriers did not exist. She hadn't been to church in a long time. Living out in Cedar and being nine months pregnant, made a trip into town on foot or on a bicy-

cle out of the question. With Sylwester at church, Janka took Krystyna by the hand and slowly walked down the gravel road beside the farm. There was nothing here to tell the world that it was Easter. In Poland the entire country celebrated this Holy occasion; church bells rang, people dressed up, special breads were baked, eggs were colored. People greeted each other with, "Chrystus Pan Zmartwychwstał .... Christ has risen from the dead." And they responded with, "Sprawiedliwie że powstał .... It is true that He has risen." Janka was overcome with grief, and wept. She thought of her family thousands of miles away in Germany and wondered what they were doing this Easter Sunday. Janka looked across the field and saw Mr. Martin on his tractor plowing his fields. No one worked on Sunday in Poland, especially not on Easter Sunday. The sight of Mr. Martin working, triggered tears that would not stop. She wiped the tears from her face and slowly walked back home. She was drained. She and Krystyna laid down on the bed and fell asleep.

She awoke when Sylwester came home, and her labour began. However, there was no rush for the baby was big and would take a long time to be born.

The Following Day
Wandzia Twyla Drzewiecki is Born

Wanda - *Wandzia* ... Vun-ja

Mr. Martin drove Janka to the hospital in Nanaimo, while Sylwester stayed behind to work and care for Krystyna; fathers were not permitted in the delivery room. Wandzia Twyla Drzewiecki was born, on Monday, April 11, 1950, a very healthy ten pounds ten ounces. She had little curls all over her head, and was gorgeous. Sylwester adored his two little girls, but believed the next one would be a boy for sure. Wandzia was the exact same birthweight as Krystyna Michalina, and looked double the size of the other babies in the nursery. Sylwester and Janka had learned that fat babies were healthy babies that survived. They were acutely aware of infant mortality in Eastern Poland, as Sylwester's parents had lost five children, and Janka's parents had lost three. They feared childhood illnesses, and believed in doctors like they believed in God.

1950 at the Drzewiecki's Home on Martin's Farm, after Wandzia's Baptism.

From Left: Wandzia's Godparents:
Tomek Radziul, and Władka Jedzieczyk holding Wandzia,
Krysia, Janina, and Sylwester

As Wandzia grew, Sylwester nicknamed her Syna - Sonny, because she was to have been his son, but she would point to herself, nod her blond curls, and correct him by saying, "Ja, ja Wandzia ... I, I Wandzia." She was cute, and Sylwester couldn't help but smile. She insisted on her real name and Wandzia became Wandzia.

Krysia and Wandzia - 1952

August 1, 1950
The Canadian Government's Labor Contract is Completed

It was a surprise to learn that their twelve month contract began the day they set foot in Canada. The two months they had spent waiting in St. Paul for a work placement, was calculated into their contract. Ten months had now passed since arriving at the Martin's farm. Sylwester was told at the Unemployment Office in Nanaimo, that his contract had been fulfilled. He could now look for work elsewhere, but he was not allowed to leave the farm until he found another place to live.

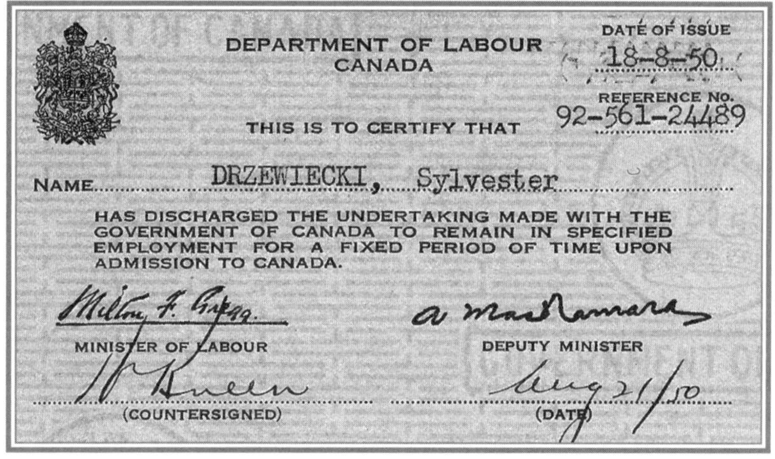

Sylwester's Canadian Department of Labour Discharge - 1950

The contract expired August 1st, 1950; Janka's 24th birthday. Sylwester went that very day to apply for a job at the newly constructed Harmac Pulp Mill in Cedar, which was owned and operated by MacMillan Bloedel Ltd. The mill was looking for hundreds of employees and Sylwester was immediately hired. He would work five and a half days a week at $1.12 per hour. The company wanted Sylwester to start immediately, but he asked if he could start the next day as he needed time to find a place to live. They agreed.

That same day, Mr. Martin drove Sylwester into Nanaimo to buy some furnishings, for they owned nothing. Sylwester bought the bare necessities from a second hand store: a bed with a metal frame for two dollars, a wood stove, a table and some chairs. They had no pots, no pans, and no dishes. The one plate they had received as a wedding gift in Germany, had regrettably broken when hot food was placed on it. They had no kitchen utensils except for two forks and knives, and one very large fork which Mrs. Martin gave them. Janka used Mrs. Martin's fork for years. *(Fifty years later, at the time of the writing of this book, she still used that fork to lift her delicious homemade pączki - doughnuts out of the hot oil.)*

There was a small cabin for rent near the Martin's farm. Sylwester and Janka rented the cabin for twenty dollars a month. It had no running water, but had a good well close by. The floor was linoleum. Growing up with clay floors in Rudnia and Omelanka, Sylwester and Janka were amazed at how clean linoleum was.

Sylwester, Janka, Krystyna, and Wandzia, moved into the rented cabin on August 3rd, 1950. Each day, Sylwester walked the pipe line, that carried fresh water to the mill, to get to work; thirty minutes each way.

Sylwester began in general maintenance, and later worked as the leadhand painter. His forty years of service at Harmac Pulp Mill, from 1950 to 1990, were accident free. He became known as the Singing Painter as he sang wherever he worked. His deep, beautiful voice could be heard as he painted the mill from one end to the other, year after year.

Sylwester at Harmac Pulp Mill

MacMillan Bloedel Limited

1075 West Georgia Street, Vancouver, Canada V6E 3R9
Cable Address: "Harmac"   Telex No. 0451471

RAYMOND V. SMITH
President and
Chief Executive Officer

Telephone 661-8490
Area Code 604

July 27, 1990

Mr.   Sylvester Drzewiecki
Site P
RR#4, Nanaimo
B.C. V9R 5X9

Dear Sylver:

On August 1, you celebrate 40 years of service with MacMillan Bloedel and I congratulate you on this outstanding achievement.   Of particular note is your accident free career, this in itself is an achievement of which to be very proud.

I understand that your son Richard joined the Company earlier this year, and I can't help but wonder whether MacMillan Bloedel will have gone through as many changes when he celebrates his fortieth anniversary, as they have since you joined the bull gang forty years ago.

I thank you for your loyalty and contribution to the company Sylver and, once again, congratulations on your membership in the 40 year club and every good wish for the future.

Sincerely,

Congratulatory letter from the Chief Executive Officer of MacMillan Bloedel's Harmac Pulp and Paper Division for Sylwester Drzewiecki's 40 accident-free years of service.

August 1, 1990

"CONGRATULATIONS"

Our congratulations go out to Silver Drzewiekci, Leadhand Painter, for achieving forty years of service today.

If you see Silver in your travels, please take the time to congratulate him on this outstanding achievement.

Congratulatory note printed in the Harmac Bulletin - August 1, 1990

Part 6 - Chapter 4

The Rented Cabin, Cedar, B.C.
August 1950 - December 1950

The Snakes and The Cooking Pot

There was a rickety old shed on the rented property, and Janka thought perhaps there might be a can in there that she could use to boil potatoes. The shed was overgrown with brush and high grass, and looked ready to topple down. When Wandzia and Krystyna fell asleep for their afternoon nap, she hurried off to find a pot. She'd be there and back in no time.

Janka ran through the field looking out for snakes. There were none today. She quickly stepped onto the door sill and looked inside the shed. It took a few second for her eyes to adjust to the dark. There, on top of a wooden shelf, was a gallon can. Janka stepped into the shed, and immediately ran out screaming. The shed was writhing with snakes! They were heaped on top of each other, twisting and turning.

The thought of the snakes crawling in the shed kept Janka running. She didn't stop until she was safely in her home. The girls slept through her panic. Janka desperately needed that can, but the thought of returning to the snake infestation made her shudder. She needed a plan.

While her phobia still consumed her, she found a very long stick, and bravely returned to the dark shed. She inched forward. Planting her feet in the doorway, and leaning inside, she knocked the can off the shelf. It fell on the heap of twisting snakes. The sight of her cooking pot on top of the nest made her sick. She rolled her pot towards the door with the stick, grabbed it, and ran home.

The girls were still asleep when Janka returned. She carefully pried open the rusted can, and was relieved to find it brand new inside. She scraped off some of the rust, filled the pot with peeled potatoes, and cov-

ered them with water. She figured if she firmly pressed down the lid, the water would come to a boil more quickly, so she forced the lid down with her hands. To make sure it was really tight, she hammered it shut. She was proud of her ingenuity. She put the pot on the hot stove, not realizing that she had created a bomb.

Wandzia was in her crib in the kitchen, and Krystyna was playing with her. As Janka worked and the children played, the trapped pressure grew.

A neighbor gave Sylwester a ride home from work that day. He had just been dropped off, and was walking towards the house, when a deafening explosion blew. It reminded him of the bombing raids during the Second World War. He ran, fearing the worst. Frantically, he yelled, "Co wybuchło? Co wybuchło? .... What exploded?! What exploded?!"

He found Janka standing in the kitchen looking up at her potatoes stuck to the ceiling. There was water everywhere. Pointing to the ceiling, with a dumbfounded expression, she said, "Zobacz gdzie kartofle, na sóficie. To miała być nasza kolacja .... Look at the potatoes on the ceiling. That was supposed to be our supper." So much for ingenuity.

Luckily, no one was burned. That was the last pot of potatoes Janka cooked with the lid hammered down. Two weeks later, Sylwester received his first paycheck and came home with *real* cooking pots.

A few weeks later
Boiled Snakes

Janka still did not believe that every snake she saw could be a harmless garter snake. What if one was poisonous? She didn't trust any of them. She was outside with her girls when she stumbled upon a snake pit close to where Krystyna liked to play. She was horrified by the sight of the slithering snakes wrapped around each other. Janka grabbed her children and fled into the house. She immediately started to boil a big pot of water to kill the snakes. In spite of her intense phobia, she took the boiling water out to the pit and poured it all over the snakes. They swiftly slithered out

in every direction. She ran into the house and locked the door. Even the smartest snake couldn't get in!

In later years Janka was embarrassed by what she did, but at the time she did what she thought was right to protect her children.

September 1950
Sylwester and Janka's First Car

Fourteen months after setting foot in Canada, Sylwester bought a 1947 Plymouth. He was transformed into someone of great importance as he drove down the road. Resting one arm on the window sill, and steering with the other, he felt superior and successful. If only the people in Rudnia could see him now!

Unfortunately Sylwester had not anticipated the economic drain his dream car would create. The car cost $1800. Sylwester had put $800 down, which he and Janka had frugally saved, and paid $70 a month towards the balance. His earnings were under $200 a month, and he soon realized he could not keep up with the payments and support a family as well. He had no option but to return the car and exchange it for a less expensive one. It seemed straight forward to him, and he was shocked when the dealership told him, "We are not in business to buy your car, we are in business to sell ours." He had no idea he would lose money in the transaction, for he had just purchased the car two months earlier. He was in a pinch and the dealership took advantage of his inexperience. They took back the 1947 Plymouth, and in return gave him a 1929 Chevrolet, plus $150. He had been swindled out of a fortune.

It was a very expensive lesson, and a financial setback for Sylwester and Janka. They continued to work and save, and were extra cautious with their future purchases.

The 1929 Chevrolet - Photograph 1952
Krysia, Sylwester, Danusia, Wandzia, and Janina

October 1950 - One Month Later
The Rudolphs Move In

At the mill, Sylwester met a worker named Charlie Rudolph. He told Sylwester that his family was looking for a place to live. The families decided to share the five-room cabin and split the $20 a month rent because Sylwester and Janka were only occupying two of the rooms. Charlie, Freda and their five-year-old son Dennis, moved in in October, 1950. The families lived well together. Dennis and Krystyna were wonderful playmates. Sylwester and Charlie repaired the well and fenced the yard. Janka still spoke very little English, and Freda began to teach her a few words.

Once in the house, Krystyna developed a jealousy for her baby sister, and when her mother wasn't looking, she would try to hurt her. Krystyna found a piece of wire and headed straight for her baby sister. Janka ran when she heard Wandzia scream, and found Krystyna standing beside the crib with her hands behind her back. Janka picked up Wandzia. The baby looked fine at a glance, but was still whimpering. "Co ty zrobiłaś do Wandzi? .... What did you do to Wandzia?"

"Nic, mamo nie zrobiłam. Nic .... Nothing, Mama. I did nothing."

"Co ty masz tam w rączkach? .... What do you have in your hands?"

"Nic mamo nie mam .... I have nothing Mama." Janka turned Krystyna around and saw the wire. She checked the baby again. Blood was coming from her mouth. Krystyna had poked Wandzia's tongue. Fortunately she didn't poke her sister's eye or ear.

Janka patiently explained how dangerously Krystyna had acted. She understood never to poke her sister with a wire again...she found other ways to torment her instead.

Part 6 - Chapter 5

The Little Brown House, Cedar, B.C.
January 1951 - December 1954

From left: Wandzia, Janka, Krysia, Sylwester holding Danusia

Introduction:
Sylwester 25 years old
Janka 24 years old

Sylwester and Janka were ingenious and frugal, and after only seventeen months since arriving in Canada, Sylwester and Janka had saved enough money to buy a tiny three room house in Cedar, about one and a half miles from Martin's farm. They purchased the property directly from the owners, Mr. and Mrs. Wager. The Wagers were an elderly farming couple who owned several hundred acres in Cedar. Sylwester and Janka paid $1200 for the house and one acre of land. It was two thirds the price of the 1947 Plymouth! In December, 1950, they gave Mr. and Mrs. Wager $200 and paid the rest directly to them in monthly instalments of $50, interest-free. In January, 1951, they said goodbye to the Rudolphs, and moved into

their little brown house. Sylwester and Janka felt like millionaires. They had a house and a car which would have taken a lifetime in Eastern Poland.

The property was in absolute wilderness. It bordered Cedar Road on the east side, but thick, dark forest surrounded them. Their little cabin was dwarfed by the massive trees. The total square footage was possibly 500 square feet, which included a kitchen, bedroom, and sitting room. There was no bathroom, no running water, and no well, but they had the luxury of electricity. They carried water in buckets from the neighbor's well for months. Selecting a well site and digging it by hand was one of their first priorities. They had no central heating, but the wood stove in the kitchen heated the tiny house. The floors were plywood, which had darkened with time. There was a driveway on the south side of the cabin which lead into a small garage. Even though their land was overgrown, they envisioned a building site for their future home, and a plot for their orchard and garden. It was beautiful, and it was theirs.

The neighbors were sparse, but there were a few spread out along Cedar Road. Larry and Beverly Fowler, Gordon and Edna McGillivray, Alex and Mildred MacLeod, and Mac and Margaret McLeod. The neighbors called Sylwester and Janka, Sylver and Jenny. Everyone was kind, and willingly pitched in and helped each other.

Sylwester was learning the English language more and more each day at the mill, but Janka had little exposure to it. She spoke Polish to Krystyna and Wandzia all day, and Polish when Sylwester came home in the evening. She would have enjoyed conversation with the ladies in the neighborhood, but she was still terribly isolated by language.

Gordon McGillivray worked at Harmac, and drove Sylwester to and from work each day. While Sylwester worked at the mill, Janka worked at home. She got up every morning and made her husband breakfast and a large, homemade lunch to take to work. His lunches quickly became the talk of the lunchroom. Janka's work was endless and she literally never sat down. She carried water, scrubbed laundry by hand and hung it to dry. She washed floors, chopped wood, sewed, mended, knitted and crocheted. She baked bread and cooked meals. In season, she gardened and preserved food. Supper was always on the table when Sylwester walked in

the door from work...and she did all this while caring for a two-and-a-half year-old and a nine-month-old baby.

After supper, they cleared their land with simple hand tools. They had no chainsaw or bulldozer, just muscle. They used an axe, saw, grub hoe, and pick axe. Trees had to be felled, stumps pulled, and the well dug. Twenty-four hours was not long enough in a day. They worked non-stop. Tommy and Mary Radziul allowed Janka to use some of their garden space, and after working all day and helping her husband after supper, Janka would rock her children to sleep and walk up to the Radziuls to tend her garden.

Hauling water was a ominous job while the well was being dug. Over the months, thousands of heavy buckets were carried from the neighbor's well from across the road, and from other sources. During the hot summer months, the neighbor's wells were very low, and they barely had enough water for themselves. Sylwester and Janka had to look elsewhere for water. Sylwester carried water in his 1929 Chevy from the huge pipeline, a quarter mile north, that supplied Harmac with thousands of gallons of water each day. They discovered fresh spring water about six miles South of Cedar, near Ivy Green Park, that gushed from a pipe installed for everyone to use. Every second day, Sylwester would fasten a barrel on the front bumper of his 1929 Chevy, between the headlights, and bring water home.

Sylwester and Janka were Cedar pioneers, working from sun up to sun down. Rest only came with sleep, which their young children interrupted. On top of it all, Janka was pregnant again and due in November, 1951.

Early 1951
The Second-Hand Ringer Washer

With a new baby on the way, Janka's workload would be even greater; especially laundry. She not only scrubbed her family's clothes by hand, she also scrubbed diapers, bedding, linens, and towels. It was an enormous job to keep everyone clean. Janka desperately needed an electric washing machine.

The family drove to Nanaimo to look for one. An old ringer washer made of cast iron was selling for two dollars, but there would be no extra money until payday. Standing behind them in the store were their neighbors, Mac and Margaret McLeod. Mac lent them the two dollars until payday, and they loaded the ringer washer into the 1929 Chevy.

The washing machine was kept in the garage, for there was no room in the house. Janka still had to haul water from across the road, into her house, heat it on the stove, and then carry it out to the machine. Laundry was still a lot of work, but it was a luxury having a machine do the washing.

The next luxury would be to have a well and indoor plumbing.

February 1951
Well Witching

The property sloped downwards on the west side, and bordered Wager's farm. There was a running creek on the farm, and Sylwester assessed that the water table was easily attainable from the lowest point on the property. He guessed that he would probably reach water at about fifteen feet. However, their house was on the highest point of the property. Since he had no knowledge of the electrical pumps that were available to pump water uphill, he abandoned that location and decided to dig the well closer to the house.

Mac McLeod was experienced in well witching and volunteered to find the best location for the well. He held the branches of a 'Y'-shaped stick in each hand and slowly walked around the property. The stick would supposedly point towards the ground where water would be found. It pointed in the driveway right beside the brown house, which would not do, but down from the house the stick pointed again. Mac told Sylwester he would hit water at fifteen feet at that exact spot. The well site was marked, and the digging began. Mac was right. They did hit water at fifteen feet, but in order for the well to hold any water, they had to dig to thirty-six feet....three

and a half stories below ground.

Digging the well was slow, back-breaking work with the pick and shovel. The dirt was hoisted out one bucket at a time. To achieve any progress, they needed the digging to continue during the day while Sylwester was at work. Sylwester hired two men who managed to go down another six feet, but money was slim and paying for labour added up quickly. They had to let the two men go.

Spring 1951
The Regulants

Stasia had written that she and her three children had arrived in Canada on April 20th, 1950, and were with Zygmunt in Val d'Or, Quebec. Janka was anxious to be reunited with her family, but they were still over 3,000 miles apart. Janka and Sylwester discussed inviting the Regulants to move west.

Janka wrote a long letter asking her sister to come to British Columbia. She described how they had purchased a three room house on an acre of land; Sylwester had built a chicken coop and they would soon have chickens; they were digging a well and would have indoor plumbing; and that jobs were plentiful in British Columbia. Janka and Sylwester offered to let the Regulants live with them until Zygmunt found employment and a home of their own.

Zygmunt had been working in Canada the same number of years as Sylwester, but was not yet able to buy a home. The Regulants lived in the bunkhouses that were provided by the government. After reading the letter, they decided to move West. A fellow Pole, Czesiek - Chester Krygier, worked with Zygmunt. *(Chester had survived the Nazi death camp of Dachau. His identification number, which had been tattooed on his forearm, was a grizzly reminder of the camp.)* Zygmunt told the Krygiers about British Columbia, and they decided to venture West too.

Stasia wrote saying that they would be selling all their belongings and moving to British Columbia. They introduced the Krygier family in the

letter, and explained that the two families would be traveling by train across Canada. They would be arriving on May 6th, 1951. Janka was elated and her spirits immediately soared. She started cleaning and planning for the visit. She needed more water. She wanted to proudly show off her home and wanted everything to be just right. That evening Sylwester attached the barrel between the headlights of the 1929 Chevy, and drove to Ivy Green Park to bring more water for Janka's cleaning frenzy.

The following day, after Sylwester left for work, Janka started cooking and scrubbing. She hadn't felt this wonderful in years. Her family and new friends would be arriving in a few days. Sylwester came home to supper on the table, and a very tired wife. She was three months pregnant and had taken on extra work that he thought was absolutely foolish. He did not understand the fuss. Sylwester scorned Janka's efforts. She was hurt and angry by his verbal jabs, and told him to go outside and dig the well. Now both of them were fuming.

"Ja nie mogę iść kopać studnię. Tam jest drabina i ktoś musi ją wyjąć .... I can't go and dig the well," he snapped. "The ladder is in it and someone has to pull it out."

"Idź. Ja wyciągnę .... Go. I'll pull it up."

The bickering couple stormed out to the well. Sylwester climbed down the ladder, grabbed the pick and started to work. Janka pulled out the ladder and left. Sylwester's anger cooled off with the hard work. He was hitting rock. Janka resumed her preparations for her special guests. She wasn't going to let her grumpy husband upset her plans. She wanted everything to be just right, and it would be. There was more laundry to do and she set to work with her ringer washer.

An Hour Later
The Axe and the Washing Machine

After digging in the well for some time, Sylwester heard Janka frantically screaming, "Sylwek, Sylwek ratunku! .... Sylwek, Sylwek help!"

Images ran wildly through his head, as his wife screamed for help. He grabbed on to the dirt walls and tried to climb up, but fell crashing onto the rocks. He tried to brace himself against the walls and walk up, but the diameter was too wide. He continued to clamber, thinking that Janka had been electrocuted. He heard her cry again, "Sylwek, Sylwek ratunku!" Bears and cougars inhabited vast territories on Vancouver Island, and Sylwester's imagination ran wild as he tried to climb out. He fell into the well over and over again. He had to think, or he would never get out. High above his head, laying across the opening of the well, was a plank. If he could just grab that plank, he could heave himself up and out. He tried and missed, and each time bashed into the rocks. Finally he caught the board and swung himself up and over. He grabbed the double-bladed axe from the chopping block close by. He sprinted, with the axe, towards his screaming wife.

Janka's hand was trapped in the ringer rollers of the washing machine. Her hand and fingers were already blue. She had unplugged the machine before her whole arm was rolled into the ringers. In his panic Sylwester ran back and forth, trying to think of what to do. He would pry the rollers apart with the blade of the axe.

The neighbors were alerted to Janka's screams. Gordon McGillivray and Larry Fowler ran like the wind to help her. They flew to the edge of the fence that separated the Fowler's and the Drzewiecki's properties, and could not believe the drama unfolding before their eyes! They saw a crazed Pole with a double-bladed axe in his hand, running towards his screaming wife. He was going to kill her! It was instant hysteria! Gordon and Larry jumped the fence like it wasn't even there.

When he saw his neighbors coming, he frantically ran towards them for help, with his double-bladed axe still in hand. Gordon ran straight at Sylwester, ready to fight, while Larry ran to rescue Janka. Gordon saw Janka's predicament and realized that Sylwester was trying to rescue his wife, not kill her! Gordon turned and ran to Janka, with Sylwester running behind, still holding the double-bladed axe.

Gordon and Larry quickly tried to pry the ringers apart, but the ringers would not budge. The old machine was made of cast iron, and was rusted. Gordon quickly told Sylwester to get a hammer. He scrambled under the garage where he kept his tool box. Gordon gave the side of the ringer a hard smack to release the locking mechanism. The spring opened and the ringers popped apart. Janka was freed, and the blood rushed back into her hand.

Sylwester took Janka to emergency for X-rays, and Edna McGillivray took over her chores. She finished the laundry, scrubbed the floors, baked the bread, and looked after Krystyna and Wandzia. Edna's kindness was never forgotten.

Janka had a very sore and bruised hand, but no broken bones or nerve damage. She hadn't realized how exhausted she was. The added trauma sent her into near collapse. She laid down, with her wrist and hand securely wrapped, and instantly fell asleep. Sylwester's whole body ached from falling against the rocks. He was thankful for his good neighbors, even though Gordon had been ready to knock him off his feet.

Sylwester Drzewiecki and Gordon McGillivray, 1979
Twenty-eight years after the Axe and the Washing Machine Episode;
Life-Long Friends and Neighbors

May 6, 1951 - Two Days Later
A Packed House

The Regulants and Krygiers had arrived! The little house was bursting with excitement and people. Janka's years of waiting and loneliness had finally ended.

Six adults, and six children under the age of seven, squeezed into the tiny, three-room house. The twelve people living in the little brown house in May, 1951, were:

The Drzewieckis:

Sylwester	Father
Janka	Mother - 3 months pregnant with Daiena
Krystyna Michalina	2 years 9 months
Wandzia	13 months old

The Regulants:

Zygmunt	Father
Stasia	Mother - Janina's sister
Krystyna	7 years old
Zbygniew	2 years 10 months
Zygmunt II	16 months old

The Krygiers:

Czesiek	Father
Lotka	Mother - 6 months pregnant with Halina
Wanda	5 years old

May 8, 1951 - Two Days Later
The Snake in the Bucket

While Sylwester worked at the mill during the day, Zygmunt and Czesiek helped dig the well. After supper, the three men went back outside. Sylwester climbed down to do the digging, filled the bucket with dirt, and the two men hauled it up and dumped it out.

A snake was in the bottom of the well and Sylwester thought it would be hilarious to scare the newcomers who had never seen Cedars' harmless garter snakes. He picked it up by its tail, put it on top of the dirt in the bucket, and gave the signal for Zygmunt and Czesiek to haul it up. As he laughed at the image of the two men jumping when they saw the snake, he did not expect his prank to backfire.

When they hauled up the bucket and saw the snake, they thought it was poisonous and instantly let go of the rope. The heavy bucket plummeted straight towards Sylwester's head. Sylwester darted out of the way in the nick of time, and the loaded bucket landed with a hard thud. Much Polish cursing and yelling ensued. So much for Sylwester's practical joke, it could have killed him!

The Next Day
The 1929 Chevy's New Parking Spot

The temptation of trying to drive the 1929 Chevy, while Sylwester was at work, was too hard for Zygmunt and Czesiek to resist. They didn't know how to drive, but climbed in, with Zygmunt at the wheel. He started the engine, put the car in gear, and off they went. It would have been a good idea to figure out how to stop before they started to go, but a tree stump on the property did the job for them.

When Sylwester came home, Zygmunt and Czesiek were working extra hard in the well. The dirt was flying. Sylwester was impressed, until he saw his car parked on top of a stump. Sylwester decided to give the two adult, juvenile delinquents a driving lesson.

May 10, 1951

The Crown Zellerbach Company was hiring in Ladysmith, south of Nanaimo. The hiring foreman for the loggers lived on the Cedar Road, and Sylwester went to talk to him about possible employment for Zygmunt and Czesiek. The man wanted to see them the next morning.

In order to drive his two guests to the Crown Zellerbach office in Ladysmith, Sylwester took the following day off work. Zygmunt and Czesiek were immediately hired and remained with the company for the rest of their working years. They looked for accommodation, and rented two small cabins near Ivy Green Park. In less than one week, the Regulants and the Krygiers had found work and a home in British Columbia.

Sometime Later
The Dynamite

Zygmunt and Czesiek continued to help dig the well on their days off. Nine feet down into the well they hit hardpan. They had to use dynamite. Sylwester was a self-taught handyman and knew a little about electrical power. Krygier seemed to know a little about blasting. Between the two of them, they figured they knew what they were doing....but they were wrong.

Holes were drilled in the rock and dynamite shoved in. Sylwester took the wires from the detonator and connected them to the main light switch in the house. Rather than stand guard, he hurriedly told Janka to be sure the children didn't touch the switch or the dynamite would blow!

Krystyna was three years old and overheard her father specifically say that the switch was not to be touched, and wondered why. Sylwester and Zygmunt had just climbed out of the well, and were extending their hands to help Krygier off the last rung, when Krystyna flicked the switch. Everything blew! The ladder and Krygier went flying! Everyone ran out of the house, except for Krystyna, who made herself scarce.

All three men were lucky they had not been killed. Sylwester stormed into the house, and hollered at his wife for not watching the children. Later he realized how foolish he had been for he had created a very dangerous situation.

Cabin at Ivy Green Park - 1951
Sylwester Drzewiecki, Czesiek Krygier, Zygmunt Regulant

Seven months and thiry-six feet later, Sylwester and Janka had running water. It was a miraculous feat, not only to have accomplished it, but to have emerged unharmed.

November 2, 1951
Daiena Filipina Drzewiecki is Born
Daiena - Danusia...Da-noo-sha

Slowly more and more land was cleared and there was enough space to plant an orchard near the well. Autumn was the perfect time to plant the trees, and Janka set to work. With her two girls by her side, she paced out where the nine trees should go. There was a variety of plum, apple, cherry, and pear. She was nine months pregnant and due any time- but ignored her condition, and started breaking the soil with the pick and shovel. Hour after hour she dug and planted. The incredible physical exertion set the baby into motion. Labour pains began, but she had time. It was another big baby.

With the trees planted and watered, she then went into the house, heated water on the stove, bathed the girls and herself, packed a few essentials for the hospital and made dinner. Once Sylwester was home, Gordon McGillivray took her to the Nanaimo hospital. Danusia Filipina Drzewiecki was born at 9:30 p.m. weighing ten pounds ten ounces, just like her two sisters. They were thrilled with their third healthy daughter, but Sylwester was certain the next one would be a boy.

Drzewiecki Family Photograph 1952
Danusia seated in the yellow baby buggy which was brought from Germany.

Poor Danusia suffered from colic, and cried incessantly. Nothing alleviated her discomfort, or her screaming. Janka and Sylwester were up all night. The colic subsided after four noisy months, but sleepless nights continued with three youngsters taking turns waking them up.

Spring 1952
Krystyna Discovers Scissors

Having watched her Mother give her father a haircut many times, Krystyna thought it would be fun to play barber. Little Wandzia was her big sister's shadow, and did whatever Krystyna wanted her to do. Krystyna took her two-year-old sister, and the scissors, into the garage. Wandzia had the most beautiful golden curls. A curl came off here, a chunk there, more on this side, and a little on that side. When Krystyna was done, a pile of Wandzia's blonde curls were all over the garage floor. Taking her little sister by the hand, she proudly ran to her Mother. "Mamo, ja uciełam włosy dla Wandzi! .... Mama, I cut Wandzia's hair!" Poor Wandzia had clumps of hair missing all over her head. The hair would grow back, but in the meantime Krystyna needed another talk. She never cut her sister's hair again...she found other things to cut, like her mother's curtains.

Setting out fabric and the scissors on the kitchen table, Janka went to remeasure the living room windows one more time before she cut. Krystyna eyed the sewing project, and Janka told her not to touch. That was a mistake.

Krystyna picked up the scissors and cut the material every which way. The fabric was totally useless when she was done. She left her masterpiece and hurriedly ran outside. She was no fool. Janka returned to shredded fabric and a missing culprit. She hid the scissors thus ending Krystyna's scissor capers.

Summer 1952
The Well Runs Dry

What a disappointment when the well went dry the following summer. Water was once again hauled every two days in the barrel secured between the headlights of the 1929 Chevy, but it was not enough. A man was hired to deliver water to fill the well; it cost fifteen dollars which was almost two day's wages. With water once again in good supply, laundry and bathing resumed.

Before bed Sylwester checked the water level of the well and found it had gone down substantially. In the morning the well was dry again. It was simply too shallow to hold the water in the summer months, and digging continued year after year. However, at forty feet, the water shortage continued. A new well site was chosen in 1955 and the digging started anew. Now knowing about electric pumps, the second well was dug where Sylwester had originally wanted to dig in 1951. Water was reached at fourteen feet.

Later that year, the Regional District knocked on their door informing them that a water main was planned for installation in the Cedar district. There was a one hundred dollar connecting fee. Sylwester and Janka immediately signed their names and their days of digging wells, and water problems, ended.

Between the two wells, they had dug fifty-four feet into the ground; an equivalent of five stories. They undid their years of hard work by filling in the wells to keep the children safe.

Spring 1953 - Wandzia 3 years old
The Oldsmobile

The 1929 Chevy was replaced with an Oldsmobile, purchased from a neighbor for three hundred dollars. The old car was made of thick steel and was as solid as a rock. The two back doors, opened towards the rear of the car.

Driving home from church, the girls were treated to candy. However, they had to wait until they got home to change out of their Sunday dresses. Wandzia could hardly wait to get home and out of the car. As Sylwester slowly guided the car into the garage, he reminded the girls not to open the back doors until the car was completely stopped. However, a very excited Wandzia was opening her door as her father spoke. The door flung backwards, hitting the garage with a thud, scaring everyone.

Now it was Wandzia's turn to have a talk even though car and building survived the crash.

The Oldsmobile
Note that the back doors open to the rear.
From Left: Cousin Zyg Regulant, Krysia, Marysia,
Danusia, Wandzia, Sylwester - 1955

Part 6 - Chapter 6

The Brick House, Cedar, B.C.
1953

Introduction:

The Drzewieckis were quickly outgrowing their little brown house. Daiena was a toddler and Janka was pregnant again. The trees had been cleared to build their new home. Sylwester drew out the floor plan, making an extra large kitchen for it was where company visited. Food and company were synonymous.

The concrete for the basement was poured early in 1953. The foundation looked the size of a palace compared to the little brown house. Logs from their land were used as supporting beams for their brick house. Brick and mortar stood the test of time in Europe. Brick by brick the new house went up with Janka and Sylwester working together every step of the construction.

With no schooling in English, language was a continuing challenge. On one occasion, Sylwester went into a store to buy *candy* for

Krystyna, and he came out with *candles*. Krystyna was not impressed. Another time Sylwester had a flat tire and needed a jack. By the time Janka reached the neighbor she forgot the word *jack* and used a much better descriptor, *bumper jumper*.

My siblings and I became proficient at understanding our parents, whether they spoke Polish, English, or a mixture of the two. As we grew and adopted the English language, our parents spoke to us in Polish and we replied in English. This was the source of much confusion when friends came over to play. Eventually my parents began speaking English to each other.

July 1953
Daiena Climbs the Ladder
Twenty Months Old

By July, the walls of the brick house were standing and the construction of the roof started. The girls played close by, while their parents worked. Krystyna, being the eldest, made sure her little sisters played right where they were told. A pregnant Janka was on the roof, hammering side-by-side with Sylwester.

It was time to check the girls. Sylwester climbed down from the roof and treated them to some candy. He hugged and praised his girls for playing so nicely, and told them to stay right where they were as he climbed back up the ladder. Daiena's watchful eye did not miss a thing. She knew her father had put the rest of the candy in his pocket. She wanted more, and she knew where to get it.

The spaces between the rungs of the ladder were huge compared to Daiena's height. Krystyna and Wandzia didn't notice their baby sister slowly climbing up to the roof. Her tiny arms pulled with all their might. Her knee, then her foot reached the next rung. The thought of more candy in her father's pocket kept her going.

Daiena's tiny hands held the sides of the ladder, her little feet were planted on the top rung, which was above the roof line, and a big smile was

on her face. She was one and a half stories above the ground. Janka and Sylwester stopped breathing. They talked quietly to Daiena, trying not to startle her. "Trzymaj się mocno Danusiu. Tatuś da ci cukierek .... Hold on tight Daiena. Daddy will bring you candy," he coached as he gently stepped towards her. He grabbed her and carried her down to safety. The tension ended in tears of relief. Emptying his pockets, he said, "Więcej cukierków nie mam .... No more candy."

Forty-five years later, the vision of twenty-month-old Daiena standing at the top of the ladder, wearing a little yellow dress, smiling, and holding on tightly, still made Janka and Sylwester shudder.

1953
Krystyna is Lost

Swings that Sylwester hung from a tree in the yard provided hours of fun for Krystyna and Wandzia. They sat on the wooden seats and pushed each other, or laid on their bellies and spun around and around. They were in the midst of fun when Wandzia fell off, and the wooden seat hit her in the back of the head. Frightened at the sight of blood, and by Wandzia's wailing, Krystyna ran and hid. It was perfect five-year-old logic, but terrifying for the parents and neighbors who could not find her.

Janka was the first to notice Krystyna's disappearance. Her parents frantically searched for her calling, "Krysia, Krysia!" The neighbors joined in the search and everyone spread out, calling and looking. They went through the house, and around the house, calling her name. They went into the forest; down the road; to the creek; but she was nowhere to be found. They were two hours into the search, and began to panic as night was falling. She could be anywhere in any direction.

The windows and doors were not yet installed in the brick house, and there were many places in the construction for a clever five year old to hide. Everyone had run through the house many times. Mrs. Fowler saw a little head of dark hair slowly peek over the window sill, look out at the rescue party, and then quickly hide again. Krystyna had scared the whole

neighborhood, and had been hiding in the new house the whole time! She needed another talk.

I, the author, was the next child to be born.
Therefore the rest of this book is written in first-person.

December 25, 1953
I, Mary Anna Drzewiecki, am Born
Mary - Marysia...Ma-ree-sha

As with her previous pregnancy, my mother ignored her need to rest. In addition to her endless chores and three preschoolers to watch, she was pounding nails in the roof when she was seven months pregnant with me. She skipped meals and rested little, right up to the day I was born.

My family had a traditional Polish Wigilia - Christmas Eve dinner at the Radziuls, and at noon on Christmas Day, the Radziuls came to our house. My mother had been cooking traditional Polish foods for days, and was preparing dinner, when her labour began. The contractions were close together and she knew I would soon be born. She apologized to our guests, and readied herself for the hospital. My father took my three sisters to the Regulants in Ladysmith and took my mother to the Ladysmith hospital. I was born at 6 p.m., weighing seven pounds, ten ounces; three pounds less than my other sisters. Poor Mom missed Christmas dinner at home and in the hospital, but she had me as a consolation.

The phone rang at the Regulants telling my father that he had a fourth daughter. He was so disappointed not to have a son, that he didn't visit my mother and I for two hours. He entered the nursery, which was full of screaming newborns, and wondered which one was his. He hesitantly walked up to the window and noticed one infant quietly looking at her hands, wiggling her fingers in front of her face. He was intrigued as he walked over to the newborn, and read 'Drzewiecki'.

My father felt terrible for not wanting to see me, and tells me because of his initial rejection at my not being a boy, he was extra protective of me during my childhood. He had always wanted a daughter named Mary, and Mary was his first choice for any one of my sisters. My mother did not particularly like that name, but because I was born on Christmas day, my father finally got his wish....I wonder if I would have been named Joseph, had I been born a boy.

The Four Drzewiecki Sisters - 1954
Standing: Krysia - Seated From Left: Wandzia, Marysia, Danusia

December 10, 1954
The Brick Palace

My family moved into the unfinished palace on December 10th, 1954. The house had three bedrooms, a large kitchen, a living room, and a bathroom with a full-sized bathtub. There was a large cold storage room downstairs, for my mother's hundreds of jars of preserves from the orchard and garden. Later, my parents had two huge freezers packed full of meat and homegrown fruits and vegetables. Dad was an outdoorsman, and there was also plenty of fish and venison. Wartime experiences had a lifelong effect on my parents. Food always had to be in an abundant supply, and nothing was ever wasted.

My father's dream of having sons finally came true in 1955 and 1961. Richard Sylwester was born September 28, 1955 and Roman Jan on January 13, 1961 in Ladysmith, BC. They too, like my sisters each had a birthweight of 10 lbs, 10 oz. My mother certainly grew big babies.

My father celebrated for days after my brothers were born. If he wasn't raising a glass with friends, he was raising a glass to himself in the mirror.

Rysiek - Richard, 1957

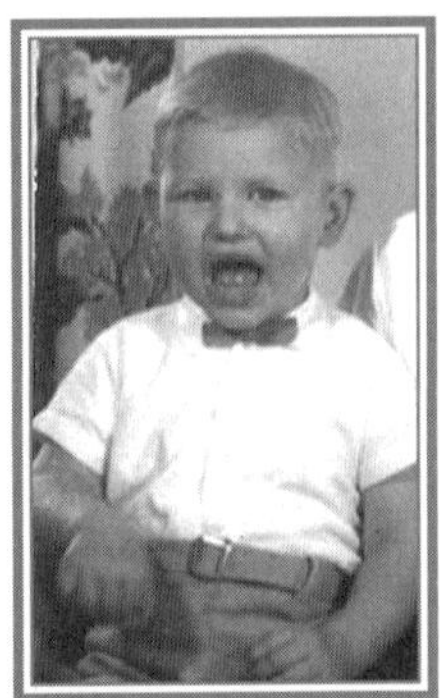

Roman - Ron, 1964

Drzewiecki Family Photo, 1967
Back Row From Left: Danusia, Krysia, Rysiek, Wandzia, Marysia
Front: Janina, Roman, Sylwester

The Old Barrel Furnace

In the basement of our brick house stood a double-barrel wood furnace that kept the house warm through the damp Vancouver Island falls and winters. One of my earliest childhood memories is of sitting around the furnace with its door wide open, watching the fire as my father told stories of his youth. My sisters and brothers all gathered round, seated on wooden benches and chairs. My mother would come downstairs and join us with mugs of hot chocolate and freshly baked treats. We were captivated by Dad's amazing tales of growing up in Eastern Poland and surviving the labour camps in Germany in the Second World War. It was difficult for us to relate our peaceful and comfortable lives to his of poverty, starvation and war. Here we were in Canada only one generation later, with comforts my father could only dream of as a child; plenty of food, warm clothes, medical care, and education.

It is now the year 2000 as I finish writing my parents' amazing epic. Mom and Dad still live in the brick house. They are now in their mid-seventies, have six children, fourteen grandchildren, and three great-grandchildren. My father's photographic memory is as remarkable as it ever was, and the stories continue to unfold around the kitchen table.

Janina and Sylwester Drzewiecki
April 2000

Moi Kochani Rodzice - My Dear Parents,

I am so thankful that you immigrated to Canada, and I am grateful for all you endured in your pursuit of a better life for yourselves and for your children. You are my teachers and my friends, and I owe you so much.

Dziękuję Mamo i Tato. Ja bardzo kocham was i jestem dumna że jesteście moimi rodzicami ..... Thank you Mom and Dad. I love you dearly, and am proud that you are my parents.

With Much Love Always,
Your Youngest Daughter, Marysia Anna Drzewiecki

Marysia - 1958

Love not things, but each other;
For when we pass from this earth,
All that truly matters,
Are those whose hearts we have touched with love.

- Mary Drzewiecki, 1994

Epilogue

Born and Raised
Under a Straw Roof
A True Legacy of the Human Spirit
WOLYN
Lucke
Krakow
POLAND - 1939
Mary A. Drzewiecki

Epilogue

On April 7th, 1997, my parents celebrated their 50th wedding anniversary, with my mother still wearing her silver wedding band which Zygmunt had made from a Polish two złoty coin; my father's ring was lost years earlier somewhere at Harmac. *La Gondarina* played at the party and they were moved by the memory of coming across the Atlantic in 1949 on the SS Scythia.

On July 25th, 1999, my parents celebrated fifty years since their arrival in Canada. The celebration was held in their park-like backyard, in the orchard that my mother had planted the day my sister Daiena was born. They were surrounded by family and lifelong friends. It seemed impossible to them that fifty years had passed since they docked in Quebec City, yet seeing their grown grandchildren, and their growing great-grandchildren, it was obvious that it had; sadly, a grandson died in infancy in 1977. How their lives had changed since Rudnia and Omelanka, in Eastern Poland, where they were *Born and Raised Under a Straw Roof*. My parents will be forever grateful to have lived and raised their children in Canada and see their successive generations live in the country they adopted, and love.

The two dollars my parents were given in Vancouver in 1949, when they disembarked from the train, was the only money they ever collected from the Canadian government in all their years in Canada. My father never collected any funds from Unemployment Insurance during his forty years at Harmac, and he seldom took a day off sick. My parents still have the old galvanized bath tub, the black scissors, the tin bowl, and the meat grinder they brought across the Atlantic with them. The old yellow buggy was used to rock all six of their babies to sleep. As we grew, we played with that buggy until it fell apart; the wheels were transferred to many a go-cart. Incredibly my mother still has her official birth certificate which she took from her home in Omelanka when she fled into the forest; the blanket was lost somewhere in their journeys. The barrel furnace stands behind the well that Mom and Dad dug by hand in the early 1950s. It has been reduced to one barrel by corrosion, but continues to be used as an incinerator.

The Retired Double Barrel Furnace by the Old Well

The Polish picnics, which I enjoyed so much as a child, slowly diminished as the wave of post Second World War immigrants aged, and their children became adults.

Polski Piknik - Polish Picnic,1957

The little brown house is gone. The thick forests near my parents' brick house have been cut down for housing developments, and there has been a dramatic decline in the snake population in the area. My mother's distaste for snakes never changed; only one snake ever made it inside the house.

Once my mother acquired real cooking pots and cooking utensils, she became an incredible cook. She has prepared countless feasts, without any more potatoes stuck to the ceiling. Guests drop in unannounced and my mother will instantly produce an array of food that is pleasing to the eye and to the palate. She never seems to concern herself with how many people stay for dinner, just whether or not there are enough chairs. My mother's passion is in the kitchen, and she continues to experiment with recipes.

My father realized his dream of living near the ocean and becoming an avid sports fisherman and outdoorsman. His fishing and hunting tales are endless. He continues to fish the waters of the Georgia Straight in his fourteen foot aluminum boat.

Sylwester Drzewiecki the Outdoorsman
Northern British Columbia - Silver Lake 1989

Moose Hunting 1979
Prince George Area

Fishing the Georgia Strait 1995

"I'm going fishing, and if I catch a fish it's a bonus."
- Sylwester Drzewiecki, 1995

Proud Canadians

Janina and Sylwester Drzewiecki's Canadian Citizenship Papers

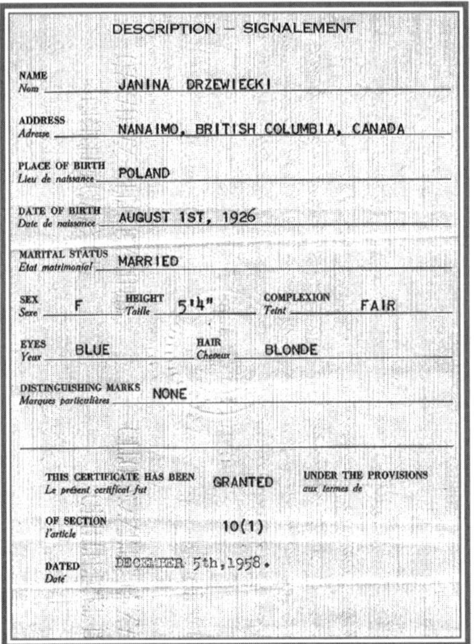

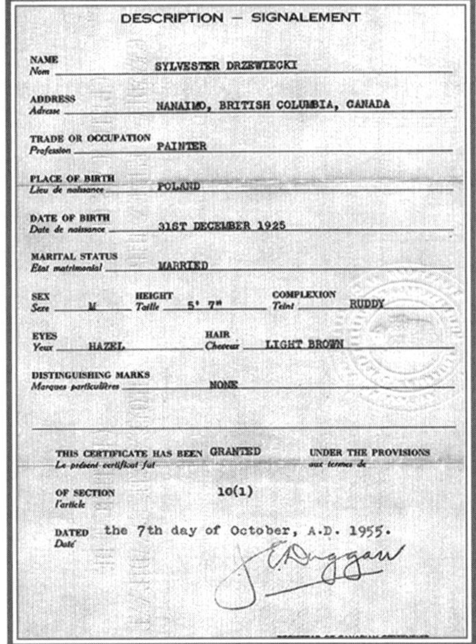

My parents are true Canadians, and proudly fly the Canadian Flag in their front and back yards. My father became a Canadian citizen on October 7th, 1955, and my mother on December 5th, 1958.

Adam and Filipina Horoszkiewicz

Adam and Filipina Horoszkiewicz, 1980

Adam and Filipina Horoszkiewicz's application to come to Canada through government sponsorship was rejected in Germany year after year. By 1954, the Drzewieckis and the Regulants had enough resources to sponsor them. They applied through Canadian immigration in Victoria, B.C., and Adam and Filipina were approved. On October 20th, 1956, Adam and Filipina left Germany on the ship the Arosa Sun, and arrived in Quebec City on October 31st. They then travelled by train across Canada.

Even though I was very young, I remember my excitement at seeing my grandparents for the very first time. They presented us with watches, leather backpacks, toys, and other special gifts from Germany. They eventually built a lovely home in Ladysmith, from the salvaged materials of two demolished houses. Their home and yard were immaculately kept. Babcia's - Grandma's vegetable and flower garden were second to none. Roses trailed over the entire length of her fence, and people would drive by to admire her flowers.

Dziadziuś - Grandpa worked at a variety of small construction and farming jobs, until he was hired by the city of Ladysmith, where he worked for parks and grounds maintenance. He did not retire until the age of 70.

Babcia and Dziadziuś became Canadian citizens on April 1st, 1966.

Descendants of Adam and Filipina Horoszkiewicz: The Drzewieckis and The Regulants, 1998

We are all candles in the wind;
Our flames briefly flicker, and are gone,
But if our light warms the hearts of others,
Our dance lives on.

- Mary Drzewiecki , 2000

Zygmunt and Stasia Regulant

Zygmunt and Stasia, 1974

Zygmunt died suddenly from a heart aneurysm in 1978. He was only sixty-four years old, and was looking forward to retiring the following year. He worked for Crown Zellerbach for 27 years, from 1951 to 1978, the logging company that hired him when he came to British Columbia. On the day of his funeral, his grandson, Zygmunt Regulant III, was born. He is buried in the Ladysmith Cemetery.

Zygmunt built two homes in Ladysmith. Stasia still lives in the last home her husband built. She worked at the Ladysmith hospital for 34 years, from 1954 to 1988.

By the year 2000, the Regulant's family of three children grew to include eight grandchildren, and five great-grandchildren. Sadly, their son Zbigniew - Bill died of a heart attack in 1984 at the young age of 36 years.

The Regulant Children - Zygmunt II, Krystyna, Bill, Ladysmith, 1953

Bibliography

Bibliography Citing Book Sources:

1. Lukas, Richard C. *Forgotten Holocaust: The Poles under German Occupation 1939-1944*.
   New York: Hippocrene Books, 1990.

2. Pfeiffer, Christine. *Poland: Land of Freedom Fighters*.
   Minneapolis, Minnesota: Dillon Press, Inc., 1984.

3. *National Geographic, Atlas of the World: Seventh Edition*.
   Washington DC: National Geographic Society, 1999.

4. *The Times Atlas of the World Volume II: South-West Asia : Russia Mid-Century Edition*.
   London: The Times Publishing Co. Ltd., Printing House Square, 1959.

Bibliography Citing Internet Sources:

1. Cunich, P. and Deli, Peter, Department of History,
   University of Hong Kong. (1999). Lenin and the Russian Peasants.
   Available: http:hkuhist2.hku.hk/firstyear/Deli/delie10.htm

2. Klopotek, Mieszysław A. The Second World War in Poland.
   Available: http://www.ipipan.waw.pl/klopotek/pl//ww2.htm

3. Fiodorov, Ivan D.I. (2000). Tsar Nicholas II emperor of all Russia 1894-1917.
   Available: http://www.ticino.com/usr/ivand/Tsars/Nicholas_II.htm

4. German Resistance Memorial Center, Topic 12, Stauffenberg and the Assassination Attempt
   of July 20,1944: The Attempt on Hitler's Life.
   Available: http://www.gdw-berlin.de/b12/ausstellung/b12-ein-e.htm

5. Rudek, Mieczysław, Hetman Magazine. (1998). The Battle of Warsaw 1920.
   Available: http:/www.perfekt.net/hetman/pages/bit1920ang.htm

6. Poland 1921-1939 Map.
   Available: http://www.pgsa.org/images/Pol1921.gif

7. The Abdication of Nicholas II.
   Available: http://www.pp.clinet.fi/~pkr01/history/abdic.html

Books of interest written in the Polish language, about the Ukrainian uprising in Wołyn, Eastern Poland:

1. Ozarowski, Filip. *Gdy Plonal Wołyn* (trans: *When Wołyn was in Flames*)
   To order: Punkt, 2619 Post Rd., Steven Point, W154481, USA

2. Piotrowski, Czesław General. *Gdies Miendzy Horyniem i Styrem* (trans: *Somewhere Between the Horyn and Styr Rivers*). Warsaw 1991

Point of Interest:
   General Czesław Piotrowski, the author of *Gdies Miendzy Horyniem i Styrem*, went to school with Stasia Horoszkiewicz-Regulant in Huta Stepanska in 1939.

Index

PART VI - CANADA

Sylwester and Janina - Moje Rodzice - My Parents

About the Author

Mary Drzewiecki earned a Bachelor's Degree from Simon Fraser University and teaches elementary school. She has a variety of interests in the visual and performing arts, and worked for many years as a professional fine artist. She has a zest for life and loves the outdoors.

Mary can honestly say that her daughters, Annette and Marysia, have been the wind beneath her wings. Mother and daughters continue to encourage each other to believe in themselves, and to reach for the stars.

From Left: Annette, Mary and Marysia, 2000

I Am,
And no one knows.
I hear, in the silence of my soul;
I see, where blindness befalls others;
I sing from the heart, without words or music;
I find beauty and treasures, in the simplicities of life;
I feel joy, in the love and laughter of children;
I fly, without putting myself above others;
I play a part, in the orchestra of life;
I am, and no one knows,
But me.

- Mary Drzewiecki, 1994

From Left: Marysia, Mary and Annette, 2000

Born and Raised Under a Straw Roof is Mary Drzewiecki's first book, and the fulfillment of a dream to preserve her parents' legacy, and her roots, for generations to come. If you have cried, laughed, and celebrated with her parents, then they too have touched your heart.